The
Ferriby Boats

The Ferriby Boats

Seacraft of the Bronze Age

Edward Wright

London and New York

First published 1990 by Routledge
11 New Fetter Lane, London EC4P 4EE
29 West 35th Street, New York, NY 10001

©1990 Edward Wright

Typeset, printed, and bound in Great Britain by
Butler & Tanner Ltd, Frome and London

British Library Cataloguing in Publication Data
Wright, Edward
The Ferriby boats.
1. Prehistoric wooden boats. Archaeological
investigation Humberside. North Ferriby
I. Title
623.8′21

ISBN 0–415–02599–0

Library of Congress Cataloging in Publication Data
Also available

This work is dedicated, first, to my brother with whom I shared the first decade of the project; second, to all those who have endured the ordeal of cold, mud, stench and exhaustion on the river-bank to bring to light evidence of some of early man's most remarkable technical achievements; and not least to my wife, family and friends who have shown the greatest tolerance towards my lifelong obsession with my subject.

Contents

Illustrations

Scales

A variety of scales have been incorporated in the author's photographs over the years, including trowels and spades. In the earlier ones the most frequent is a two-foot carpenter's folding rule graduated in inches, sometimes open and sometimes folded. From 1946 onwards there appears a short plank graduated in centimetres/10 centimetres. Thereafter, except Figures 3.9 and 4.22, scales are all metric and readily interpretable.

Tables

Abbreviations

Ant.   *Antiquity*
Ant. J.   *Antiquaries' Journal*
ARC   *Archaeological Research Centre*
Arch.   *Archaeologia*
Arch. J. *Archaeological Journal*
BAR   *British Archaeological Reports*
IJNA   *International Journal of Nautical Archaeology*
MM   *Mariner's Mirror*
NMM   *National Maritime Museum (Greenwich)*
PPS   *Proceedings of the Prehistoric Society*

Preface

This book is the fruit of a long gestation process and even then cannot represent the last word on the subject since information is still being garnered and research continues. Nevertheless it aims to provide as up-to-date an account as is possible at the end of 1989, or fifty-two years after the first discovery in 1937. In the interval all the major finds from the site have been or are about to be published, but this is the first attempt to bring all the strands together under one cover and therefore represents my testimony of half a century's work in the investigation and exposition of one of Britain's more remarkable archaeological phenomena and one still less widely known than it deserves, a situation for which this book aims to provide the remedy. While it is designed to give all the information required by the specialist maritime archaeologist, it has been written with an eye also to the general reader. Thus technical terms are kept to a minimum and where used their meaning is explained in the glossary. It relies heavily on illustration in preference to verbal description: on line drawings with adequate captions and the use of photographs, the latter in part to validate the reliability of the drawing and also to convey impressions of the remarkable finish which was still preserved in the finds when first exposed to view. Regrettably, despite advances in the methods used to conserve waterlogged and degraded wood, not even the more recently found artefacts retain all the signs of careful workmanship evident

on first excavation, while the earlier ones recovered before modern techniques became available are in a sorry state. It needs to be said however that if they had not been lifted when they were, they would have been lost altogether owing to the tidal erosion of the deposits in which they were embedded.

The scheme of the work is a logical one; the first three chapters are a narrative account of the discoveries and the action taken in consequence of them. As will be seen, these fall naturally into three phases: the finds and investigations before and during World War II; the postwar surge of activity and the first radio-carbon date giving an indication that the boats were works of the Bronze Age; and finally the third large find, which was followed by progressively more thorough and scientific research still continuing up to the present day. Having set the scene, the fourth chapter gives detailed descriptions of the actual boat-finds with sufficient information to enable them to be replicated as found. The following two chapters go beyond the actual finds: Chapter 5 tackles the hypothetical reconstruction of a complete boat, again in sufficient detail for actual building to be undertaken and to estimate its performance; and Chapter 6 considers the materials identified and the methods by which the boats might have been built. To complete the picture, the accumulation of other artefacts from the site is described in considerable detail in Chapter 7, some of them being of direct relevance to the operation or construction of boats. Evidence for the ancient environment, that for the age of the boats and discussion of the archaeological background for the period are set out in Chapter 8. In the final chapter discussion turns to the nature of the group of finds and their possible purpose, and concludes with an attempt to relate them, at this stage of knowledge somewhat speculatively, to what is known of boatbuilding comparable in age or technique elsewhere in the world. Chapter 5 is the joint work of J. F. Coates and myself and he has also contributed significantly to Chapter 6. The refinement of the reconstructed design which we offer is the fruit of prolonged collaboration between us and owes much to his skills as a professional naval architect and to his experience of ancient forms of boatbuilding, while his passage dealing with performance is based on his extensive calculations, the mathematical detail of which we did not consider appropriate for inclusion in the present work but which we aim to publish with other technical matter separately. For those professionally interested, arrangements will be made for large-scale prints of the drawings of record and of the lines and reconstruction drawings to be available on application to the author.

My brother and I approached the challenge presented by the earlier discoveries as palaeontologists rather than archaeologists. The finds had characteristics of size and complexity comparable with those of fossil dinosaurs and we treated them accordingly. When we started, our ignorance of boats and boatbuilding was total and we learned as we went along with the project. For many years there was no specialist body of technique on which to draw and the narrative describes some of the pitfalls into which we fell. I have little doubt that another major find in a similar situation would receive better treatment than that meted out to Boats 1 to 3!

Although the impression may be given that the project has been something of a solo effort on my part, I must acknowledge support and help from many quarters over the years. I cannot include the names of all who have contributed during the half century of activity and many have already received acknowlegement in reports published at intervals. The efforts of the National Maritime Museum, The British Museum, and Hull Museums under successive directors before and immediately after World War II are referred to in the text. As far as the National Maritime Museum is concerned it has been a continuing process, in which initially the late G. P. B. Naish was principally involved. From 1970 onwards Basil Greenhill, by then Director, gave the impetus needed to ensure that 'Ferriby studies' were made a key area of concern for the emergent Archaeological Research Centre (ARC) and without his direct encouragement this book would not have developed in the form that it has done. Sean McGrail and his staff in ARC have been towers of strength and have provided the base facilities without which the work would have foundered. He himself has applied characteristically stringent criticism to the text itself at two stages of its preparation as well as writing the generous introduction. While we have not always agreed on matters of interpretation, I owe him a great debt for the stimulation to greater accuracy and precision which has resulted from our exchanges. While ARC was still in being Veryan Heal never failed me in providing access to records held at the museum and she has also contributed to the study of wood-working tools of the Bronze Age embodied in the book. Chris Gregson and others have been ever willing to cope with questions of conservation and to receive awkward specimens of degraded wood into their care. Since the demise of ARC, Gillian Hutchinson has shouldered the task of support from the National Maritime Museum entirely on her own and I am more than grateful for all the help I have had from her, this despite the multitudinous demands on her time from many quarters.

Most of the archive is already lodged at the National Maritime Museum, Greenwich.

This includes the originals of all field records and drawings and duplicates of all photographic negative material. One of my remaining tasks is to see that this is so ordered and annotated that the record need no longer be dependent on my own memory of events.

One of the great benefits of the initiatives of the National Maritime Museum in the 1970s and 1980s has been the series of gatherings of like-minded workers in the maritime aspects of archaeology from all over the globe. This has enabled me to establish contacts in Europe and elsewhere which have greatly improved my grasp of the background necessary to understand my subject adequately. Many have also been most helpful in providing direct help in answer to queries as well as a much-needed sounding-board for the airing of theories. I should mention especially Arne Emil Christensen in Norway, Ole Crumlin Pedersen in Denmark, Henry Forssell in Finland, Detlev Elmers in West Germany, Wolfgang Rudolf in East Germany, Béat Arnold in Switzerland, Ottavio Filgueiras in Portugal and Richard Steffy in the USA. To these and many others I give my thanks.

That the book has been driven to completion for publication, much is owed to Barry Cunliffe who both encouraged me to finish the task and opened doors to ensure publication. His ready support is most warmly acknowledged.

A project of this kind relies heavily on a range of disciplines in parallel with archaeology, all of which contribute towards amplification of the picture to be derived from study of the artefacts themselves. The first such contribution came from Kew with the identification of the materials in F1 before World War II. In 1946-7 help was provided by the Sub-department of Quaternary Research at Cambridge and its founder Sir Harry Godwin. The Research Laboratory at the British Museum under Dr Harold Plenderleith not only tackled conservation of timber but provided the first radio-carbon date for Ferriby material. In 1963 Cambridge again came to our aid with D. M. Churchill's first serious investigation of the environmental conditions and more radio-carbon dates, among which Godwin's own name figures in the list of references together with that of his successor R. G. West and of V. R. Switsur, whose personal contribution to the problems of dating the boats has been and continues to be of fundamental importance. Following Churchill's work, Paul Buckland, now of Sheffield University, has shouldered the load on environmental studies and Jennifer Hillam of the same university has made great strides towards unravelling the prospects of absolute dating by dendrochronological methods with the declared intention of achieving eventual success for all three of the major boat-finds. Richard Darrah's readiness to share his unrivalled experience of replicating ancient methods of working timber has been invaluable. To these and all others who have worked on 'Ferriby studies' my warmest thanks are given.

Colin Burgess's help is referred to in the text; but his contribution of a comprehensive, tabulated scheme for the British Bronze Age has not only injected much-needed clarity into my own attempts to describe the archaeological background for my subject, but will, I hope, provide valuable service to prehistorians generally. In earlier years I owed a debt to Grahame Clark, Christopher Hawkes and Stuart Piggott for archaeological coaching and support. C. W. Phillips's contribution in 1946 was of crucial importance.

Illustrations have been culled from various sources, and authorship is acknowledged appropriately. Most recently the production of accurate reconstruction drawings by J. F. Coates has made a notable improvement in the quality of what is offered to the reader; based on these he and I were able to brief John Craig to generate the lively depictions of separate features and the complete boat in action. Where not attributed to others the photographs and drawings are my own work.

I like to think that the fascination of exposure to the astonishing artefacts themselves has been sufficient reward for those who over the years have endured the ordeals of work on the river-bank. It has always been both arduous and disagreeable but never dull. I am proud to share the common bond of achievement with what is now a declining number of fellow-toilers.

Finally my thanks are due to my daughter Caroline who typed the first draft of the text and to Mrs Susie Henderson who made order out of the much mangled final version. Their patience has been exemplary!

EDWARD WRIGHT
Beaconsfield
1989

Acknowledgements

I should like to express my thanks for permission to reproduce the following material: M. S. Anwar: Figures 6.16, 6.17; Allen Binns: Figures 3.3, 3.4, 3.6; British Museum, London: Figure 6.1; J. F. Coates: Figures 5.15, 5.17, 5.18a and b, 5.23, 7.13; John Coles: Figure 6.2c; D. R. Crowther: Figure 7.21; Richard Darrah: Figure 6.10b; Detlev Ellmers: Figure 8.6; Hull City Museums and Art Galleries: Figure 5.4; Illustrated London News Picture Library: Figure 6.5; Instituut voor Prae- en Protohistorie and B. Donker: Figure 9.5; I. J. McInnes: Figures 3.7b, 7.16; Eero Naskali: Figure 6.12; National Maritime Museum, Greenwich: Figures 2.17, 3.8, 3.10, 6.3, 6.4, 7.8, 7.18a, 7.20, 9.8, 9.12, 9.14; Norsk Sjofartsmuseum, Oslo: Figure 7.10; Patrice Pomey: Figure 9.9; Quintin Wright: Figures 7.23, 7.24. M. W. Barley: extract from his 'Lincolnshire rivers in the Middle Ages'; P. C. Buckland and his co-authors: extracts from their paper on the paleœnvironment of the Ferriby site; C. B. Burgess: for his hitherto unpublished 'Chronological table for the Bronze Age in Britain' reproduced on p. 179. The publishers and I have taken all possible care to trace the ownership of copyright material and to acknowledge it fully.

Introduction

The three Bronze Age boats from North Ferriby may not be so spectacular as the Anglo-Saxon ship burial from Sutton Hoo with its royal grave goods – nor lend themselves so readily to crowd-pulling displays as the Viking Age Skuldelev vessels from Roskilde Fjord, Denmark, nor be so evocative of a period of history as the *Mary Rose*, yet they are undoubtedly of greater significance than any of these to maritime archaeology and to our understanding of early boatbuilding and boatmanship in north-west Europe. Indeed, the Ferriby boats are of worldwide importance, being surpassed in age only by the third millennium BC planked boats from the vicinity of the royal pyramids at Giza and at Dahshur in Egypt.

Sixty years ago, before the Ferriby boats were first encountered by E. V. and C. W. Wright and before the Hjortspring boat from Iron Age Denmark had been excavated by Rosenberg, little was known about the early history of the building and use of water transport in north-west Europe. Indeed, despite much indirect evidence for man's use of rivers and the sea from early times, little thought was given to the matter: Paul Johnstone's remark in the 1970s that, 'it is surprising in how many otherwise excellent works one can look in vain in the index under "boat", "ship", "canoe" . . .' applies with even more force to the period before World War II. Such speculation as there was in those days focused on the logboat (dugout canoe) and very occasionally on the hideboat (wicker coracle): the use of planked boats of advanced design was thought to have been possible only in the great civilizations of the early Middle East and Mediterranean, and not in north-west Europe until Roman times. The discovery, recording, and excavation of the Ferriby boats changed all this, revealing, as it did, boat-building of a standard and complexity not previously thought achievable in the Bronze Age of that region.

This book – Ted Wright's *magnum opus* – chronicles intermittent but purposeful research on the North Ferriby material from 1937 to 1989. We read of the difficulties of intertidal excavation: heavy, glutinous clay; limitations imposed by the tidal regime and the hours of daylight; and the complications of lifting and extracting substantial waterlogged timbers. We learn of perseverance and ingenious solutions to these problems, and of the use of 'modern' techniques to sample the environment of the boat-finds, and to record the boats within a metric grid. The position of the pith and the pattern of rings and rays in the cross section of timbers were noted – a most useful source of information about early methods of selection and conversion of trees which has regrettably not yet become standard practice elsewhere. A comprehensive photographic record was compiled, plaster casts were taken of toolmarks, and timber was salved so that at some time in the future innovative techniques might be used to recover information from it – forethought which paid off when dating by radio-carbon assay became possible. Analogies were drawn between twentieth-century examples of sewn plank boats and the Ferriby remains, and experimental methods were used to throw light on Bronze Age methods of boatbuilding. In their use of such archaeological techniques the Wright brothers were as much in advance of their times as were their namesakes in aviation.

The Ferriby archive is of a standard comparable with those compiled today from similar contexts, and of the highest standards when measured against those generally achieved in the middle decades of this century. Thus, even though the remains of boats 1 and 2 were damaged by the conservation techniques used, the Wright records were sufficiently detailed for models of what was found to be built for display at Hull and Greenwich. These records also provided a firm basis for further research to determine what the boats had been like before they were abandoned in fragmented form on the North Ferriby foreshore. As Ted Wright describes in Chapter 5 of this book, his research led increasingly to dialogue with curatorial staff at Greenwich, in one instance even to 'vehement argument' – some indication of the enthusiasm with which he pursued his research, and a sure sign of the value of decades of work. His infectious enthusiasm not only induced others to examine facts and theories about the Ferriby boats, but also directly or indirectly stimulated the location and excavation or examination of other prehistoric craft, logboats as well as planked boats, and also led to important excavations of prehistoric sites on the Humber foreshore at Melton, Welton, and North Ferriby and on the higher ground at Redcliff, including the recovery of environmental evidence.

I have known Ted Wright for almost twenty years and during that time we have not infrequently discussed and re-discussed the hypothetical reconstruction of these boats – that is, what exactly was missing from them when they were found, how had they been propelled and steered, and what sort of performance had they had? Whilst not necessarily agreeing with all aspects of the Wright solution to these problems, I do entirely agree that the Ferriby boats are the most important maritime finds in north-west Europe to date. Their excavation was a significant milestone in the progress of archaeological research and their documentation a benchmark by which to measure the standards of subsequent boat excavation. I commend this book not only to those interested in the past, be it maritime matters, woodworking techniques, environmental history or trade and transport affairs, but also to those who wish to learn how archaeologists work in the field and at their desks and drawing boards. They will find much to instruct and to entertain in this account of one man's pioneering work, and learn how his perspicacity and determination over fifty years opened eyes to aspects of man's past not previously thought of and encouraged others to follow.

SEAN McGRAIL
Institute of Archaeology
University of Oxford
1989

1

Site, surroundings and discovery

North Ferriby lies, as does its counterpart South Ferriby, tucked under the western side of the chalk escarpment of the Yorkshire and Lincolnshire Wolds where this is cut by the tidal estuary of the Humber (Figure 1.1). On the north bank the area is partially covered by a mantle of glacial till and at Ferriby itself there is today a low tongue of glacial deposits running south-west towards the shore of the estuary leaving a shallow re-entrant to the east before the chalk reaches the river-bank at Hessle and another deeper to the west between Ferriby and Brough-on-Humber (Figure 1.2). Where this tongue of glacial deposits reaches the estuary it forms a cliff some 10 m high, aptly named Red Cliff (Figure 1.3). Once tides in the estuary approached their modern levels, each of the two re-entrants became a catchment for deposition of the accumulated silts of the flood-plain of the Humber, and the ridge between provided an additional route of access from the water's edge to the high ground inland: to the east the chalk of the Wolds, then the glacial tongue and to the west what is left of the oolitic Jurassic escarpment at Brough which is a minor feature compared with its counterpart, the Lincoln Edge to the south. Across the estuary opposite North Ferriby, the Lincolnshire Wolds fall steeply towards the shore with a thinner covering of glacial till than that on the north bank (Figure 1.4). The low ground between the Wolds and the Edge forms the valley of the River Ancholme which drains north into the Humber at

South Ferriby Sluice. Upstream of the Jurassic escarpment the flood-plain broadens out as the Vale of York to the north and west and the river Trent catchment to the south and there is no high ground to provide convenient crossings for a number of miles inland. In historic times the stretches of land between Hessle and Brough on the north bank and Barton and Winteringham on the south have for centuries been significant for north–south communication. The main link in Roman times was that between Winteringham, the road terminal north from Lincoln, and Brough which in turn gave access north to Malton and north-west to York by way of the Escrick moraine which provides some elevation above the vale. In medieval times regular crossing places were numerous as witness the extensive use of ferries on Lincolnshire rivers reviewed by Maurice Barley:

> Bridges were few and so inadequate that ferries were at least equally important, nor do the former necessarily indicate the main routes into and out of the county. Domesday gives ferries over the Humber at Grimsby (two – presumably over to one or other of the lost villages within the arm of Spurn Point), Barton-on-Humber, South Ferriby (two) and Winteringham. It is clear that by this time the main road north from Lincoln crossed the Ancholme at Brigg and the Humber at either Barton or South Ferriby. . . . These make it highly probable

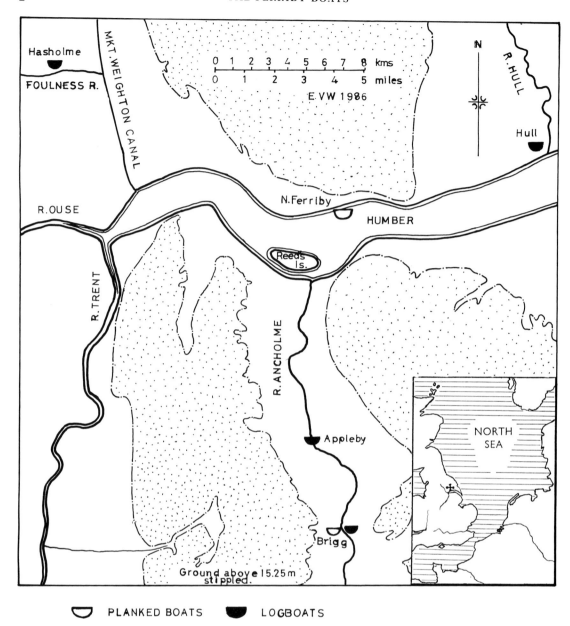

Figure *1.1* Location of the North Ferriby and other boat-finds in the area.

that the pre-Roman trackway along the western edge of the Wolds was the most frequented. Certainly from the 13th Century the main crossing was between Barton and Hessle. (Barley 1936)

It can fairly be assumed that the area was equally important in pre-Roman times for passage north–south where the estuary is narrow and it is possible to avoid the carr-lands inland to the west. This is not to say

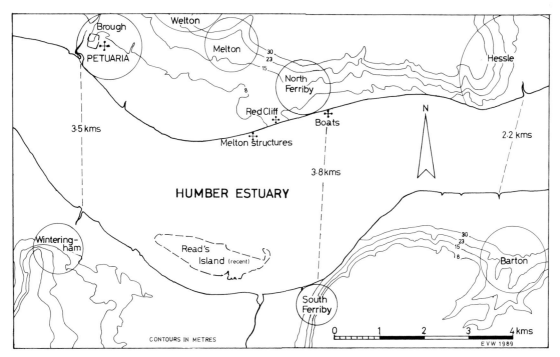

Figure 1.2 Map of the middle Humber showing areas of high ground bordering the estuary. Modern villages circled.

Figure 1.3 The 10-metre-high Red Cliff with section of glacial deposits. Traces of the Early Iron Age settlement were located in the 1 metre of soil at the top of the cliff edge.

Figure 1.4 View from the boat site across to the Lincolnshire shore. South Ferriby to right of centre where the woodland slopes down towards the water.

that the low-lying areas were not inhabited or accessible. Finds of prehistoric logboats in the Ancholme valley, the Trent catchment and, most recently, the Foulness river marshes all attest to utilization of the waterways as well as the land routes.

Before the landscape had been modified by deforestation, land use and settlement to something recognizably akin to its modern pattern, it is possible to visualize the area as being densely wooded on the heavier soils of the glacial deposits and more thinly so on the chalk and limestone ridges. While relative sea levels were markedly lower than today's, the penetration of tidal, saline waters inland was less extensive than now; but as they rose the flood-plain of the Humber catchment became covered first by fen-woodland, the decaying vegetation of which formed the peat deposits which cover all the valley bottoms both west and east of the high ground. The further rising of sea levels resulted in the drowning of the fen-woodland environment and its replacement by open salt marsh from the accretion of sediments from which were formed the deposits of grey estuarine silty-clay readily recognizable where it occurs from its colour and consistency. Its faunal content gives evi-

dence for the extent of tidal penetration, bringing salt water well inland up the river systems. Conditions such as these prevailed along the edges of the Humber estuary proper and well up the valleys of the rivers draining into it and they are exemplified by the deposits in the re-entrants to east and west of the tongue of glacial deposits at North Ferriby, Melton and Welton.

The peat and silts to the west which outcrop on the shore from Melton westwards (Figure 1.5) have been known for nearly a century and were observed and recorded by J. W. Stather (Stather 1896). Thereafter the vagaries of the silting processes in the Humber caused their submergence under inshore mudbanks for nearly fifty years; but in 1930 there was a comparatively sudden shift of the main deep-water channel used by sea-going shipping from the south to the north side of the estuary, and the whole of the recent silt was scoured away to reveal not only the Melton deposits once again, but also similar deposits in the eastern re-entrant at North Ferriby (Figure 1.6). Stather was still alive and active in the Hull Geological Society at the time (Figure 1.7) to witness this second emergence to view of these interesting post-glacial deposits and

Figure 1.5 Post-glacial deposits at Melton, first recorded by Stather in 1896.

Figure 1.6 The post-glacial deposits at North Ferriby first reported by Bisat in 1931.

they were reported in print by W. S. Bisat, one of the leading local experts on East Yorkshire glaciology at the time (Bisat 1932).

My brother and I, then in our early teens, were already developing our interest in the geology, and more particularly palaeontology, of the region, encouraged often by Thomas Sheppard, the Director of the Hull Museums and knowledgeable in most fields of anti-quarian and geological lore. It was he who

Figure 1.7 Visit of the Yorkshire Geological Society to the North Ferriby site in 1931. T. Sheppard on right. (*Photo:* C. W. Mason.)

Figure 1.8 'Hurdle' structure excavated by C. W. and E. V. Wright c. 1935.

first introduced us to the Ferriby deposits, and living as we did only a mile away they soon became a subject for regular study, initially for their faunal content of insects, molluscs, and animal bones about which we reported in our first published paper, a note in the local journal *The Naturalist* (Wright and Wright 1933). Regular observation of the peat and overlying clay could not fail to stimulate search for artefacts of human make, first among the widespread layer of broken flint below the peat; but this proved to be entirely of natural occurrence with the evidence pointing to late-glacial frost-fracture. In the clay above the peat, however, we soon began to find roundwood stakes with marks of cutting at the ends and both at Ferriby and Melton light horizontal structures which we came to refer to as 'hurdles' (Figure 1.8). After several years of search the peat yielded only a single well-made flint implement (Figure 1.9), subsequently lost in the wartime destruction of the main Hull Museum.

Through the middle 1930s our attention was divided between the intertidal deposits and the rediscovered late pre-Roman Iron Age habitation site on the elevated ground at Red Cliff between the Ferriby and Melton sites (Corder *et al.* 1939; Corder and Pryce 1938). However when tidal conditions permitted we maintained a regular watch on the shore, having soon appreciated that scouring by water provided a regular and only gradually destructive form of excavation by exposing to view the natural and artefactual content of the clay and peat in a way which digging could not do. We were thus engaged early in September 1937, when I saw the ends of three massive wooden planks projecting at a shallow angle from the clay and called across to my brother, who was examining the edge of the peat a short distance away, that I had found a 'Viking ship'. His initial scepticism disappeared as he too saw the planks, which could only be part of a large boat. We were as usual armed with trowels and began to explore the find. We very soon learned that the unexposed part

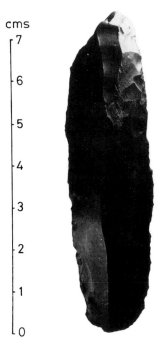

Figure 1.9 Flint tool found by C. W. Wright in the peat at North Ferriby.

retained its original fastenings, stitches of twisted fibrous material, and that the seams were packed with moss and capped with neatly finished laths of wood. The outer edges of the planks were found to be furnished with vee-shaped grooves into which the bevelled edges of the outer planks fitted closely. Other features observed in this first investigation were a variety of projections on the surface of the planks, mostly square in plan-view but including also what appeared to be a pair of lengthwise ridges. What we appreciated most clearly, however, was the problem of removing the glutinous clay matrix without damage to the wood. The few photographs of this first phase of exploration demonstrate that we had much to learn about cleaning the find to a standard suitable for adequate recording (Figure 1.10).

Our next move was to establish the total extent of the remains and this was first achieved by probing with a pointed walking stick. This indicated that the depth below the

Figure 1.10 First excavation of the eastern end of Ferriby 1 in September 1937. Note upstanding blocks (vestiges of cleats), groove in keel-plank and bevelled edge of outer bottom plank.

clay surface increased for some 6 m to the WNW and then decreased again towards the surface about 13 m away, where a knob of dark wood protruding from the clay was identified as the opposite end of the middle plank. The structure broadened to a maximum of about 1.5 m at half its length. On the next suitable combination of tide and light we undertook a more deliberate investigation of the western end. We were able to phase our excavation and cleaning, at which we soon became more adept, so as to leave adequate time for measurement, sketching, and a thorough photographic record followed by backfilling before we were driven off by the rising tide (Figure 1.11). The most important observations of this excavation were the steeply

rising curve of the end of the keel-plank evidently shaped out of the solid log (Figure 1.12) and the presence of a plank at an acute angle on the north side, although the corresponding plank on the south side was absent (Figure 1.13). Oval holes for fastening planks to the keel-plank were present along both edges, some still containing cut or broken remnants of stitching materials (Figure 1.14); and there was a transverse ridge across the plank, worn but still c. 3 cm high (Figure 1.14).

We were able to make one more exploratory excavation before the beginning of the Oxford Michaelmas term but on that occasion encountered difficulties with the accumulation of newly deposited silt as a result of the

Figure 1.11 Second excavation of the newly located western end of F1, September 1937.

Figure 1.12 The tip of the keel-plank of F1. Note the run of the grain indicating shaping from the solid timber.

Figure 1.13 Appearance of the end of the lowest side-strake in Dig 2.

windless conditions prevailing. Our planned transverse trench could not be completed in the time available and an irregular pit resulted. Cleaning too was hampered by the problem of removing the water which drained into the pit. One major new feature was exposed in the form of a substantial and intact rectilinear lengthwise ridge centred on the keel-plank together with an associated block which left a squared slot between the two protuberances (Figure 1.15). Somewhat puzzling also was a blind seam terminating in the middle of one of the side-planks, and this we interpreted as the end of a repaired crack (Figure 1.16). The siting of this excavation was chosen deliberately to cover the area previously identified by probing as that where the boat remains were buried most deeply below the surface of the clay.

My brother and I decided not to disturb

Figure 1.14 The transverse ridge across the keel-plank.

Figure 1.15 The third excavation (Dig 3) revealed what was later described as the 'saddle feature'.

Figure 1.16 'Blind' seam in the outer bottom-plank in Dig 3, later identified as a repaired crack.

the find any further while we began enquiries in an attempt to find what if any parallels there were for the methods of construction so far identified. Among others with whom we corresponded was James Hornell, who was later able to cite a single ethnographic parallel for the tongue-and-groove edging of the planks (Figure 1.17) in the Gujerati boats from India (Hornell 1930). In the following spring, the Hull Geological Society made an excursion to the Ferriby and Melton sites and a photograph of the eastern end by their indefatigable photographer C. W. Mason survives in the archive (Figure 1.18). During the summer of 1938 a small team consisting of Maurice Barley, Anthony Congreve, Revd Thomas Romans, my brother and I, under

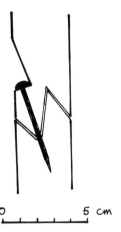

Figure 1.17 Type of seam used by Gujerati boat-builders, later put forward as the only parallel for the Ferriby pattern by James Hornell in 1946.

Figure 1.18 View of eastern end of F1 during visit by the Hull Geological Society in 1938. (*Photo*: C. W. Mason.)

Figure 1.19 Dig 4 in August 1938.

the direction of Philip Corder, had spent a week trial-trenching the pre-Roman Iron Age site to the west at Red Cliff and took the opportunity of a favourable tide and clean conditions on the bank to carry out a more extensive excavation across the middle of the boat-find. With the extra resources a stretch 2 m long was excavated, cleaned to a higher standard than previously achieved, adequately recorded and finally back-filled (Figure 1.19). The most important new revelations were three in number: first and foremost was the appearance of five planks side by side with fastenings and seams intact, the outer edges of the outer planks being furnished with cut or broken stitches, some caulking moss surviving in the grooved edges and lengths of the capping laths still in position. Second, a transversely placed lath across the keel-plank with its ends tucked under the lengthwise ones over the seams (Figure 1.20) indicated the presence of a joint in the keel-plank. Finally there was an additional array of upstanding blocks to the east of the joint in the keel-plank generally similar to those already observed at the extreme eastern end (Figure 1.21) as well as a short isolated lengthwise ridge or pair of ridges at the eastern end of the excavation.

I have gone into some detail about the progressive recovery of information derived from the first four investigations because it represented the sum total of evidence about the construction of our Ferriby boats available for the ensuing two years during which our

Figure 1.20 The transverse joint or scarf in the keel-plank.

Figure 1.21 Upstanding blocks on the planks, later identified as the remains of cleats and other features.

way of life was about to be changed by the outbreak of World War II. In the winter of 1938–9 we maintained our watch on the boat and made two more finds from the estuarine clay nearby: the first being the well-preserved blade of a paddle (Figure 7.11) and the second a substantial forked timber with a variety of worked features (Figures 7.4 and 7.5). The paddle was very soft and fragile and was immediately recorded after lifting and before shrinkage or distortion could begin. It was then copied in the form of an accurate replica in softwood by G. K. Beulah on behalf of Hull Museums. Finally it was made the subject of an initial experiment in conservation by a friend in the local timber industry, G. S. Wade, and treated by pressure-impregnation

with creosote. The outcome was reduction to dried, curled fragments and these were returned to the museum where they were subsequently destroyed by enemy action in the 1943 fire raid. The wood was unfortunately not identified; but later information suggests that it was possibly of ash (*Fraxinus*). The forked timber was deposited without any attempt at conservation at the museum and likewise disappeared in the fire. Its possible nature is discussed in Chapter 7.

The final pre-war activity was the removal of c. 2m of the eastern end of the keel-plank and the corresponding pieces of the adjoining outer planks which had become dangerously exposed by the continuing erosion of the shelf of surrounding clay. The pieces were sawn

Figure 1.22 The eastern ends of the planks of F1 after removal in the winter of 1938–9.

off, lifted and photographed, badly as it turned out (Figure 1.22), and then stored in the cool, damp environment under the staging in a north-facing fern-house at our home, where they gradually dried out with some distortion and considerable cracking of the outer surfaces.

With war imminent and no certainty of what might follow, it was thought prudent to commit to print some record of what had been learned of the find and, with the ready encouragement of O. G. S. Crawford, a brief illustrated note was published in *Antiquity* (Wright and Wright 1939). By then the wood used for the planks had been firmly identified as oak (*Quercus*) and the material of the stitches as withies of yew (*Taxus*). Some tentative ideas were advanced about the original shape of the boat, in particular the belief that it had been built with a rounded transverse section but had slumped flat after abandonment

(Figure 1.23). Based on the evidence of the 1938 excavation, it was thought that there had been five planks, with fastenings present for at least one more on each side and a sketch of a reconstructed transverse section therefore shows a keel-plank with three strakes on either side of it. A rough sketch illustrating the relationship of the boat to the stratigraphy of the beds around it shows a profile generally curved fore-and-aft but with the accentuated upward curve of the well-preserved western end prominent. My brother and I then went our several ways into military service in the belief that there was little more to be done until peace returned.

In fact we were both wrong since intermittent leave from military duty provided opportunity for maintaining observation of the river-bank. In my own case leave in April 1940 was the occasion for the find of a bronze knife or dagger blade (Figure 7.25) which did at least point to the possibility that some of the contents of the estuarine clay might be of prehistoric date although the conditions of deposition of such an artefact left its exact provenance uncertain. Subsequently a further spell of ten days of leave following commissioning in November 1940 brought even better opportunities when, with good clean conditions and a favourable tide, the sawn eastern end of the boat was well displayed. Further erosion had exposed a curved seam in the southern outer plank and this showed that a piece or 'stealer' had been fitted into the outer edge of the main side-plank which would account in part for one of the extra seams observed in the 1938 excavation. The exposure was measured, sketched, and photographed (Figure 1.24). On searching to the westward I next came upon the end of another broad plank some 50 m away and projecting close to the edge of the shelf of peat and clay at that point. I was able to clear a c. 2 m length of it, which was evidently a keel-plank of another boat similar to the first (Figure 1.25). The find lay roughly N–S, that is at right angles to the bank, and as far as could be

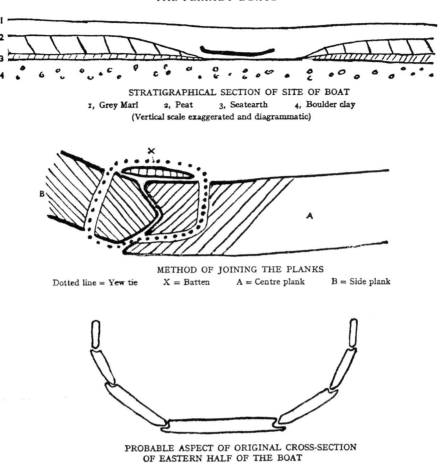

STRATIGRAPHICAL SECTION OF SITE OF BOAT
1, Grey Marl   2, Peat   3, Seatearth   4, Boulder clay
(Vertical scale exaggerated and diagrammatic)

METHOD OF JOINING THE PLANKS
Dotted line = Yew tie   X = Batten   A = Centre plank   B = Side plank

PROBABLE ASPECT OF ORIGINAL CROSS-SECTION
OF EASTERN HALF OF THE BOAT

Figure 1.23 Sketches of F1 included in note in *Antiquity* (Wright and Wright 1939).

determined by probing was narrow and c. 10 m long. The exposed southern end was plainly incomplete and a small sounding at the northern end showed that that too was broken or cut off short and also revealed the end of a cleat similar to that at the south end observed in the first dig. Although the ends were incomplete and lacking the upward projection of the western end of the first boat (F1), the surface was better preserved and at each end displayed a lengthwise ridge or cleat pierced by transverse squared holes. It was readily apparent that the two groups of rough projections found on the eastern half of F1 were the worn down vestiges of just such cleats.

During the same week, I excavated a further 2.26 m length inland of the first and confirmed that there were no other planks present. A squared slot between two upstanding blocks was found in this stretch, comparable to that seen in the third dig on F1 but differing in that the two blocks were of equal size and height and the whole feature longitudinally symmetrical in plan-view (Figure 4.14). A measured sketch was made but no photographic record as darkness was falling and there was only just time to complete backfilling of the excavation. From these early investigations of F2 at least one major advance had been made with the revelation of the existence of cleats on both boats, complete on

Figure 1.24 Exposure of southern corner of F1 in 1940 after the 1938–9 cut showing end of plank let into the outer bottom-plank.

Figure 1.25 Discovery of F2 in November 1940, the first excavation (F2 Dig 1). Note the intact cleat and oval holes.

Figure 1.26 F2 Dig 3 (April 1942).

one and damaged on the other, and likewise squared open slots; but the purpose of both features remained obscure. It was not until April 1942 that another opportunity occurred to investigate F2 further, and on that occasion with the help of a young nephew and one of his friends I opened a trial trench covering the estimated middle area of the plank (Figure 1.26). The results were rewarding since two complex cleat systems were exposed on either side of a well shaped box-scarf between the northern and southern components of the keel-plank. More important however was the presence of comparatively slender transverse timbers in all the holes in the complete cleats exposed. These were of oak and uniformly shaped with the lower side flat and the top rounded, width being c. 45 mm and thickness c. 30 mm. In several instances the ends showed chopmarks suggesting deliberate cutting along the line of the edges of the plank (Figure 1.27). The joint in the keel-plank was contrived with an overlap of 0.133 m and was

caulked with moss (Figure 1.28); but unlike that seen in F1 the capping lath was missing. Conditions for recording and especially photography fortunately were good and once again the excavation was back-filled for the better preservation of the find.

Meanwhile during 1941, my brother had been impelled to cut off and remove another length from the eastern end of F1 which was by then at risk, the curved end of the stealer which I had observed in November 1940 having already been washed away. He made a measured sketch of the pieces and deposited them at Hull Museum, where they were later destroyed by fire. This exposure completed the accounting for the appearance of four seams in the 1938 excavation, since the eastern end of the northern seam proved to be blind as in the case of that in Dig 3 (1937) and was clearly also a repair to a long crack. We thus had evidence for a keel-plank made up of two components scarfed in the middle and two long outer planks of which the southern one

Figure 1.27 Transverse timbers through the cleats, showing marks of cutting on the ends (F2, Dig 3).

Figure 1.28 The scarf in F2 (F2, Dig 3).

had been made up with a stealer of unknown length and the northern one contained a long repaired crack. How the stealer related to the repaired crack in the southern plank and how the presumably complete western ends of both the outer planks were terminated remained obscure although we had surmised that the northern one tapered in plan-view, believing, wrongly as it turned out, that we had located its end in the second excavation in 1937. The final act relating to activity during the war years came with my removal in the winter of 1943–4 of a further 1.0 m from the exposed ends of the two parts of the northern outer plank and the keel-plank, their southern equivalents having already been washed away. This was done in dire emergency and regrettably no record was made, although the pieces survived with those already stored at our home in North Ferriby. These records for F1 have been combined in Figure 5.9.

It will thus be seen that by 1944, when the outcome of the Second World War was still very much in doubt and conditions for any form of archaeological work virtually impossible, much information had been accumulated about these two boat-finds of an apparently unique kind. Much however remained unknown and the remains themselves were increasingly at risk by reason of natural erosion of the bank. This had of course been accelerated by the disturbance of the deposits caused by our own investigations; but in the process some parts had been salved which would otherwise have been lost, although regrettably some of these had in turn been destroyed through enemy action. The situation was such that rescue action was necessary just as soon as conditions permitted.

2

Operations after World War II

With the end of hostilities, my brother moved back from employment on the army staff to his old career as a civil servant based in London while I was working on the Rhine Army staff in Germany until demobilization in June 1946. With no pre-war career to resume or any opening immediately available, I was able for a limited period to maintain myself on my savings and gratuity on demobilization and to try to complete the excavation and recording of my boat-finds. Support was scant, for I was not in close touch with the re-emergent archaeological establishment; and the Hull Museums' organization was in some disarray following the destruction of their main museum and its collections in 1941 and the death in 1945 of Tom Sheppard, who had been their moving spirit for many years. His successor J. B. Fay and assistant W. B. Southern, however, gave me both moral and practical support albeit with severely limited resources, the main benefit being the regular release of Southern from other duties to join my excavating team which was completed by P. E. Slack, the student son of some old friends (Figure 2.1).

The scene when we began operations had been depressing, as even more of the seaward side of F1 had been washed away since my last rescue of 1943–4. Fortunately most of the parts lost had been covered by records made in 1938. Some 0.6 m of the seaward end of F2 had likewise disappeared, but that too had been recorded in 1940. Much of what

Figure 2.1 Peter Slack and the late Bill Southern, 1946.

remained of F1 was dangerously exposed and liable to further damage or loss especially if subjected to another winter as severe as those of previous years. So during the summer of 1946 the three of us set out to excavate and record what was left of F1 (Figure 2.2) and leave plans for partial or complete removal to be developed after recording was done. We took the view that F2 was less at risk and

Figure 2.2 Fı during the excavations by E. V. Wright with P. E. Slack and W. H. Southern, July–August 1946.

could safely be left for later attention. As a minimal objective we had in mind the recovery of key samples of the remains to illustrate details of construction. When tide and daylight permitted we began work and in the intervals I began to renew contact with the few people I knew who might assist the cause. One of these was C. W. Phillips, with whom we had corresponded during the early years of the war following his excavation of the Sutton Hoo ship and the royal burial deposit contained in it. When he became temporarily free of other commitments I prevailed on him to pay a visit to Ferriby, and on 27 August 1946 he and my small team spent a momentous day working together on the site. This was a major turning point for the whole venture and I cannot write too warmly of the

favourable change in our pitifully weak attack on our formidable task that resulted from his support and influence.

Once it became likely that we might receive a visit from Phillips we had reserved for attention the hitherto unexplored area to the east of the 1937 Dig 2, since this if any was likely to display intact the best preserved features of construction. In the event the results of that day's excavations surpassed our best expectations. First we found that the tapered plank-end located in 1937 did not link up with the northern of the outer bottom-planks but was part of the first strake of the side of the boat and that the angle between it and the transversely flat bottom-structure survived apparently intact (Figure 2.3). This was largely determined by the fact that the tapered

Figure 2.3 Excavation of the western end of F1 with C. W. Phillips on 27 August 1946.

end was shaped most ingeniously with a three-dimensional curvature so as to fill the space between the steep side and the flat bottom while tapering in plan-view down to join with the edge of the keel-plank (Figure 2.4). Not only this, but the western cleat system with its transverse timbers and their fastening wedges was found intact (Figure 2.5). When all had been cleaned ready for recording, Phillips sat on the edge of the excavation trench and pronounced

Figure 2.4 Shaped end of lowest side-strake (S-S1).

Figure 2.5 Intact cleat system.

with great earnestness and authority 'something must be done about this' – and it was!

In preparation for what might follow we made certain critical decisions; the first was to suspend further excavation and cleaning of F1 from which much of the overburden had already been removed, our expectation being that if we were able to lift it intact, final cleaning could be carried out under controlled conditions ashore. The second was to concentrate on making an accurate plan of what was already exposed. While this was going on, Phillips would use his influence to stir the archaeological fraternity into action in support of our small-scale campaign. His first approach (Appx 2.1) was to T. D. Kendrick, then Keeper of the Department of British & Mediaeval Antiquities and later Director of the British Museum, who referred us to H. J. Plenderleith, Keeper of the British Museum Research Laboratory. His second contact was with Sir Geoffrey Callender, the Director of the National Maritime Museum (NMM) at Greenwich. Callender was readily persuaded that the enterprise was one which was of proper concern to Greenwich and sent one of his staff, Reginald Lowen, up to Ferriby to discuss what facilities we might need to effect an immediate rescue operation. With Phillips, Plenderleith, and Lowen, I then laid plans. Greenwich provided access to naval resources which were made available through the agency of the Director of Naval Construction at the Admiralty and through them also to civilian ship repairers who at the time were still operating very much under wartime governmental controls. Where funds were needed Sir James Caird stood behind Callender with his ever-generous financial support of the causes of the NMM. The eventual bills came to a substantial sum and were met without demur. When it became apparent that a powerful winch was required my brother prevailed on the then Deputy Engineer-in-Chief at the War Office to make an army vehicle available through the Central Ordnance Depot at Chilwell. In the event the first that they sent up were a pair of medium artillery gun-tractors which I thought too light for the task, and with willing co-operation they then substituted an immense 'Diamond T' tank-recovery tractor.

Following Phillips's visit and having been coached by him, Slack, Southern, J. B. Fay and I set about making the detailed plan of the visible remains of F1, laying out a metric grid of cords, and plotting co-ordinates at 50 mm intervals with a light square of laths and a plumb line, the results being transcribed on to cartridge paper to a scale of 1:10. Working from west to east, the early results were good and have proved consistent with other records. But we were not sufficiently careful in rechecking our datum from one day's work to another and the eastern parts of the plan show some manifest distortions when compared with the *in situ* photographic evidence (Figure 5.9). The programme then had to await the next period of suitable tides in daylight hours and this enabled us to assemble the team of excavators and support facilities. For archaeological excavation, our local team was augmented by Phillips, Plenderleith, J. W. Brailsford, and William Watson, the last two seconded by Kendrick from the British Museum, and for part of the time my brother was also able to join us. I assumed direction of the enterprise, with Plenderleith providing technical support and Phillips taking responsibility for the excavation of F2 (Figure 2.6) while preparations were made for the extraction of F1. The visitors were all housed at our home in North Ferriby where my mother was helped on the domestic front by Mrs Plenderleith. It should not be forgotten by today's generation that catering in those days involved all the complications of food rationing – no mean problem when it came to feeding a houseful of hungry excavators. An event of note on the first day was the near loss by drowning of Plenderleith, who slipped over a sharp drop in the bank, was carried away by the tide and had to swim ashore, hampered by oilskins and gumboots.

Figure 2.6 Excavation of F2 under Phillips's supervision September 1946 (*L. to R.*: Phillips, Watson, Brailsford, fireman, and Plenderleith).

After much discussion, heart-searching and with direct telegraphed encouragement from Callender (Figure 2.7), the method eventually adopted for the extraction of F1 was to deepen the trenches on either side so as to leave the boat isolated on a plinth of clay (Figure 2.8) and then slice it off complete with the plinth on a steel platform which would then form a sledge which could be dragged up the bank above high-water mark. There it would be possible to work continuously to lighten the load and reinforce and protect the find for transport to Greenwich where detailed cleaning and recording could be carried out and plans made for conservation. It must be recognized that the art of conservation of wet and degraded wood was then in its infancy and Plenderleith's enquiries in Scandinavia and elsewhere had established that the best technique known was immersion in an increasingly concentrated solution of glycerine. It was envisaged that if the find could be extracted intact it would be necessary to build a conservation tank around it; but planning for this was left to wait on events.

The labour of deepening the trenches and constructing the platform was in the hands of a gang from the Globe Engineering and Boilerworks Co. of Hull led by its charge-hand Stan Wilson. They were strong and experienced men and were soon as interested in the work as the archaeological party. The platform was built of quarter-inch steel plates (6.25 mm) bolted together and strengthened by inverted T-section stringers (Figure 2.9). We realized that it would be desirable to reduce the friction and ease the passage of the platform through the plinth and to this end a slab of half-inch (12.5 mm) plate was provided, which was to be pulled through

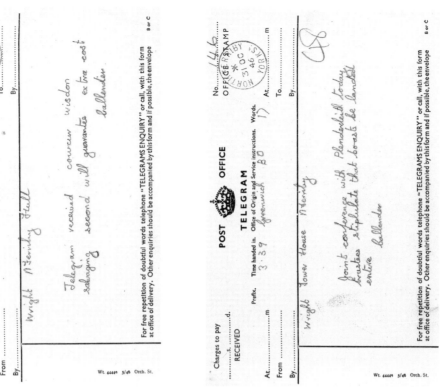

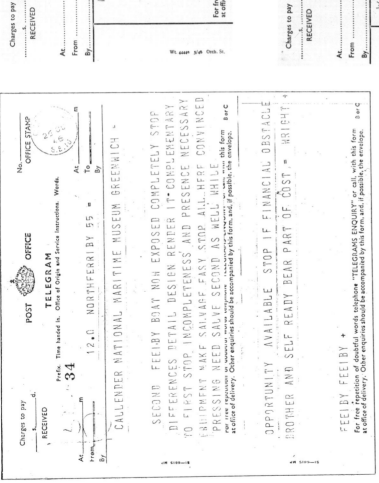

Figure 2.7 Telegrams to and from Sir Geoffrey Callender, Director of the National Maritime Museum, authorizing the lifting of F2 and urging entire rather than piecemeal extraction of F1.

Figure 2.8 F1 on plinth.

Figure 2.9 Construction of the platform for lifting of F1.

before moving the platform itself. A spreader of two-inch (50 mm) diameter steel bar was also prepared to ensure that the loop of cable attached to the front of the platform did not foul the plinth. Finally a bent 'prow-piece' was made ready for bolting to the nose of the platform after insertion so that it could ride up out of the trench. The tractor could not be brought along the strand in order to give a direct, straight pull from SSE to WNW along the axis of the boat. The nearest point of access was on made-up ground in the area of the old brickyard some 50 m north of the flood-bank in a position which required a ground anchor for a block round which cable could be passed to give a pull in the required direction. To secure the anchor a slab of half-inch steel plate was driven into the bank to reinforce one of the piles of the old brickyard landing (Figure 2.10). The strong man of the Globe squad, whose name was Tommy, drove the plate in with a 28 lb. sledge hammer which

came to be known among us as 'Tommy's Toffee Hammer' when he demonstrated his capacity to use it with one hand! Steel wire rope of two-inch (50 mm) circumference was prepared for the pull. The final technical preparation was the provision of pressure water hoses for clearing silt from the excavation trenches. The local fire service was contacted and in those carefree days attended daily with a mobile pump under the guise of a 'training exercise', another of the many facilities available at no cost to the project (Figure 2.11). For the benefit of any future excavation it should be mentioned that the experiments which we made in using hoses to remove clay and expose timber were unsuccessful, as the pressure was altogether too violent and tended to blast away wood, if anything more easily than clay.

The first pull was applied to the plate designed to cut ahead of the platform but it proved impossible to control and as it tended

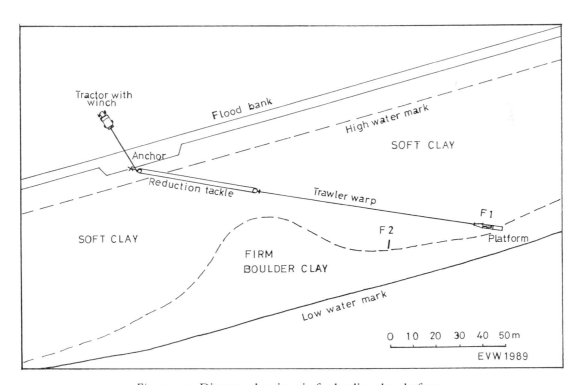

Figure 2.10 Diagram showing rig for hauling the platform.

Figure 2.11 Hosing new silt from excavation trenches of F2; H. J. Plenderleith assisting firemen.

to ride up and risk slicing into the boat its use was abandoned. The tackle was then switched on to the platform itself, and when all was ready the first trial pull was made using an arrangement of double blocks up against the anchor so as to give a 2:1 reduction between tractor and tow, whereupon the two-inch steel wire rope promptly parted. The Globe party then decided that what was needed was a 3.5-inch (87.5 mm) 'trawler warp' and concluded that one could be borrowed from 'Mr 'udson' of the Hull trawling firm of Hudson Brothers. This proved to be the case and their truck duly turned up on the following day with this massive rope: the only problem was laying it out on the then very slippery bank, a task which required the work of all hands, including the archaeologists. The first test showed that the rope was of ample strength and the platform was moved up to the edge of the plinth. When the extra load was applied as it began cutting into the clay, the spreader-bar folded up like a hairpin but the bridle just cleared the boat timbers and no damage was done. The pull then continued but after the leading edge had penetrated nearly half-way

under the boat the plinth began to show signs of breaking up. We continued very slowly, but with the tide turning and a rising easterly breeze behind it, time was running out: I could not risk the possibility of rough water carrying away the already disturbed boat from its bed. I therefore decided to saw off the western part of the boat and drag the platform through to the plane of the cut so that the leading edge could be exposed and the steel prow bolted in place for the haul out of the trench and then up the bank. This was one of the hardest decisions of my life and when I had completed the cut, according to one eyewitness, I laid my head on the boat and wept. All this took time, and the rising tide was lapping the seaward end of the platform before we could resume pulling. From then on it was a race with the tide and later with darkness. As the blocks closed on each other the reduction-tackle had to be let out four or five times before the platform was drawn up to high-water mark. A dozen or more heavy deal planks on which the platform had been erected had to be recovered in case they were washed against the boat, and by then it was fully dark and all hands were quite exhausted. We had not prepared for work in the dark but fortunately the local constabulary who had come down to help keep the spectators in order – and in particular out of danger from breaking cables – carried torches so that as best we could we secured everything for the night. It was an epic day and full of lessons for anyone attempting any similar makeshift recovery operation, which in our case had come close to complete disaster. The following morning I was early on the scene; but only a few minutes ahead of the first souvenir hunters. As soon as possible therefore I organized the piecemeal removal of the disturbed fragments to the security of my home where they were covered with wet sacking in an attempt to reduce drying and shrinkage. The trawler-warp was recovered and returned to its owners and the platform and other tackle removed; but for years afterwards the strand was littered with fragments of rusted wire cable, shackles and other abandoned metal. In 1984 I could still identify part of the prow plate, and the slab of plate driven into the bank for the anchor can still be seen as the last remaining memorial of the event which had cost us so much effort and anguish.

While all this was going on, Phillips and the archaeologists had been excavating F2 so as to expose it for recording and thereafter removal. During the excavation several finds were made of rudimentary structures of roundwood poles near and under the southern end of the plank (Figures 2.12 and 2.13). Nearby a single wooden artefact was found which was thought to be some sort of tool used in the stitching process (Figure 7.15a). On the surface of the plank another artefact was obtained in the form of part of a roughly conical sinker or weight of baked clay (Figure 7A4). The southern end of F2 to a length of 0.6 m having been carried away and lost at some unknown date between 1943 and 1946, otherwise the plank was found to be in good condition and, aided by judicious hosing of

the excavation trench to remove silt, the excavation was carried through without serious problems to the point where the majority of the clay round it was removed to reveal all main features, detailed cleaning of the wood being left until later (Figure 2.14). Removal of clay near the remains was done with the hands rather than tools in the interests of safety. The results were measured by Plenderleith and myself and then drawn and photographed on 26 October 1946. The drawing (Figure 2.15) was a tolerably accurate plan of the upper surface and the various features on it, but recorded only such features as were visible. One general error was the assumption that all the stitch-holes were of oval section similar to but smaller than those observed at the southern end whereas later detailed cleaning revealed that all but the southern four or five in each side were of square section. A similar error had been made concerning those in F1. What we did not appreciate at the time was that there was a significant degree of bending or curvature fore-and-aft in each of the two parts of the plank and we did not record the profile *in situ*. The significance of this, as described in Chapter 5, did not emerge for many years afterwards.

The near disaster with F1 had taken place when suitable tides in daylight were already occurring too late in the day to be practicable for continued working on the bank. The next satisfactory period came round two weeks later. Several days were also needed for clearing up after the removal of F1. It was apparent however that any attempt to lift intact each of the two separate parts of F2, divided as they were at the central scarf, entailed unacceptable risks. It was therefore decided to cut each half of the plank into pieces of length convenient for lifting and manhandling up the bank. A suitable wooden stretcher was prepared for carrying them and in the event removal presented no serious problems other than the fact that the combined weight of the stretcher and each of the slabs of waterlogged wood was

Figure 2.12 Structures of roundwood stakes encountered just west of F2 during excavation.

Figure 2.13 c. 90 mm–diameter trimmed log under southern end of F2.

Figure 2.14 F2 on completion of excavation.

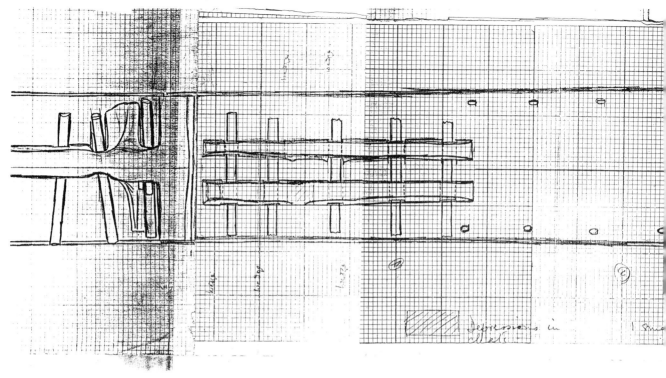

Figure 2.15 Part of *in situ* plan of F2 measured and drawn by Plenderleith and the author on completion of excavation.

Figure 2.16 Key diagram of pieces of F1 delivered to the National Maritime Museum in October 1946, including those stored at the author's home between 1939 and 1943.

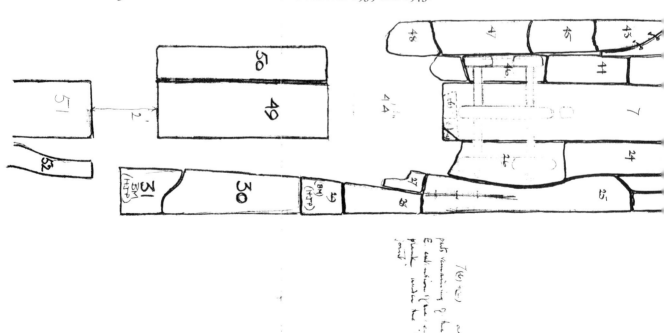

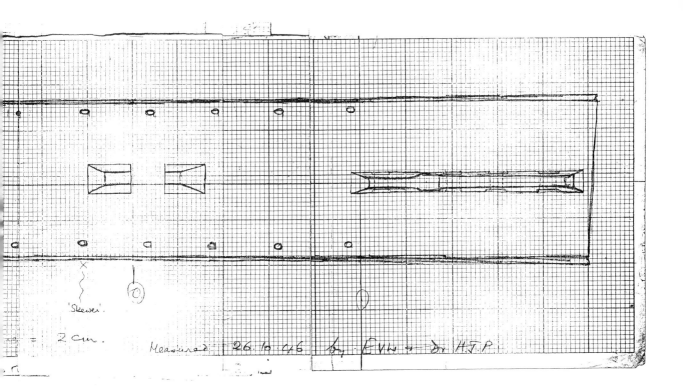

'Skewer'.

⊢ = 2 cm.

Measured 26.10.46 by EVW & Dr HTP.

FERRIBY.

MAJOR TIMBERS.

E.V.W.   5. NOV. 46.

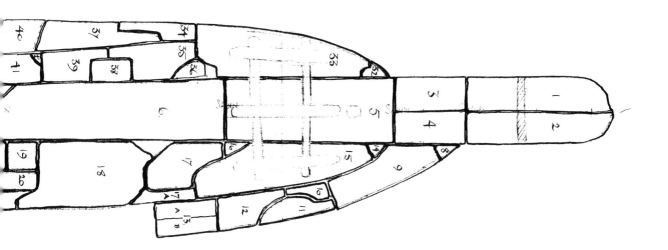

quite as much as eight strong men could lift and carry up the slippery foreshore.

Meanwhile, calamity had struck at the National Maritime Museum when on 6 November 1946 Sir Geoffrey Callender had collapsed and died in the museum. It is not a reflection on those of his staff who were left to say that our enterprise thereafter was handicapped by the loss of his drive and authority. Plans for transport to Greenwich however went ahead without delay. Before loading, I prepared key diagrams of the parts of each boat which were marked with numbers embossed on zinc garden-labels nailed to the wood (Figure 2.16). I also cut full-sized patterns of all pieces out of bitumen-coated paper so that the actual parts would not need to be moved more frequently than necessary when reassembling the remains. Wood-wool was provided free by the Hull firm of timber merchants Horsley Smith to pad the beds of the three trucks made available by the Admiralty for transport to Greenwich, and when all was ready the convoy set off, shepherded by myself in my own car which just staggered to London having run three out of four big-end bearings in its engine. On arrival the timbers were offloaded on level ground alongside the Neptune Hall where the Bargehouse now stands, and with the aid of a party of warders I soon laid them out in their correct order for recording, the piece of the lowest side-strake and the upturned end of the keel-plank being propped up to approximately the correct angle with dunnage and wedges. It was at this time that the shapely carved cleat and lengthwise grooves under the tip of the keel-plank were first recorded (Figure 4.6). The first complete plan was drawn to a scale of 1:16; but this was found to be too small for easy resolution of lines and a second plan was then built up on squared paper to a scale of 1:8. Profile and section drawings were made as well as representations of the rays and growth rings of the wood to illustrate the position in the log from which the planks had been hewn. The quality of the many photographs which I took was marred by problems of development in an unheated darkroom during the bitterly cold winter that followed. Some photographs of good quality but of somewhat generalized aspects were taken by the museum's photographer (Figure 2.17). During the cleaning process a number of interesting and clear toolmarks were revealed and two sets in particular, one on F_1 and the other on F_2 (Figures 2.18 and 2.19) were recorded by means of plaster casts which regrettably disappeared from the care of the museum at some time in subsequent years.

Most of my records were completed before the end of the year, survived loss on a London Underground train and were recovered from the Lost Property Office at Baker Street; but during late November and early December there were severe frosts which did no good to the unprotected wood as it lay in the open at Greenwich. A few weeks of damp and warmer weather followed but by mid-January 1947 there was a further cold spell and a little snow. During this time I paid a further visit to fill in a few gaps in the photographic record and the frost can be seen in the photographs (Figure 2.20). At the end of January there followed one of the coldest spells ever recorded in this century and this persisted until early March, which exacerbated the degradation of the wood. Unfortunately there were delays in the procurement of suitable tanks for conservation and it was not until June 1947 that the wood was committed to the conservation processes. From then the steeping procedure went forward in increasingly strong concentrations of glycerine but the tanks were uncovered and, not surprisingly, in hot weather the smells that came off were disagreeable. Plenderleith at the British Museum remained in touch with G. P. B. Naish, who was by then in charge of operations at Greenwich, and continued to monitor the process of conservation using two sample pieces taken from the northern of the two outer bottom planks. After several years the state of the contents of the tanks had

Figure 2.17 F1 reassembled at Greenwich: note especially the wavy edges of the keel-plank with the outer bottom-planks trimmed to fit. (*Photo:* NMM, Greenwich.)

become so unpleasant that the trustees gave instructions that the timbers be removed and the tanks drained and dismantled. The con-

dition of the pieces of F1 was less satisfactory than those of F2 and the latter in any case represented a more tractable artefact. The

Figure 2.18 Toolmarks recorded on F1: squared outlines c. 25 mm across.

Figure 2.19 The only measurable toolmark recorded on F2: consistent with the scar left by an axe with curved, double-bevelled edge c. 75 mm broad.

Figure 2.20 The end of S-S1 in F1 showing the flange and signs of frost on the surface, winter 1946–7.

decision was therefore taken to coat the pieces of F2 with a specially prepared epoxy-resin-based varnish devised by Plenderleith to protect the glycerine-impregnated wood from the atmosphere and more particularly from moisture. Each separate piece was then placed in a substantial glass-topped wooden case with the idea that they might be available for viewing by the public. Orders were given that what was left of F1 should be disposed of, but happily Naish thought otherwise and contrary to instructions stored away the more substantial pieces in the basement of the museum where they survived until attitudes changed and adequate research facilities became available. Moreover the pieces treated in the British Museum Research Laboratory also escaped destruction and have been returned to join the remainder of F1 in the museum's reserve collection. After 1947 my own connection with the finds had lapsed as I tackled the learning phase of a career in industry.

It was not until the 1960s that I found out that most of the pieces of F1 had been discarded and it was not until I became a Trustee of the National Maritime Museum in 1972 that I was informed that some had survived. This was of course a better outcome than I had at one time feared; the utmost credit is due to Naish for his insubordination, since what survived of F1 has provided much important information and especially material for dating and the study of the production of planks from tree-trunks. Nevertheless the state of the pieces of both finds is a sorry one since the wood is much shrunken and cracked and in neither case suitable for public display.

APPENDIX 2.1

9. Madingley Road,
Cambridge,
August 28th, 1946.

Dear Kendrick:-

I want to present you with a few remarkable facts and learn your reaction to them. In the last two days I have been down at North Ferriby on the north shore of the Humber five miles upstream from Hull looking at the two boats which C. W. and E. V. Wright of that place began to examine in 1939 and had to abandon because of the war. C. W. has now gone into the War Office, but E. V. is having a longish spell of leave after demobilisation and is now having another crack at the problem.

I knew something about the boats from the short preliminary notice given in Antiquity, 1939, p. 349 and had been in correspondence with the excavators, but had not seen for myself. Yesterday I worked like a black between the tides and exposed some of the most vital parts of one of the boats as well as studying the conditions in which they rest in Humber mud, etc. etc. Without getting unduly excited I can now say that it will be a most unfortunate matter if the better preserved of the two boats is not got out whole, pickled, and kept as a real treasure of the country's archaeology. The wood is in pretty good shape considering that it must have been in situ for at least 2000 years, and a large lump has not shown undue shrinkage after being on the floor of a greenhouse at the Wrights' place for seven years with no treatment or extra dampness.

The technical details of the boat are astounding, and are all perfectly preserved. The fundamental feature is an immense keel plank running from one end to the other, about 2 feet wide and at least three inches thick. It swerves up markedly towards each end and has not been bent but dug out to this shape. It is supported on each side by two other flat planks of the same thickness which makes a chevron joint with it on each side. These joints are caulked with moss and are covered on the inside of the boat by long battens of split oak which are tied down to their work by the great yew wood stitches which are the only general means of holding the planks together employed. There is, however, a special device for bracing the three bottom planks together, and that is in the form of strong wooden bars run through trios of large parallel cleats cut out of the solid plank (see sketch).

At least three strakes were raised from this composite bottom, and by a great piece of good fortune one of these, the first, is still in place, and all its junction details at the forward end are perfectly preserved. It is this part of the boat which, in default of any other, *must* be preserved. The plank is an amazing piece of cutting, swerving in to tumble home against the bottom with a sweep like a ploughshare. This beautiful curve has been cut out of the solid, and the second and third strakes must have done the same at each end, one, two, and three being in turn each longer than the other.

This boat is a most remarkable transitional vessel between the dug-out and the clinker built boat, and I know of nothing at all like it except the Hjortspring boat which is quite a minor thing compared with this monster. No associated finds have been made, but although the boat is probably Iron Age I see no obvious reason why it should not belong to the Bronze Age.

The other boat is, or was, of much the same type, but has certain strange features such as the use of two pieces of plank butted together to make the fundamental keel, and also a different and probably more accomplished type of edge-to-edge joint for the planks. This second boat seems to me to be close to some ancient pier or dock, for I can see very suspicious pile ends poking out of the mud.

Do you think that there is any hope of getting the first boat out in one piece? It will be a big job, but much bigger have been successfully accomplished, and in its present state with much of its stern (or bow?) gone and almost all the upper strakes absent it is not more formidable than a big dug-out, and nothing like such a monster as the late Brigg boat, though of course its character is less massive, and it would want a lot of support in being moved.

I do not suppose that there is any money for anything, but I am sure that if this was found on the shores of Denmark no effort or expense would be spared to get it into Copenhagen. It would certainly be a most remarkable relic of ship-building – in fact, the most interesting in European prehistory as far as my knowledge goes.

Would it be possible for Plenderleith to go down and make an examination and report? He would be very hospitably entertained by the Wrights who are most charming and cultured people full of every kind of creditable interest.

I am no engineer, but I think I could see how the thing could be moved along the mud to a road which terminates at a little beach about a quarter of a mile to the west.

You will pardon me for feeling very strongly about this matter, but I think you can trust me not to let you down, or to give a gross overestimate of the importance of this boat.

If you want to see me I can come to Town. Is it any good approaching South Kensington, the Office of Works, and the National Nautical Museum?

Yours sincerely

C. W. Phillips

3

Boat 3 and later developments

The sequence of events leading up to the finding of the third Ferriby boat-fragment F3 goes back to the early 1950s. It was in 1951 that Willard Libby's revolutionary process was announced for the absolute dating of organic materials by calculating the extent of decay of their content of the radioactive isotope of carbon, C14, and the British Museum Research Laboratory was one of the first institutions in this country to be equipped with the facilities to effect determinations. It was natural that my brother and I were eager to resolve the uncertainty about the age of the boat-finds as soon as possible; but capacity at the British Museum was limited and demand was high. It was therefore several years before Plenderleith consented to accept Ferriby material for dating. One of the initial problems was that only material uncontaminated by preservatives was then eligible for processing and this immediately disqualified all the wood of F1 and F2, which had by then been impregnated with glycerine. I therefore set about trying to find fresh material from the site which could without question be related to one or other of the boats. In 1953 I was able to locate an area some 10 m to the south-west of the excavation trench from which F1 had been lifted, which yielded among other debris a regular supply of typical pieces of the oak sealing laths used for covering the seams. Quite incidentally it also produced numerous short lengths of twin-strand cord of a type represented previously by only one small frag-

ment found in the neighbourhood of F2 in 1946. I delivered a sufficient quantity of sealing lath to the Research Laboratory in 1955 and thereafter waited in high expectation for the results of the determination. This came in 1958 (Figure 3.1) and to our amazement set the age of the material at 750 ± 150 BC (BM58), or somewhere in the middle of the local Late Bronze Age. The date was the more remarkable because a number of prominent archaeologists had been sceptical of my earlier deduction from association with what was known of comparable deposits and their arte-factual contents that the boats dated from the pre-Roman Iron Age. Indeed Sir Lindsay Scott, the President of the Prehistoric Society, had argued strenuously in the discussion following my lecture to the society in 1947 that the boats hailed from what were then known as the 'Dark Ages' now termed the 'Early Mediaeval' period. In fact the new date, even allowing for due caution in building on a single isolated determination from timber probably but not absolutely certainly derived from a Ferriby boat, made better sense of the stratigraphical sequence and such artefacts from the site as were broadly datable than did attribution to the Early Iron Age. Nevertheless an indication of so great an age for constructions of such complexity was a startling development.

For the next few years I did little to pursue the study of the boats beyond paying occasional visits to inspect the site, finding

Research Laboratory,
British Museum,
LONDON, W.C.1.
13 Nov 1959

Dear Mr. Wright

    The result of the radiocarbon dating measurement on
your sample ref. BM58   is given on the attached report
form.   The age is in years before present time and is based
on a value of 5568 ± 30 years for the half-life of carbon 14.
The error term has the significance of a standard deviation.

    The result is released for your immediate use and
publication but on the understanding that it will also form
part of date lists from this laboratory which will be published from time to time in the British Museum Quarterly and
the Radiocarbon Supplement of the American Journal of Science.

    The latter journal is now the recognised central organ
of publication for all results from dating laboratories, and
its editors require the results to be prepared in a standard
form.   In order to facilitate the preparation of results for
this publication, our report has been set out in the form of
a questionnaire, and I should be very grateful if you would
supply the additional information required by completing items
NoS, 3 — 9 inclusive.   on the duplicate copy of the
form and returning it to the above address.

        Yours faithfully,

        Harold Barker

E.V. Wright Esq.
FRESHFIELD
ELLOUGHTON - BROUGH   For KEEPER, RESEARCH LABORATORY
EAST YORKSHIRE.

Figure 3.1 Letter reporting the result of the first radio-carbon determination and demonstrating that the boats dated from the Bronze Age.

conditions for examining the peat and estuarine clays generally much less favourable
than previously. Early in 1963 I had spent
some weeks on a business trip to the Indian
sub-continent when during spare periods I
missed no opportunity of visiting places where
some of the most notable examples of conservative boatbuilding practice in the world
still survived in everyday use. As a result of
this stimulus I began to speculate about the
spread of primitive techniques in both time
and place. On my return I found East Yorkshire still in the grip of another of the severest
winters on record and when the thaw eventually came in mid-March I perceived that conditions for observation were likely to be better

than of late. Finding that the tide was also favourable, on a Sunday afternoon I felt impelled to take some of my family down to Ferriby to see what could be seen. The bank was too muddy for my youngest son of four years old, but I was able to reach the clean stretch of clay near low water with his seven-year-old brother. When we reached the area from which samples had been obtained for radio-carbon determination nearly a decade earlier, I saw two converging alignments of cut or broken withy stitches protruding 15–25 mm above the surface of the clay. This phenomenon could only mean the presence of planks beneath the surface and I asked my son to stand still until I could tell him where to put his feet without treading on the evidence. A minimum of trowelling revealed the edges of planks under the clay and the apparent outside limits of the find; and a quantity of metal rods conveniently available on the foreshore were collected to mark its outline. On our way home we called at the house in North Ferriby of J. E. Bartlett, the Director of Hull Museums, to report the find which he promptly went to see for himself before the tide covered it. During the following two weeks he and I concerted plans for its excavation and recovery. Our excavating team was drawn mainly from the East Riding Archaeological Society reinforced by additional acquaintances (Figure 3.2). The engineering side was largely catered for *ex gratia* by Priestman Brothers Ltd of Hull, not least by the provision of a powerful 'Caribou' mobile crane and winch.

Figure 3.2 Excavating F2 in April 1963 (*L. to R.*: Bartlett, Naish, Mackey, Binns, Daae, Spalding, and author). (Photo: *Yorkshire Post*.)

Figure 3.3 F3 isolated on plinth of clay with temporary supports to prevent planks sagging outwards. (*Photo:* Allen Binns.)

Having painful recollections of the experience with F1 in 1946, I had argued strenuously in favour of piecemeal extraction of the new find in sections small enough to be manhandled, but eventually I yielded to persuasion that an attempt should be made to remove in a single lift the main part of the fragment consisting of two planks joined together for some 5 m of their length. The plan adopted was to clear the remains so that they were isolated on a plinth of clay as had been done with F1 (Figure 3.3), but then to build a rigid cage of tubular steel scaffolding around and under the boat-fragment which would be supported by plywood sheeting inside the framework (Figure 3.4). The cage was designed to be strong enough to be hauled bodily from its bed, winched up to high-tide

line to bring it within reach of the crane, and lifted on to a waiting truck for transport to a prepared holding tank in the storage area of Hull Museums. There it could be kept submerged in water and available for detailed cleaning and recording pending arrangements for long-term conservation.

The initial excavation yielded several interesting features, the first of which was that the planks represented were part of an outer bottom-plank of shape similar to those in F1, together with the related part of a lowest side-strake which differed from its counterpart in F1 in that the hollowed-out end was finished with a sharp internal angle instead of the rounded section of the earlier find. Nearly half of the length of the outer bottom-plank consisted of a long splinter still in place but

Figure 3.4 F3 in tubular scaffolding 'cage' (*L. to R.:* Bartlett, Cutts). (*Photo:* Allen Binns.)

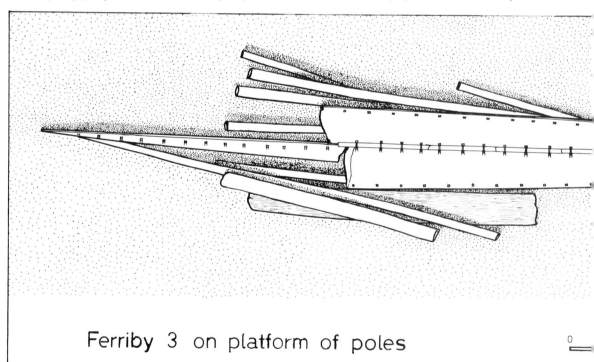

Ferriby 3 on platform of poles

Figure 3.5 F3 *in situ* on 'hard' of roundwood poles.

no longer attached to the remainder, having apparently been chopped off in antiquity. The fragment of boat had been laid on a prepared bed of poles or 'hard', evidently to prevent it sinking into the mud (Figure 3.5). At a distance of c. 1.0 m from the eastern end careful excavation also revealed a complex of twisted material, some of it of cords and some a loop of withy including a recognizable knot or lock (Figure 7.16). Both the cut-off splinter of outer bottom-plank and the loop complex were lifted out separately by hand and, after three days of increasingly toilsome work as the surroundings became ever softer and more puddled, work began on the construction of the scaffolding cage. A trial pull was made towards the end of the fifth day and the cage and its contents were dragged half-way up the ramp prepared to ease the path out of the excavation trench. As the tide came up, a

vertical scaffold tube was attached to the structure to give some warning to passing river traffic that there was an obstruction in the channel. As tide fell the following morning the marker was found to have been bent over, doubtless by a blow from a barge passing over it (Figure 3.4). After that the haul up the strand was achieved without incident until the final stages when the silt surface of the strand gave way to shingle and the angle steepened. This disturbed the cradle containing the boat but not, in the view of those in charge, dangerously so. That they were wrong was soon demonstrated when the cradle opened during the vertical lift and a number of fragments of the boat timbers were deposited on the ground. None however were lost and all were transported quickly to the holding tank.

While the necessarily rapid and at times drastic programme of excavation and extraction took place, we had not overlooked the need to secure material for at least a minimal study of the relationship between the boat remains and the surrounding sediments with a view to more precise dating than had been achieved in 1946. To this end help was sought from the Department of Quaternary Research at Cambridge, and its founder and head Sir Harry Godwin FRS sent one of his staff, D. M. Churchill, to Ferriby to participate in the exercise. Churchill was able to procure most of the samples necessary for his studies and returned with them to Cambridge. His report on these was incorporated with the author's in a joint article published in the Proceedings of the Prehistoric Society (Wright and Churchill 1965). Before dating-material from the boat itself could be provided after its removal to Hull, the expected problem had arisen of preventing the development of deleterious or obnoxious organisms in the holding tank. An organic compound preservative was added to the water, thereby disqualifying all wood so treated from acceptance for radio-carbon assay. It was only subsequently that the Cambridge laboratory developed methods of 'washing' ancient

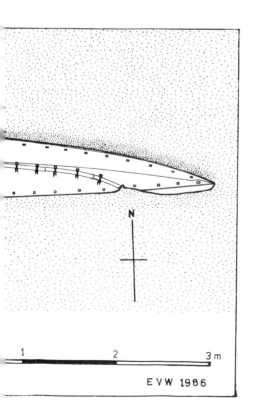

1   2   3 m

EVW 1986

Figure 3.6   F3 after tide fell when haulage from excavation trench half completed. (*Photo: Allen Binns.*)

organic material to remove such preservatives.

During the succeeding weeks, I was able to spend sufficient time at the museum to make scale drawings of the pieces of F3 and assemble them into a complete plan of the remains. Sections were recorded at convenient breaks and a profile representation drawn, but still working as in 1946 on the assumption that the outer bottom-plank had been flat fore-and-aft. The museum staff meanwhile had completed the washing of the fragments and photographing toolmarks where they were preserved. A novel detail which emerged at this stage was the discovery that in the vee of the groove cut in the outer edge of the outer bottom-plank there was bedded a twin-strand cord of fibres similar to the fragments found in the immediate area since 1953 and the single small piece noted during the excavation of F2 in 1946 (Figures 3.7 a and b). This had evidently been inserted as part of the caulking procedure in combination with the wadded moss familiar from F1 in which caulking rope had not been used. Another significant observation was the complete absence in F3 of any trace of cleats in the positions on the surface

Figure 3.7a Cord of fibres of hair moss used for caulking in F3.

Figure 3.7b Cord in place in seam in F3. (*Photo:* Hull Museums.)

of the outer bottom-plank, where by analogy with F1 and F2 they might have been expected to occur.

In due course arrangements were made by Hull Museums in co-operation with Dr R. M. Organ of the British Museum Research Laboratory to procure apparatus and facilities to conserve the fragments of timber by impregnation with polyethylene glycol (PEG). A start was made with pieces of the long splinter, on the justifiable grounds that it was of less structural significance than the main parts of the planks which had been fastened together when found, the seam between them having

been complete with caulking, stitches, and sealing laths. The programme of impregnation was monitored by Organ and in its latter days, acting on his advice, additional heating was applied to accelerate the driving off of the remaining moisture. This experiment was in the event unsuccessful since the timbers so treated became severely distorted; the remaining pieces of the main planks were in due course processed at the original slower pace and emerged several years later stabilized without serious distortion. A representative sample is displayed in the Hull Town Docks Museum and the remainder held in reserve

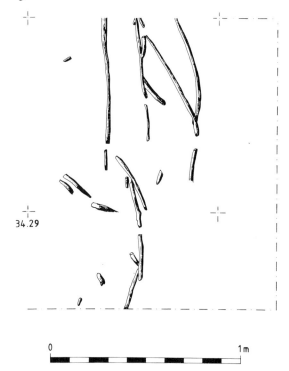

34.29

```
0 ▰▰▰▰▰▰▰▰ 1m
```

Figure 3.8 Structure of roundwood stakes to north of F2 excavated by ARC, Greenwich, samples of which showed a radio-carbon age contemporary with that of the boats. (NMM, Greenwich.)

storage at the National Maritime Museum at Greenwich.

Since the 1960s work on the site has taken two principal forms: several seasons of organized excavation by the Archaeological Research Centre of the National Maritime Museum; and fairly regular observations by colleagues and myself of the surface of the deposits as and when tide and erosion have produced favourable conditions. The former were directed to the recovery of evidence of the environmental conditions prevailing around the boat remains at the time of abandonment and submergence and extended to the investigation of the traces of a somewhat flimsy structure of roundwood (Figure 3.8) observed from 1946 onwards immediately to the north of F2 (McGrail 1983). This programme was less fruitful than might have

been hoped in terms of structures positively identified but yielded worthwhile evidence for interpretation of the ancient environment. Samples of roundwood from the structure were subjected to radio-carbon assay and yielded dates consistent with the range for the

Figure 3.9 F4 *in situ.*

Figure 3.10 Replica of western part of F1 in the Archaeological Gallery at the National Maritime Museum. (*Photo:* NMM, Greenwich.)

boat material itself. The writer's own searching has yielded small finds of perishable wooden material from the estuarine clay at least one of which can be associated confidently with the boats and which collectively add to the assemblage of boat-related debris from the same stratigraphical horizon.

Subsequently, in November 1984, I found and recovered from a position 150 m to the west of F2 a short length of plank which has the appearance of being a broken part of a wash-strake from an ancient boat (Figure 3.9). It displays several interesting features of relevance for the reconstruction of a Ferriby boat. Radio-carbon dating suggests that it could be as much as one thousand years later than the middle date accepted for Ferriby 1, 2, and 3. Interpretation of the fragment and its possible connection with the other three, as well as the dating implications if F4 does indeed belong to the same group, are covered in the appropriate later chapters, as are the other smaller finds.

Intermittent work on the boat-remains themselves was also undertaken by the Archaeological Research Centre. The most important has been dendrochronological study of the timber, by Jennifer Hillam of Sheffield University, from which tree-ring curves have been developed of the oak logs used for making the planks and more detailed estimates made of the relationships between planks and parent logs than my own superficial records in 1946. The significance of these studies is set out in Chapter 6. Otherwise there has been some examination of the method of stitching by the museum's staff and by the writer which is also treated later. At the time of writing the by now sadly decayed remnants of F1, the somewhat better preserved pieces of F2, and the stable but not fully reconstructed fragments of F3 are all held in the reserve collection of the National Maritime Museum, Greenwich, the last having been generously transferred there from Hull so that the whole assemblage could be available in one place for future reference. F4 is still going through the process of conservation. The main impetus has been towards the ordering and study of the contemporary records of excavation and post-excavation work in the interest of deriving from them the maximum information now obtainable for the preparation of the most reliable and informative representations of the finds. Some of this has already been applied to the construction of a replica of a large part of F1 as it might have appeared in an excavation setting in 1946 (Figure 3.10), and this has been on display in the Archaeological Gallery of the NMM since 1978 with a number of related exhibits to demonstrate details of construction, hypotheses for reconstruction and, by no means least, the problems associated with excavation and recovery of very large artefacts from a situation such as the muddy shore of a fast-flowing tidal estuary.

By way of postscript to this chapter, after the text was in the hands of the publishers I paid my customary visit of inspection to the site on 6 April 1989 in company with Mrs V. H. Fenwick, Chairman of the Committee for Nautical Archaeology of the Council for

Figure 3.11 F5: fragment of a cleat similar to but larger than those in F1 and F2, found by Mrs Valerie Fenwick in April 1989 c. 50m north-west of F2.

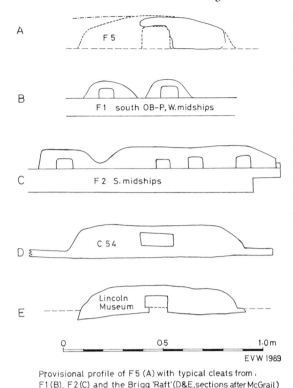

A   F 5

B   F 1   south OB–P, W.midships

C   F 2   S.midships

D   C 54

E   Lincoln Museum

0   0.5   1.0 m

EVW 1989

Provisional profile of F 5 (A) with typical cleats from :
F 1 (B), F 2 (C) and the Brigg 'Raft' (D&E, sections after McGrail)

Figure 3.12 F5: measured drawing of F5 with other cleats for comparison.

British Archaeology. Aside from examining any effects of winter erosion, our purpose was also to obtain information to support a submission for having the site scheduled for its better protection. Our scan was fruitful when Mrs Fenwick spotted a piece of worked timber which on excavation, lifting, and cleaning proved to be a detached fragment of a cleat presumably broken away from a plank similar to those in F1 and F2 (F3 has no trace of cleats). The cleat (Figure 3.11), now referred to as F5, would have been somewhat larger than any in the earlier finds and the transverse hole is estimated to have been nearly twice as wide and high as those in F1 (Figure 3.12). The fragment is being recorded and investigated at the National Maritime Museum, Greenwich and a report will be published as soon as studies are complete. It lay much further up the strand than any of the previous finds and therefore higher and presumably later in the deposits. It will be interesting to see how this is reflected when its age has been determined.

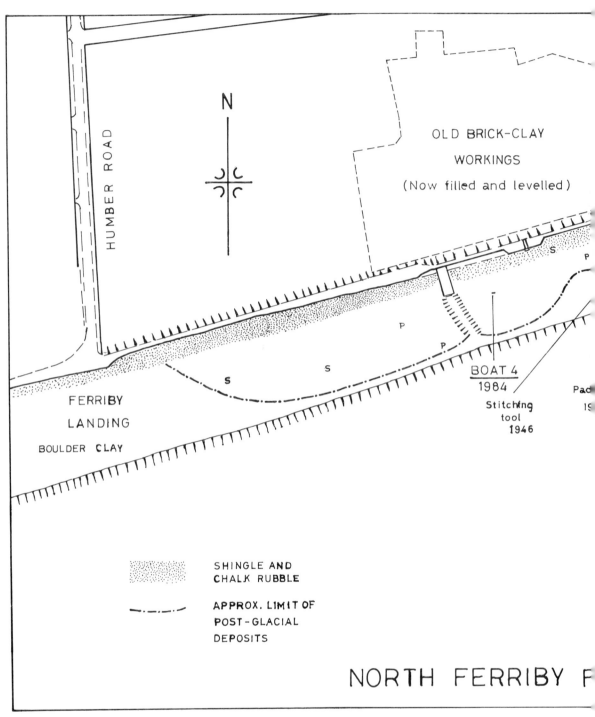

Figure 4.1 Site-plan showing locations of all recorded finds.

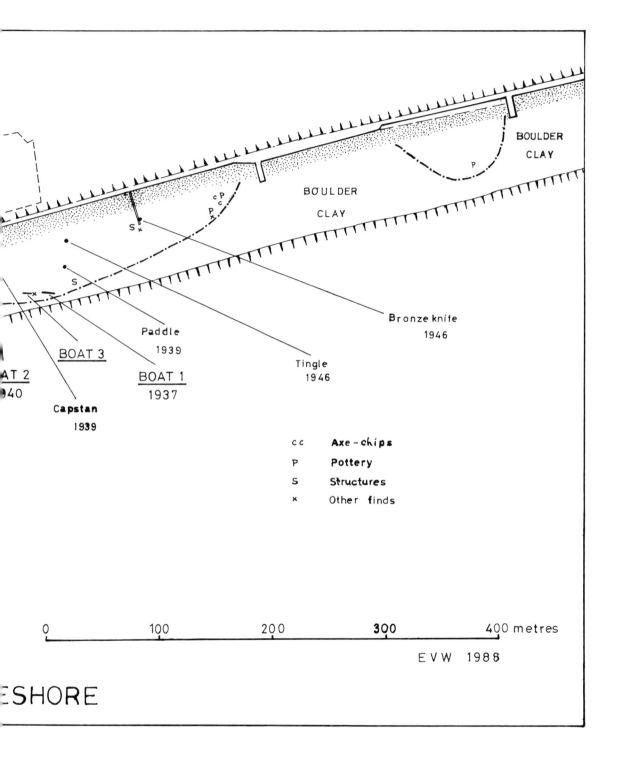

BOULDER
CLAY

BOULDER
CLAY

Bronze knife
1946

Paddle
1939

BOAT 3

AT 2
40

BOAT 1
1937

Capstan
1939

Tingle
1946

c c	**Axe-chips**
P	**Pottery**
S	**Structures**
×	Other finds

0   100   200   300   400 metres

EVW 1988

ESHORE

4

Description of the boat-finds

As the account in the three preceding chapters has shown, parts of three boats had been found in what appeared, superficially at any rate, to be a single homogeneous deposit of estuarine sediment and in close proximity to each other (Figure 4.1) with a fourth somewhat further away. The evidence that they could not have been parts of a single or only two boats is discussed later in this chapter. Using the descriptive terminology adopted for the preliminary reports (see glossary) the components represented are:

– two keel-planks (F1 and F2)
– three outer bottom-planks (F1 and F3)
– two lowest side-strakes (F1 and F3)
– a wash-strake of alder (*Alnus*) (F4)

The planks in F1 are shown in diagrammatic plan-view in Figure 4.2, and the three in plan-view together in Figure 4.3, from which it will be seen that all were fragmentary. All the planks recorded, except F4, were of oak (*Quercus*). The detailed description that follows will concentrate on F1, which was the most complete of the three finds, and then go on to explain ways in which F2 and F3 differed

from the first. Since there is no way of determining with certainty which were the bows and which the sterns of the boats – indeed it will be argued later that they were in fact more or less equal-ended – I have adopted the points of the compass for the direction in which they lay *in situ* to indicate relative positions of features. The descriptions are heavily dependent on the illustrative drawings, photographs being provided to validate the reliability of the drawings and to illustrate the texture and surface finish of the timber and fastenings. They cannot unfortunately recall adequately the qualities of workmanship observed by the few of us who over the years worked on them or saw them on first exposure from their surrounding matrix of clay and before further degradation occurred.

F1

The find (Figure 4.4) consisted of a nearly complete bottom-structure, the eastern ends of all three component planks being missing when first observed in 1937; together with a short length of the lowest side-strake on the

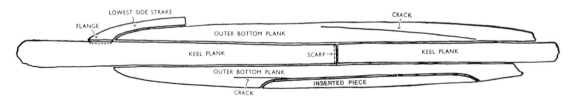

Figure 4.2 Diagrammatic plan of component planks in F1.

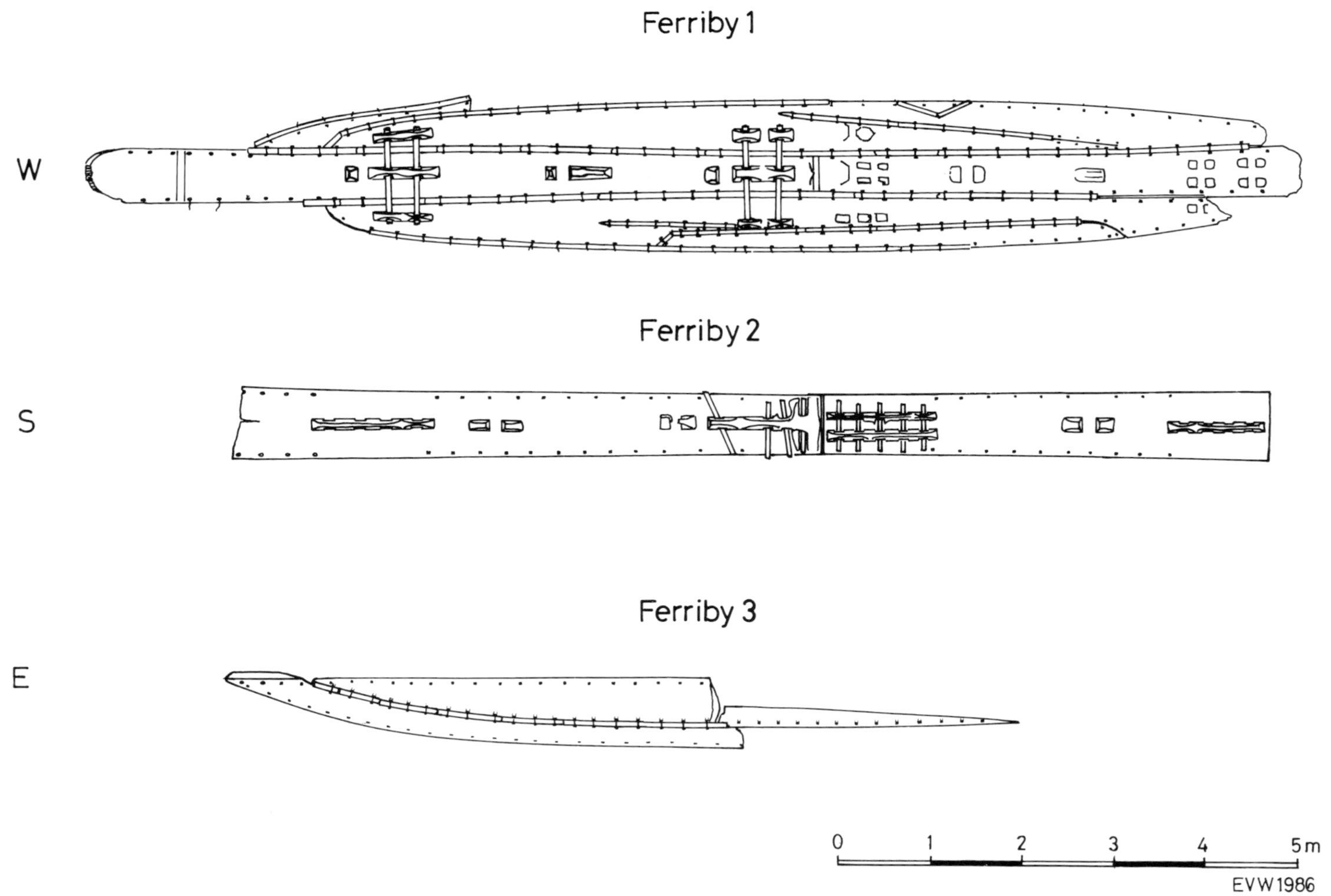

E

Ferriby 1

W

N

Ferriby 2

S

W

Ferriby 3

E

0   1   2   3   4   5 m

EVW 1986

Figure 4.3 Simplified plan-view of Fs 1, 2 and 3 in their correct relative positions.

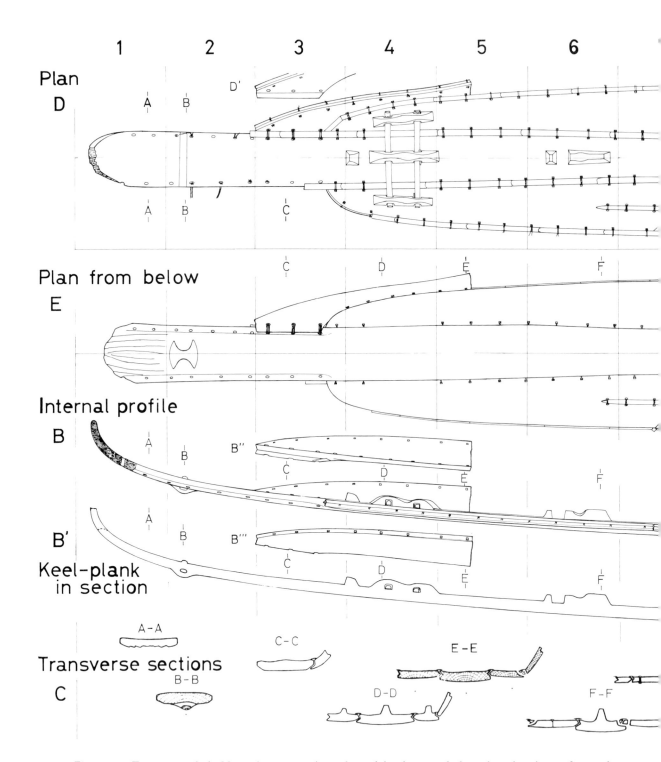

Figure 4.4 F1 as recorded. *Note*: the convention adopted in these and the other drawings of record (except those of F4) is that the artefact is depicted as stationary with the viewer moving position to

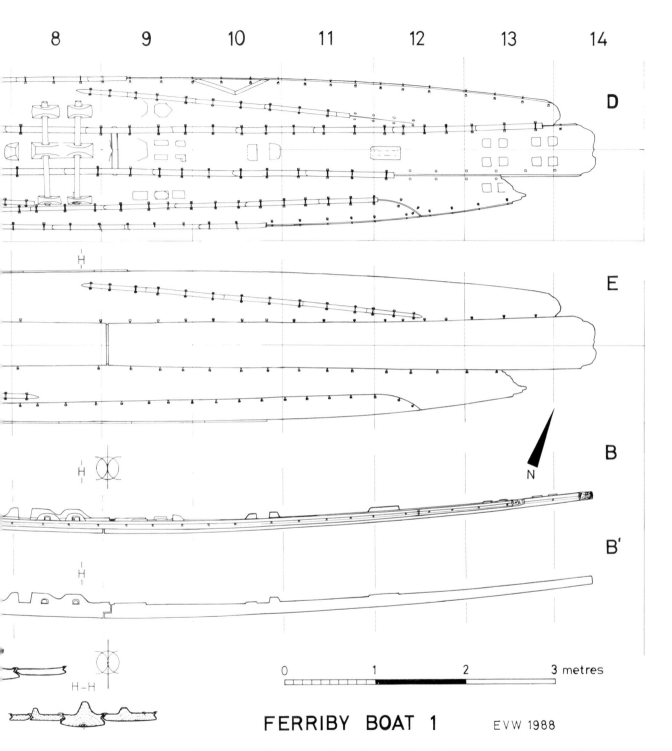

FERRIBY BOAT 1   EVW 1988

portray different aspects rather than the alternative of rotating the object itself. Thus north, east, south, west, up, and down remain constant through the series.

north side at the western end. The total length *in situ* was 13.32 m and the maximum breadth of the 'bottom-structure' as measured in 1938 (Dig 4) was 1.67 m. The emphasis on the bottom-structure as a structural entity to which sides were attached at a later stage of construction is deliberate and will be discussed in greater detail later.

The keel-plank consisted of two planks joined together with a box-scarf amidships, each plank increasing in thickness and nar-rowing in breadth towards the scarf. Fore-and-aft curvature or 'rocker' was contrived in the keel-plank by a combination of shaping and bending, aided marginally perhaps by taking advantage of the tendency of a newly split trunk to bow away from the central axis as a result of differential release of tensions in the wood itself. In addition to curvature achieved by bending, the more complete western end was shaped by hewing out of the solid, giving a markedly increased upward

Figure 4.5 F1: western tip of the keel-plank in 1937 with the edge intact on the right hand (northern) side almost to the mid-line.

curvature, apparently designed to provide the maximum height that could be worked out of the parent half-log. The original edge of the extreme tip was preserved on the north side nearly to the centre line (Figure 4.5). Westwards from the plane of the ends of the outer bottom-planks the edges of the keel-plank were squared but carved with a marked bevel of the lower sides of the edges. The eastern half of the keel-plank had lost any equivalent to this part, assuming that it had once existed, either by ancient breakage or later erosion before discovery and it is therefore impossible to say with absolute certainty how it was finished, but for purposes of reconstruction it has been assumed that it approximately

matched the surviving western end, giving thereby an equal-ended hull. The underside of the western end was carved with a pattern of converging grooves (Figure 4.6) to serve some purpose which is still the subject of debate. Suggested possibilities are discussed at the end of Chapter 5.

Immediately east of the end of these and again on the underside, an elaborate cleat had been carved out of the solid wood, pierced with an oval transverse hole and shaped with long tapering 'wings' which would serve to protect from abrasion whatever might have been passed through it. Above the cleat on the upper side of the plank, a comparatively low and much worn transverse ridge spanned

Figure 4.6 F1: underside of the western tip of the keel-plank showing the 'winged' cleat and the convergent, lengthwise grooves.

it from edge to edge (Figure 1.14). The remaining features on the upper side of the keel-plank, all worked out of the solid when the planks were shaped, will be described in the following pages.

From a point 2.65 m from the western end the edges of the keel-plank were cut with vee-shaped grooves to receive the edges of the outer bottom-planks which were bevelled to fit. In plan-form, the ends of the outer bottom-planks were curved, initially fairly sharply and then more gradually, to reach their maximum breadth at the plane of the midships scarf and then tapering again towards their damaged eastern ends. Assuming that the finish was similar to that surviving at the western ends, their estimated length complete would have been 10.5 m, of which 10.3 m survived in the northern plank. The fit between the outer bottom-plank and the keel-plank was a close one, but the seam did not follow a straight line, the edges of the outer bottom-planks evidently having been trimmed to mate with the sinuous edges of the keel-plank (Figure 2.17) during construction. As will be seen from the section drawings (Figure 4.4C) the outer bottom-planks were keyed into the keel-plank somewhat above the median line so that on the underside the keel-plank projected below the rest of the bottom-

structure, this effect being most marked towards the middle of the boat. Apart from the various protrusions referred to later, the upper surface of the bottom-structure was generally flat from side to side, but evenly curved fore-and-aft to give significant 'rocker'. The northern outer bottom-plank had been cracked during the life of the boat, the fracture being 3.7 m long, and repaired in antiquity. The southern outer bottom-plank had evidently received even more severe damage, necessitating the cutting out of a 5.05 m length of the outer edge and the insertion of a new plank to replace the part removed. In addition there was a repaired crack running lengthwise some 1.45 m westward from the cut-out section. As will be discussed later, these repairs and replacement could have been effected either at the time of initial building to remedy defects in the original planks or at any time subsequently to put right damage incurred during service, the latter being the more likely interpretation. In plan the assemblage of keel-plank and outer bottom-planks was approximately symmetrical about the centre line. The outer edges of the outer bottom-planks were again cut with vee-grooves to accommodate the strakes of the side of the boat, the lower arm of the vee projecting further than the

Figure 4.7 Part of a yew-withy stitch.

upper to give protection to the stitching (Figure 4.4C, F–F).

With the exception of the two parts of the keel-plank which came together at the scarf but were not otherwise secured to each other, all planks were edge-fastened by means of stitches made out of withies of yew branch (*Taxus*) (Figure 4.7). A withy is a length of pliable branch prepared by twisting to separate the fibres so that it is flexible enough to be used for binding. Most records, ancient or modern, refer to hazel (*Corylus*), various sorts of willow (*Salix*) and birch (*Betula*) as the materials of choice and the use at Ferriby of yew is, if not unique, then certainly the most spectacularly extensive example known. The subject of withies and the technique of stitching is treated in greater detail in Chapter 6. All the seams in F1 were caulked with moss, identified as predominantly of two common woodland species, *Neckera complanata* and *Eurhynchium striatum*, which on dismantling emerged as compacted wads up to 15 mm thick and still retaining some greenish colour. The seams and scarf were capped by laths of

oak, ranging according to situation from 70 to 100 mm wide, of neatly cambered section up to 12 mm thick and in lengths up to 1.3 m. The repairs to the cracks were likewise caulked and capped by laths, all being intact at the time of first discovery as were the fastenings and seams between the main planks. The five different types of seam are shown in the sections in Figure 4.4 and diagramatically in Figure 4.8a–f.

The fitting of the lowest side-strake to the bottom-structure represents an example of remarkable skill in the working of timber. Where it mated with the grooved edge of the outer bottom-plank it was bevelled to fit into the vee-groove so as to give the correct angle between the two planks at the chine; but where it was fastened directly to the keel-plank beyond the end of the outer bottom-plank it was itself grooved in such a way that the resulting lower flange lapped under the bevelled edge of the keel-plank. The change in shape required to effect the transition smoothly was achieved by hollowing out the hood-end of the side-strake so that in F1 it

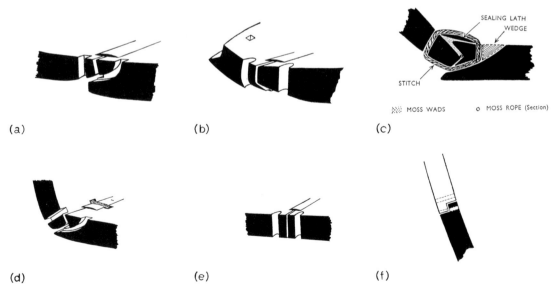

Figure 4.8 (a) Seam between keel and outer bottom-planks; (b) Seam between keel-plank and S-S1; (c) Seam between outer bottom-plank and S-S1 in F3; (d) Seam between outer bottom-plank and S-S1 in F1; (e) Repaired crack in F1; (f) Seam between S-S1 and S-S2 reconstructed.

Figure 4.9 Outward kink in
eastern end of the surviving
piece of S-S1 in F1.

was finished with double curvature inside and
out. In this way within a length of 1.5 m the
slope of the side-strake increased from zero to
c. 60° to the horizontal. Hewing of the ends
of the side-strakes out of the solid must have
provided added stiffness in the structure over
the length so affected and there is evidence
suggesting that with the relaxation of stress
near the broken eastern end of the piece of
side-strake in F1 the plank had warped outwards (Figure 4.9) after abandonment. The
outer (upper) edge of the lowest side-strake
was finished with yet another form of jointing,
a simple type of half-joint which would have
given a smooth finish inside and out (Figure
4.8f).

The variations in and ingenuity displayed

by the jointing, boring, and stitching of the
planks in different situations are such as to
justify separate description. In the seams
between outer bottom-planks and keel-plank
and the outer bottom-planks and lowest side-
strakes the stitch holes were cut with a section
of 25 mm square. The inner holes in each
situation were cut with a curved path so as to
come out in the edge of the plank. In this way
the stitches were buried almost completely
within the thickness of the seam and consequently the outside run would have been protected against abrasion on grounding. The
same technique was employed in the seam
between the inserted plank and the southern
outer bottom-plank. It was evidently not
found practicable to contrive the burying of

Figure 4.10 Stitch across lower surface of flange at the western end of S-S1 countersunk in a groove.

the stitches in the case of the repaired cracks, since a way had not been found to obtain access to the inside edges as would be required to work the holes from both ends, although the problem was solved in the Egyptian Cheops ship by boring holes obliquely into the seams (Lipke 1984: Figure 48). Consequently the holes were bored straight through and the stitches were left projecting on the outside. Along both cracks the stitch holes were of oval section c. 25 mm on the long axis and c. 15 mm on the short. Moving to the joint between the hood-end of the lowest side-strake and the keel-plank, in both planks the holes which were of oval section, c. 35 mm by c. 25 mm, were bored straight through the edges of the planks, but grooves were cut in the lower side of the flange lapping under the keel-plank so that the stitches were countersunk and thereby again protected from abrasion (Figure 4.10). With the exception of the repaired cracks therefore all stitching on the bottom of the boat which might be damaged on ground-

ing was given complete or partial protection. This consideration evidently did not affect the sides of the boat since the paths of the stitches round the half-joint were carried through to the outside. No evidence survived to show whether or not the seams in the sides were caulked or capped with the sealing laths used elsewhere in the hull. There are some significant variations in the distribution of stitches: notably their absence in the seams between keel-plank and outer bottom-planks in the way of the intact groups of cleat systems in the western half. The run of stitches at the normal intervals is, however, uninterrupted in the way of the vestiges of cleats in the eastern half. All but a few of the 98 intact stitches observed in F1 had the two strands of withy running parallel over the sealing-lath. The exceptions were three stitches towards the western end of the repaired crack in the southern outer bottom-plank and in these the strands were laid together rope-fashion (Figure 4.11). Finally on the subject

Figure 4.11 One of only three stitches in F1 where the strands of withy were laid as in rope rather than running parallel with each other. (Top seam in view beyond western end of inserted plank.)

of stitching, there was a single, stopped hole on the keel-plank on the north side near to the western end of the outer bottom-plank not matched by a corresponding hole on the opposite side of the seam, although it might just have accommodated a stitch into the corner of the second side-strake.

Next we come to groups of features distributed over the bottom-structure, the systems of cleats carved in the solid out of the logs in the making of the planks and their related transverse timbers. The term 'transverse timbers' now accepted as standard for such components might be misleading in the Ferriby context as giving the impression that they were substantial and of structural significance in the complete boat. As will be explained later, I have come to the view that they were more likely to have had a purpose in the process of construction than to have been of any significant use in the end product.

In the western half of F1 these 'cleat systems' comprising cleats and transverse timbers were represented by two intact pairs linking the keel-plank with the outer bottom-planks on each side (Figures 4.12 a and b). The transverse timbers, which were in section c. 60 mm wide and 35–40 mm thick, flat on the bottom face and rounded at the shoulders, were of such lengths and stiffness that they could not have been inserted through the holes in the cleats once both lowest side-strakes were in position, as was clearly demonstrated by the westernmost pair. In four cases out of the twelve represented, the timbers were secured in the holes in the cleats by wooden wedges. Unlike the rest of the wood used in the boat, the timbers present in F1 were of ash (*Fraxinus*) and when first exposed showed a fresh finish with the marks of the tool used for trimming still clearly visible. In the eastern half of the boat the cleats were all worn or cut

Figure 4.12a F1: the western group of cleat systems as reassembled at Greenwich and the western block (forward-facing).

Figure 4.12b F1: the western midships group of cleat systems with slot.

away and only vestiges survived. From these however it was possible to identify that two pairs of systems had been provided originally but that those on the keel-plank differed from those in the western half by having the cleats doubled. The sets nearer the middle of the boat showed clear traces of having been cut back, in some cases nearly flush with the surface of the planks.

There remain a number of other features distributed along the keel-plank on the centre line. Working inwards from the ends there are, first, matching single blocks or chocks, the outboard face of which is in each case cut flat at an angle of 105° to the surface of the plank, the inboard face being faired off. The one on the western half was perfectly preserved (Figure 4.12a) and the plane of the outboard face was at a distance of 2.85 m in from the western end and 0.22 m in from the plane of the ends of the outer bottom-planks. That on the eastern half which was reduced by decay to a pair of long ridges but can be restored with some confidence was 2.0 m in from the estimated plane of the restored ends of the outer bottom-planks but the position

in relation to the eastern end of the boat remains conjectural.

Next, on the western half there was a combination of a block in the shape of a truncated pyramid and a lengthwise ridge with a clearly defined slot in between, 0.13 m wide at the bottom and broadening to 0.15 m at the top (Figure 1.15). The ridge tapered to 0.05 m wide along the top; but a third of the way from the western end had been shaped down to form a rounded saddle with the surfaces showing signs of wear. On the eastern half there were the vestiges of a pair of blocks surrounding a similar slot, the mid-point of which was 1.67 m from the scarf in the keel-plank compared with 2.77 m in the case of the western slot. The western slot was 2.57 m inward from the plane of the western ends of the outer bottom-planks and the eastern 1.76 m from that of their estimated eastern counterparts.

Finally, the central cleat in the group to the west of the scarf projected to the west some 0.37 m further than its fellows on the outer bottom-planks and a slot was cut down through it to a level flush with the surface

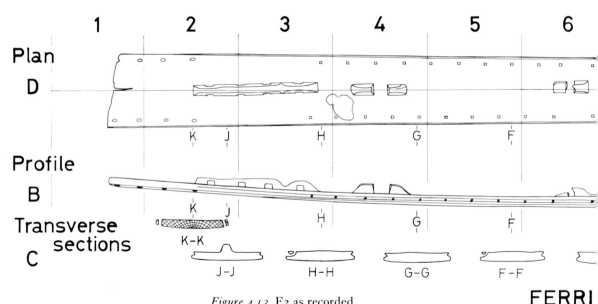

Figure 4.13 F2 as recorded.   FERRI

of the keel-plank, similar in character and dimensions to the two slots described earlier (Figure 4.12b). In the bottom of these slots were the only really well-defined toolmarks observed on F1. These were of an even width of 25 mm (1 inch), parallel-sided and rectilinear at the closed end (Figure 2.18). They could thus have been made only with an adze or chisel-type tool with a squared cutting edge.

To complete the description of F1, some comment is called for about the condition of such relatively fragile or easily detachable components as the loose ends of cut or broken stitches and unfixed sealing laths along the edges. As will be seen from the photographs of the remains *in situ* (e.g. Figure 1.19), these were still generally present when the find was first exposed, suggesting that the period was short between the removal of side-planks and the silting up of what was left of the boat, and further that the removal was part of a deliberate process of dismantling, since the fittings would be unlikely to have survived if the missing planks had been left to be carried away by weather and water action.

F2

F2 lay approximately north–south with only the southern or seaward end protruding from the clay. The find consisted of much of a keel-plank but with both ends missing (Figure 4.13). The total length present was 11.4 m made up of the southern 6.44 m to the scarf and the northern 5.10 m with an overlap of 0.14 m. The width was some 0.16 m greater than that of the equivalent member in F1 and the planks lacked some of the marked decrease in width and increase in thickness towards the scarf present in F1. The transition from grooved to plain edges and from squared to oval stitch-holes occurred at a distance of 0.94 m from the southern end or 5.5 m from the scarf (Figure 1.25); but the edges at the northern end were still grooved at a position corresponding closely to that of the limit of preservation at the eastern end of the keel-plank in F1 where the same edge-finish existed. The square-section stitch-holes mostly contained the remains of withy stitches although there were none remaining in the typically large oval holes at the southern end.

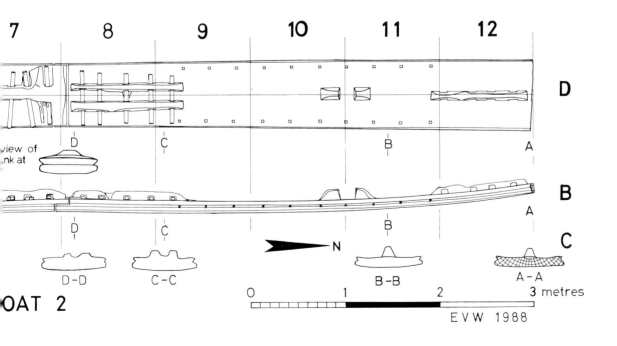

7   8   9   10   11   12

D

view of nk at

D   C   B   A

B

A

D   C   B

C

D–D   C–C   N   B–B   A–A

0   1   2   3 metres

OAT 2

E V W   1988

Figure 4.14 F2: one of the two independent slots.

As in the case of F1 the square-section holes were cut so as to emerge within the thickness of the plank whereas the oval holes passed straight through to the outside along the edge of the bevel on the underside. As also occurred in F1, the run of stitch-holes was interrupted in the way of the cleat systems except for the provision of holes on each side of the plank in two situations along the southern of the midships groups of cleat systems. The fore and aft spacing of these is still wider than the normal for the rest of the plank.

The array of features on the upper side of the keel-plank bore a close resemblance to those in F1 but the cleat systems were more highly developed (Figure 1.26). Where F1 had four groups each with two transverse timbers, in F2 the four groups were arranged 4-5-5-4. Where timbers were present, in the midships groups, they were of oak (*Quercus*) and of smaller section than those in F1. The ends in several instances showed the marks of chopping, suggesting deliberate dismantling. There were two examples of paired blocks surrounding slots of a size similar to the three

in F1 (Figure 4.14). There is a gap in the southern midships run of cleats on the keel-plank which matches the position of the midships slot in F1 but, unlike that, only on the northern face is there the clearly defined shape of the other examples of this feature, the southern face being rounded. Although there are several significant dips in the tops of the cleats there is no obvious equivalent to the carefully shaped saddle in the ridge in F1. Nor are there direct equivalents to the free-standing blocks provided in F1. It is noticeable, however, that the outermost ends of both the southern and the northern cleats were both cut with a flat face at an angle similar to that in the blocks in F1 whereas all other cleat-ends were faired (Figures 4.15 and 4.16).

In profile view both parts of the keel-plank in F2 were curved longitudinally, being somewhat elevated about the scarf where the planks were at their thickest (Figure 5.11). When adjusted to eliminate this elevation in the middle, the longitudinal curve of the combined planks corresponds closely with that surviving in F1.

Figure 4.15 F2: steep-faced cleat-end at southern extremity.

At a position c. 2.5 m from the southern end and to the eastern side of the centre line of the plank there is an irregular patch of burning of the surface, the wood being charred to a depth of c. 10 mm. This is in such marked contrast with the finish elsewhere in all three boat-finds as to provide convincing evidence against the use of fire as an aid in the production of planks (Figure 4.17), although it could have been employed to assist bending.

During the excavation of F2 in 1946 some not clearly defined structures of roundwood were observed near the southern end (Figure 2.12). They consisted of short poles of c. 60–70 mm diameter set vertically, and of c. 40 mm horizontally. A short thick pole of c. 100 mm

diameter lay just under the end of F2 (Figure 2.13) and appeared to have been deliberately placed. The wood was not identified, but from its resemblance to the poles under F3 was possibly alder.

F3

The third find which lay roughly east–west comprised a damaged piece of an outer bottom-plank 7.7 m long and stitched securely to the corresponding piece of lowest side-strake 5.67 m long (Figure 4.20). The western 3.3 m of outer bottom-plank was represented by a fractured splinter, the eastern end of which appeared from the axe marks on both faces to have been deliberately severed from the rest of the plank although still lying in its correct relative position. The western end tapered away to a point at the northern edge. The western end of the piece of lowest side-strake had been broken off rather than chopped through; but the eastern end was intact and displayed the customary projecting lower flange familiar from the example in F1 (Figure 4.18). However it differed from that in the hollowing out of the inside of the end to an angular rather than rounded section so that for a length of 2.67 m the lower part extended the plane of the surface of the outer bottom-plank and the proper angle between side and bottom was thereby preserved, being shaped out of the solid wood. The upper surface of the outer bottom-plank was not furnished with cleats, nor were there any traces to suggest that these had previously existed and been subsequently cut back. Moreover the run of stitch-holes on the inner edge was uninterrupted. The edging of the planks was in all respects similar to that in F1 and F2.

There were certain differences from the pattern of F1 in the cutting of the stitch-holes. First, the inner three holes on the end of the lowest side-strake were of square section and only the easternmost was of the oval section observed in both F1 and F2. Second, the holes

Figure 4.16 F2: steep-faced cleat-end at northern extremity.

Figure 4.17 F2: charred patch on surface of southern plank.

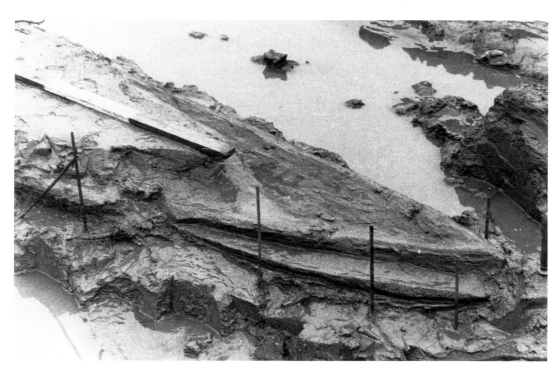

Figure 4.18 F3: flange on S-S1.

Figure 4.19 F3: caulking.

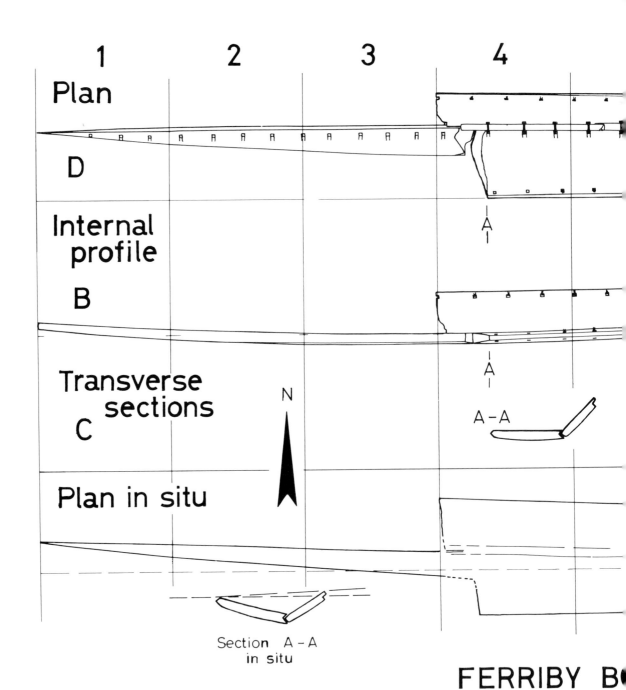

Plan

D

Internal profile

B

Transverse sections

C

A-A

Plan in situ

N

Section A-A
in situ

FERRIBY B

Figure 4.20 F3 as rec

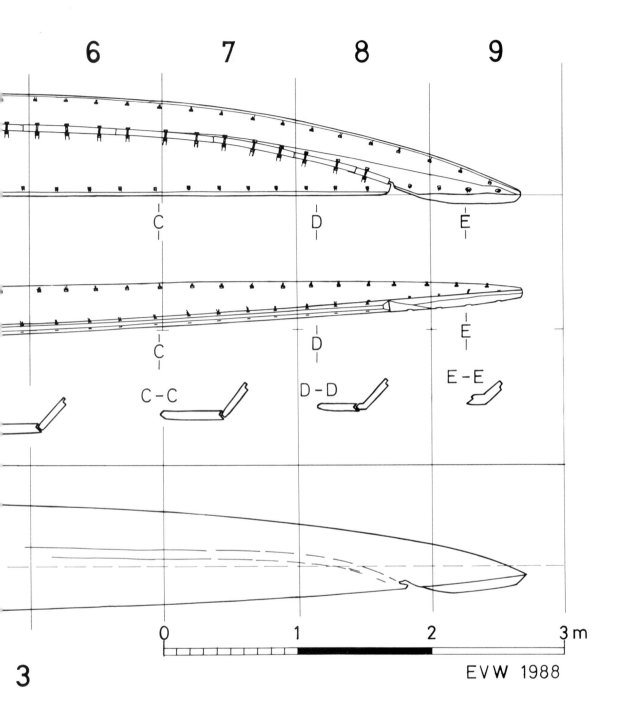

6   7   8   9

C   D   E

C   D   E

C-C   D-D   E-E

0   1   2   3 m

EVW 1988

3

on the outer edge of the outer bottom-plank were cut with a slope or ramp on the inner side, presumably to ease the angle of pull when tightening the stitches. The empty space was then stopped with a material not now identifiable (Figure 4.8c). The caulking too showed a variation in technique, being made up, first, of a continuous two-strand cord or rope made of the long fibres of the common hair moss (*Polytrichum commune*) and laid in the angle of the vee of the seam (Figure 4.19). Above this the seam was packed with the layers of wadded moss recorded from F1 and F2.

The boat-fragment had been supported on a rough platform or 'hard' of alder poles (*Alnus*) among which also was a much worn plank of oak (*Quercus*) and lay canted over at an angle of 15° to the horizontal. Drawn in profile initially with the outer bottom-plank flat fore-and-aft, it later became apparent from photographs that in fact it had been evenly curved (Figure 3.3). Unlike the situation of F1 and F2, it has not been possible to make a measured estimate of this curvature and it has therefore been redrawn with the same profile as that of the equivalent part of F1.

Before going on to describe F4, this is the appropriate place to consider whether the first three finds might be parts of the same boat, since the dating evidence could support the premise that they were contemporary (see Chapter 8). First, it is clear that F1 and F2 could not be from one boat since the keel-plank represented in F2 is present and even more complete in F1 (Figure 4.3). Again the part of outer bottom-plank in F3 has its equivalent in all four possible stations in F1, so that F3 could not be a missing part of F1. There remains the possibility that F3 might have belonged to F2. This can be dismissed on two counts: first, F2 is liberally furnished with cleat systems and these must have extended over the outer bottom-planks; but none at all are provided on the appropriate part of the outer bottom-plank in F3. Second,

the run of stitch-holes in F2 is interrupted in the way of the cleat systems, whereas they are evenly spaced along the inner edge of the outer bottom-plank in F3. The conclusion must therefore be that three separate boats are represented in the three fragments.

F4

The arguments for identifying the fragment of alder (*Alnus*) plank shown in Figure 4.21 as part of a boat are rehearsed in full elsewhere (Wright *et al.*, 1989) and this account proceeds on the assumption that the identification is correct. Whether it is part of the same sort of boat as the other three is more debatable; but the adoption of features derived from it has been of help in solving problems in completing the hypothetical reconstruction of a Ferriby-type boat in a manner consistent with the evidence recorded in the first three finds. There is to me at any rate a convincing case for interpreting the fragment as part of a sheer strake, that is the uppermost strake of the side, from a version of the kind of boat exemplified by F1, F2, and F3. Questions arising from the evidence for age are discussed in Chapter 8.

The timber which lay SE–NW is c.1.0 m long and worn or broken at each end, the west with a jagged break and the east with signs of wear leaving the surfaces rounded. The northern edge is intact for the full length; but of the southern only 0.48 m survives undamaged. For purposes of interpretation, it is assumed that the plank was fitted vertically so that the plan-view shows it edgewise with the northern edge uppermost. This upper edge is shaped with a broad flange or rail along one side so that in section the shape is that of a letter P and it has been deduced that the rail faced inboard. As can be seen in the *in situ* photographs taken before lifting (Figure 4.22), there are two openings in the southern or lower edge, one a clean cutout where the edge is intact and the other less regular and probably part of a near circular hole towards the eastern end. The timber lay with the out-

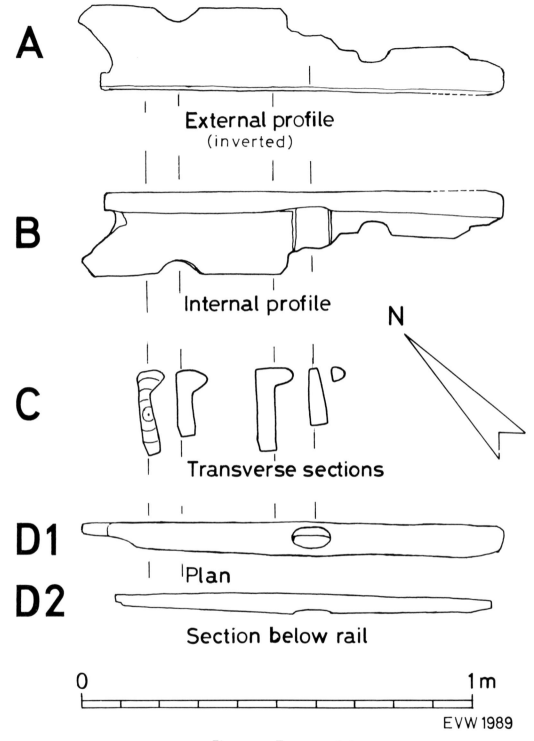

A

External profile
(inverted)

B

Internal profile

N

C

Transverse sections

D1

Plan

D2

Section below rail

0   1 m

EVW 1989

Figure 4.21 F4 as recorded.

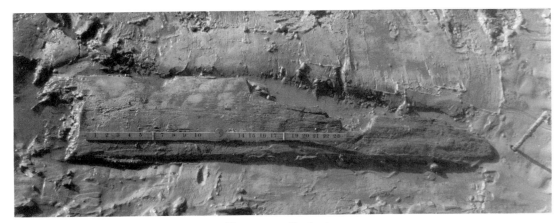

Figure 4.22 F4 *in situ.*

Figure 4.23 F4: the outboard face.

board face upwards and consequently the rail is not visible in these first pictures. When the plank was lifted – and broken in the process – it was revealed and found to have an oval hole cut vertically through its thickness and penetrating partly into the face of the plank as a shallow trench. These features are referred to respectively as the 'cutout', the 'horizontal hole' and the 'vertical hole'. There was no trace of provision for fastenings along the surviving length of the lower edge.

The finish of the outboard face of the plank (Figure 4.23) was comparatively smooth but there are a number of irregular scorings on it which are taken to be the result of ancient or modern accidental damage (Figure 4.24). In plan it has a detectable slight but distinct convex curve which supports the view that this is the outboard face. The finish on the inboard face is by contrast noticeably rougher with scoop-marks visible from the tool used

for its shaping (Figure 4.25). In section it tapers upwards so that it is only c. 30 mm thick along the bottom of the rail. There is a distinct bevel cut along the outer bottom edge to an angle of 17° from the vertical.

The rail appears originally to have been continuous beyond the ends of the timber although at the western end the slope shows two overlapping scars, suggesting that it was chopped down (Figure 4.26). The eastern end is too worn to show whether it was similarly treated. The possibility was considered but rejected that the feature might have been a cleat with shaped ends.

The cutout, which is not strictly an arc of a circle in outline, is 0.11 m long and penetrates 0.035 m into the edge of the plank. It was worked by chopping with a blade at right angles to the plank-edge and the marks are still quite sharp (Figure 4.27) even on the lands where wear from working might be

Figure 4.24 F4: marks on outboard face.

Figure 4.25 F4: the inboard face.

Figure 4.26 F4: the end of the rail, surface believed to be the result of natural wear and tear.

Figure 4.27 F4: cutout in the lower edge, note toolmarks.

Figure 4.28 F4: incomplete horizontal hole.

expected. It has been interpreted as an opening to allow a timber or thwart to pass out through the side of the hull at the level of the top of the strake below, to which it was firmly secured, as already proposed for the hypothetical reconstruction.

The horizontal hole (Figure 4.28) is evidently only part of an opening through the plank, the lower part of which, if of similar outline to the upper, would have resulted in a not quite circular shape, being at 0.09 m slightly longer than it was high at 0.07 m. The surfaces inside what is left of this hole are not well enough preserved to enable any worthwhile deduction from them as to its purpose. Placed as it is with its estimated centre 0.12 m above the projection of the complete lower edge and being as large as it is, it is unlikely to have been for the purpose of edge-fastening to the strake below. No convincing structural purpose has been offered for a hole of this size in such a position, which leaves its use as a point of attachment for a rope as one possible explanation.

The vertical hole is a feature of considerable significance (Figure 4.29). It is 0.09 m long

Figure 4.29 F4: vertical hole through the rail.

Figure 4.30 F4: inboard face within and below the vertical hole showing smoothing due to working and wear.

and 0.05 m wide at its maximum. The trench cut into the face of the plank behind it is 1 cm deep at its deepest and tapers downwards to run out in the face of the plank 0.14 m below the top edge. The effect of this is that the slope of the hole is c. 10° out from the vertical. The surface of the timber in the hole is nearly smooth (Figure 4.30) but very slight traces of toolmarks can be detected, suggesting that there was a tight contact with whatever, timber presumably, was fitted through the hole and that there was marked working between the timbers. The adjoining surfaces around the top edge of the plank were carefully studied for marks of wear or impressions of other fittings but none were found. The

most convincing purpose to account for the characteristics and finish of this feature is that it was designed to act as an anchorage for the top of a rib already postulated in the hypothetical reconstruction of a complete Ferriby boat before F4 had been examined. How this and other features of F4 are worked into the design is discussed in detail in Chapter 5.

A sample of the wood was perforce sacrificed for radio-carbon determination and the remainder is being conserved. The whole artefact has been cast in plaster of Paris so that dimensions and surface traces have been accurately and permanently preserved.

5

Reconstruction and performance

(by E. V. Wright and J. F. Coates)

Before describing the proposed reconstruction of a Ferriby boat it may be helpful first to summarize the evolution of ideas for its design over a period of fifty years since my brother and I proffered our first tentative and as it turned out wholly erroneous essay on the strength of incomplete data in 1939 (Figure 1.23).

After the discovery of cleats in F2 in 1940 (Figure 1.25) and the presence of transverse timbers through them in 1942 (Figure 1.26) I still saw no reason to depart from the idea of a rounded form although I could not fathom how the transverse timbers might be bent to follow a curved path through cleats on all planks. At that time I was unaware of the existence of the Brigg 'Raft', the published accounts of which would have pointed to the error and provided the solution (Thropp 1887). The dawn came on the day of C. W. Phillips's momentous visit to our excavations of F1 in August 1946 when a complete cleat system was displayed, with its straight, transverse timbers spanning the width of only the three bottom-planks (Figure 2.3). I then realized that the bottom-structure was built flat from side to side and with a marked angle between it and the lowest side-strake. With most of the eastern half by then removed or lost, I fell into the fundamental error of believing that the bottom was flat also from end to end between the planes of the hood-ends of the outer bottom-planks, the rise in the surviving end being obtained by shaping

plus some modest bending of the extension of the keel-plank beyond these limits. To conform with our observations of the fore-and-aft profile of F1 *in situ* as recorded in Figure 1.23, I made the assumption that the remains must have become warped after abandonment. On the strength of this belief, I recorded from the dismembered fragments the profiles of F1 and F2 with the upper face of the outer bottom-planks following a straight line until, in the case of F1, the western end of the keel-plank was shown as beginning to curve upwards west of their ends (Wright and Wright 1947: Pl. XV) and likewise with a slight rise at the extreme eastern end of the keel-plank. A similar slight rise was shown at the southern end of F2 where by analogy it would have extended beyond the outer bottom-planks (Wright and Wright 1947: Pl. XVI). When F3 came to be recorded in 1963, I followed the same convention (Wright and Churchill 1965: Pl. VII). I have gone into this in some detail, first, because much that has been written and derived from these first detailed records was based on fallacy: and, second, because the methods adopted to demonstrate and correct the situation contain a number of useful lessons.

The first serious attempt to reconstruct the appearance of a complete boat was undertaken in 1946 and was based on the reasoning that there were fastenings for two more side-strakes in addition to the only piece found up to that time, making three on each side; that

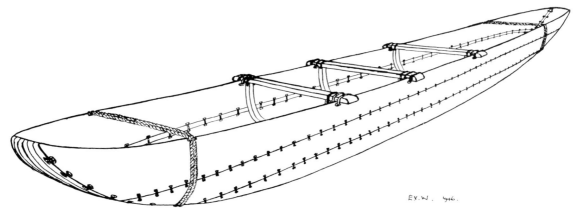

Figure 5.1 Reconstruction sketch published in 1947.

the boat was equal-ended; that it was strengthened by three ribs located in the slots on
the keel-plank and combined with thwarts
lashed to the top edges of the third strakes so
as to form frames; and further strengthened
by girth-lashings at each end passing through
winged cleats on the underside of the keel-
plank. These features were brought together
in a perspective sketch (Figure 5.1) worked
up from an oblique photograph of the remains
in situ (Figure 2.4) and this was generally
accepted for a number of years as a fair representation of what a complete Ferriby boat

looked like and was widely copied by archaeological writers. In 1947 I also made a 1:8
scale model of the surviving remains of F1
based on the 1946 drawings and presented it
to Hull Museums (Figure 5.3). A copy of this
and a similar model of F2, both at 1:10 scale,
were made by the National Maritime Museum
and their model-maker experienced great
difficulty, as I had myself, in shaping the
end of the side-strake to fit into the bottom-
structure.

In the mid-1960s and as an extension of
our work on F3, Hull Museums decided to

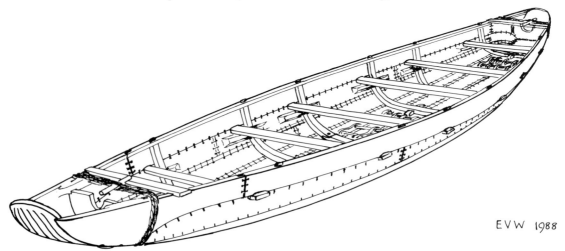

Figure 5.2 Simplified perspective sketch of complete reconstructed boat for comparison with the
discarded 1946 version.

Figure 5.3 1:8 scale model of F1 made by the author and presented to Hull Museums in 1947.

commission the making of a hypothetical reconstruction of a complete boat based on

F1. The maker was the late John Watt, one of the team who had excavated F3, and I briefed him to the best of my ability on what was required, the specification being essentially that worked out in 1946. I was not able to take much part in the exercise beyond encouraging him to stick as closely as possible to the drawings and to try to produce a result similar to Figure 5.1, this in spite of his complaints that he too was experiencing great difficulty in shaping the hood-ends of the side-strakes to mate with the extensions of the keel-plank. His model was finished just in time for a filming session with the late Paul Johnstone for one of the BBC's *Chronicle* series and I first saw it only a few minutes before we were due to begin shooting. I was appalled to see its almost grotesquely drooping ends (Figure 5.4) but when I challenged John Watt he stoutly maintained that it was entirely consistent with my own drawings. I therefore had to accept his assurance and make the best of it for the ensuing dialogue with Paul Johnstone although I had realized immediately that something was seriously wrong. Happily the film was never completed nor shown!

There then began a phase of study to find a satisfactory alternative method of 'closing the ends' without departing from the flat bottom as recorded in 1946. The most promising solution, suggested by Johnstone himself, was something akin to the style of the fishing boats which worked off the Atlantic beaches of Portugal, and he sent me photographs and directions which enabled me to see them for myself in 1970 (Figures 5.5a and b). With ideas derived from them I eventually worked out similar geometry for a Ferriby boat by experiment on the small balsa wood model shown in Figure 5.6. This was developed into various representations which owed more to the imagination than was altogether prudent, the most extreme being one shown with a paper given at a National Maritime Museum Symposium, and perhaps appropriately named 'Skylark'!

There the matter rested for another five

Figure 5.4 John Watt's hypothetical reconstruction model (1:10 scale) made for Hull Museums in 1968. The upward extensions at bow and stern have been added subsequently. (*Photo*: Hull Museums.)

Figure 5.5a Portuguese *meia lua*.

Figure 5.5b Portuguese *meia lua*: detail of planking at bow.

years until work began on the preparations for the new archaeological gallery at the National Maritime Museum. One of the three full-scale exhibits was to be a replica of a large part of F1 as found in an excavation setting, the display being amplified by a series of models; and this naturally induced in me considerable heart-searching over the quality of my own records of events thirty or more years earlier. I was also exposed to challenges from others participating in the work, the net result being that when construction of the replica, based on my 1946–7 drawing, by Kim Allen and his team was already far advanced I suddenly realized where I had erred – my records as published were wrong in showing the bottom of the boats as flat from end to end. It was clear that as found they had in fact been curved or 'rockered' and indeed this was how the profile of F1 had been depicted as long ago as 1939 (Figure 1.23); this was confirmed by our record of probing in 1937 to determine its depth below the more or less flat but sloping surface of the clay platform in which it lay. J. F. Coates was by then working with the museum and me on the reconstruction models and conceded that such rocker would result in a much more satisfactory boat than any flat version; while Allen, with experience gained from wartime photographic interpret-ation, took one look at some of my photo-graphs and pointed out the existence of pooling of water on and near to the surface to provide local horizons which proved the point. Despite vehement argument I was unable to persuade the museum to change the design for the replica and it was completed in accordance with the published records, although the dis-crepancy is not very obvious to the unin-formed eye. In deference to my strongly held views a reconstructed model incorporating an arbitrarily determined degree of rocker was included in the display together with two other alternative hypotheses. As far as I was concerned it then became my prime duty to prove my case and over the next few years I set out to review and recover the data which

would enable me to restore the original shapes of the boat remains as found, a necessary first step in providing a sound basis for methodical reconstruction.

The first action was to determine the extent to which the western tip of the keel-plank had been eroded between its first exposure and recording in 1937 and 1946 when it was again recorded both *in situ* and then after excavation. Careful study of the photographs taken in 1937 showed that at the northern side of the tip the original edge had survived almost intact round nearly to the middle line of the plank and it was simple therefore to continue this through the remainder which had broken away in antiquity. In plan-view, in 1937 we had shown the plank as parallel sided and the photographs confirmed that this was so. By 1946 not only had the end been worn down extensively, but lengthwise cracks had developed and the plank had spread, as was faithfully recorded *in situ* at the time. This too could be readjusted with confidence as shown in the latest drawings of record (Figure 4.4). The underside was not recorded in 1937 and the view from below (Figure 4.4E) is therefore based on 1946 evidence. The profile aspect of the tip presented more serious problems and the original curvature was reco-vered in the main from detailed examination of the comprehensive series of photographs of the second of our pre-war digs in September 1937. The combined results of these steps are shown in plan and profile view in Figure 5.7, a noteworthy feature being the extent of vertical erosion between 1937 and 1946 estimated at 0.30 m.

Two incontrovertible facts about the atti-tude of the find had been recorded in 1937: that the east end broke through the surface of the clay at a shallow angle and the west protruded as a small boss of timber; and that the surface of the clay platform in between was to all intents and purposes flat. Both observations are confirmed in photographs of the third of the 1937 digs (Figures 1.4 and 5.8). In 1978 it was thought to be useful as

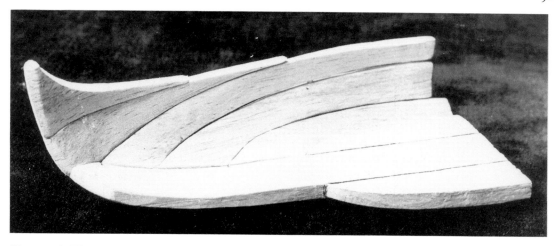

Figure 5.6 The author's experimental model in balsa wood, used to study possible solutions to the problem of closing the ends.

far as then possible to verify this evidence and I paid a rewarding visit to the site with Coates, during which we were able also to reconstruct the original gradient of the platform along the central axis of the find. This was estimated as 1:33 falling from WNW to ESE, that is obliquely to the water's edge. Coates coined the term 'the clay-line' for an imaginary line on the surface of the deposits over the middle line of the boat remains. I then set about recovering from the old records and photographs as much data as possible about the

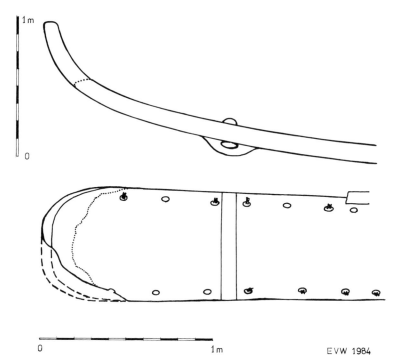

Figure 5.7 Drawing illustrating the restoration of the damaged western end (bow) of the keel-plank of F1.

Figure 5.8 Much enlarged section of left-hand end of Figure 1.4, showing angle at which the eastern end of F1 protruded from platform. Note blocks on surface to right of camera-case.

depth to which the planks had been submerged below the clay-line.

The western tip had been only just protruding above the surface by an estimated 30–40 mm and it proved practicable to estimate from the photograph in Figure 5.8 the angle at which the eastern end emerged, using the tide-line on the southern shore as an horizon. For other fixes it was necessary to calculate the height of the baulks at the ends of the 1937–8 excavations and this was done by estimating their vertical dimensions from any measurable feature in the photographs. In the end a coherent pattern was obtained and the whole was assembled into the sectional view in Figure 5.9. By extending the eastern end to match its surviving counterpart in the western end, a complete profile was then drawn. The arguments that the boats were equal-ended

will be rehearsed below. The eastern end was found to be canted slightly above the western, which was consistent with the ponding of water westwards of the mid-plane of the boat taken as being at the midships scarf in the keel-plank as could be observed in photographs of Dig 3 and of the partially excavated remains in 1946. In the reconstruction drawings the profile view has therefore been rocked so that the eastern and western tips are level (Figure 5.13B).

Attention was next turned to F2 and F3 to see if the remains as found reproduced rocker similar to that estimated for F1. In neither case were there records of the depth of exploratory excavations from which deductions could be drawn; but an oblique view of F2 after cleaning and before it was lifted showed that each half was curved lengthwise

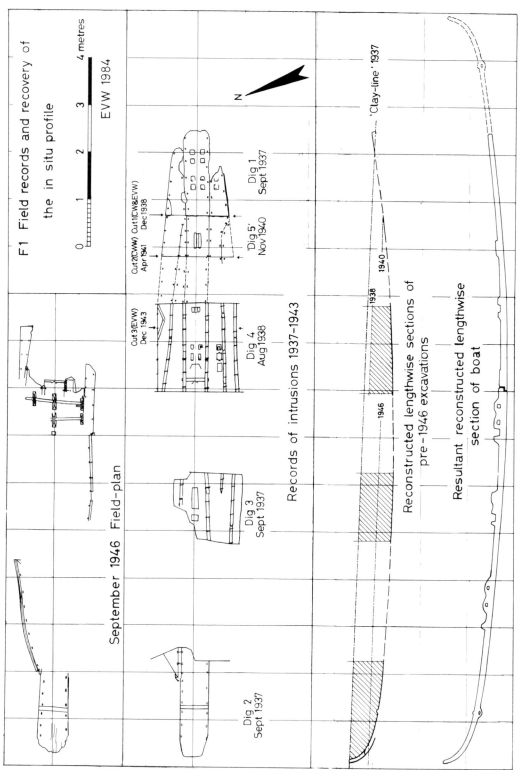

Figure 5.9 F1: pre-war and 1946 field records and reconstructed lengthwise sectional views of the pre-war excavations giving evidence of the *in situ* profile of F1.

Figure 5.10 Oblique photograph of F2 *in situ*.

in a shallow arc, meeting at a slight hump about the scarf (Figure 5.10). It was found to be feasible to draw on an enlarged photograph a quadrilateral figure joining the four corners of the find and then estimate the depths of the bottoms of each hollow below the plane of this and compare them with the known thickness of the plank-edges visible at each station

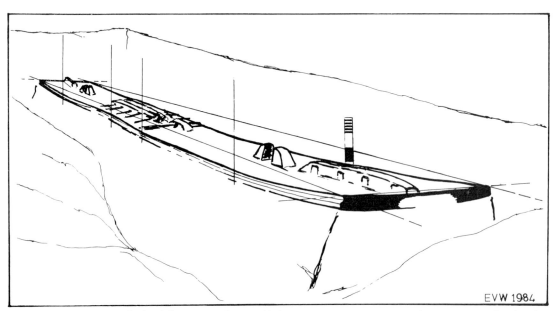

Figure 5.11 Drawing derived from 5.10 from which measurements were made to recover the *in situ* profile of F2.

(Figure 5.11). Thereby a fair approximation could be deduced of the maximum curvature of each plank and when the profiles of each were rotated so as to produce an even curve from end to end of the whole find the final result was closely in accord with that obtained by a different process for F1 (Figure 5.13). F3 proved a more difficult problem than F1 and F2 as it had lain with the outer bottom-plank tilted to the north (Figure 4.18); but it was clear that the inner edge of this plank, which in true plan-view was near enough straight, appeared in the *in situ* photographs as bowed (Figure 3.3). I have not been able to measure the extent of fore-and-aft curvature which would produce this phenomenon but have assumed for the purpose of the revised drawings of record (Figure 4.18) that it is the same as that in the equivalent part of F1.

Before proceeding further it is necessary to consider the case for the missing eastern end of the keel-plank being of the same shape and construction as the well preserved western, that is with a marked upward curve shaped from the solid. Neither F2 nor F3 give any help, since the more complete southern end of F2 stops short of what survived at the western end of F1 and the northern end does not extend as far as its counterpart at the eastern end, while the end of the lowest side-strake preserved in F3 matches its equivalent in F1 without adding to the store of evidence. The most reliable clues come from the array of features surviving on the keel-plank in F1 and F2, together with the evidence that can be drawn from the relationship between the planks and the parent logs from which they were derived.

Reference to Figures 4.4 and 4.13 demonstrates that in F1 and F2 the cleat systems, slots, and other projections broadly match each other except for the more elaborate provision of cleat systems in F2 which has groups of 4-5-5-4 compared with 2-2-2-2 in F1. The doubling of the cleats on the keel-plank to the north of the scarf in F2 corresponds with similar doubling shown by the vestiges still visible in the corresponding position in F1 (D9) (references are to the gridded drawings in Figures 4.4 and 4.13). Likewise in both cases three slots can be identified on the keel-plank, although in F1 (D6, D8, and D10) they are located closer to the middle (as represented by the scarf) than they are in F2. There are however indications that F2 may have been slightly larger than F1. There is no clear parallel in F2 for the two single blocks in F1, one towards each end of the keel-plank (D4 and D12), although it is argued that the steeply shaped ends of the cleats in F2 might serve to perform the same function, whatever that was. The 'saddle feature' associated with the western slot in F1 (D6) is unmatched in F2 although again there are dips in the ridges of the cleats which might meet a similar need. The general impression subject to minor variations in each example and some dimensional differences between the two is one approaching symmetry in the layout forward and aft.

The evidence from the timber in F1 does not deny the possibility that the ends of the keel-plank were more or less equal. The dendrochronological data points strongly to the two component planks having been derived from a single trunk, split lengthwise and each half then reduced to provide one plank. The crown-ends were arranged inwards to mate at the scarf and the stump-ends outwards, complete perhaps with some of the buttresses of the tree to give extra depth of wood for shaping of an upturned end or ends. In F1 the planks were formed from half-logs with the pith side downwards and the sapwood upwards, which would facilitate the production of two planks with matching outer ends. In F2 however the southern half was cut in the same manner as in F1; but in the northern, the plank was hewn with the half-log the other way up as described in Chapter 6. This is a strange phenomenon which is discussed in detail later. How all this might have been done and, in particular, the relationship of planks to logs as well as the extent to which the recorded profile was

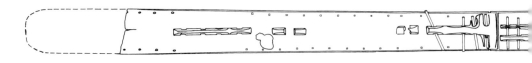

D Plan as recorded with reconstruction in broken lines

B Profile in situ

B Profile restored and reconstructed

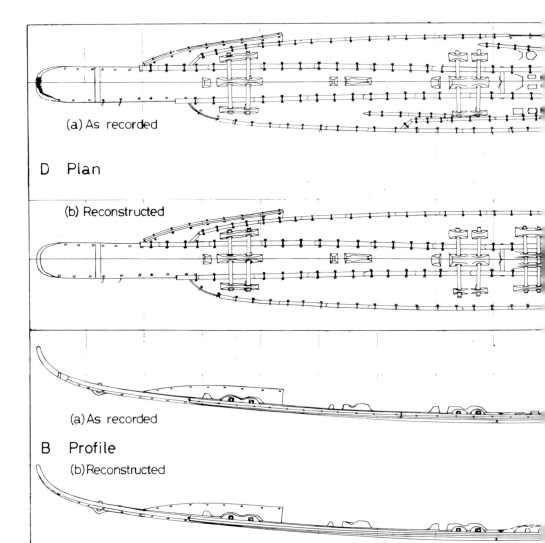

(a) As recorded

D   Plan

(b) Reconstructed

(a) As recorded

B   Profile

(b) Reconstructed

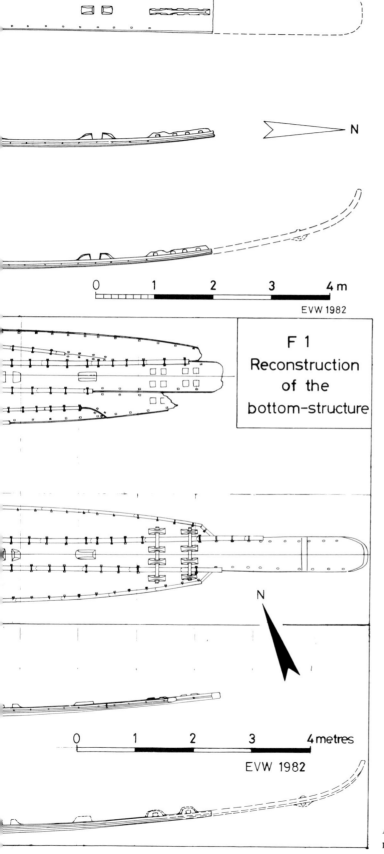

N

EVW 1982

Figure 5.12 F2 reconstructed.

F 1
Reconstruction
of the
bottom-structure

N

0   1   2   3   4 metres

EVW 1982

Figure 5.13 Bottom-structure of F1
reconstructed.

achieved by shaping, bending, or a combination of both are examined in more detail also in Chapter 6. It is estimated however that even this anomalous plank could have been fashioned with an upturned, shaped end without demanding a trunk of an unreasonably large diameter. On balance therefore I lean to the view that both had been equal-ended and the reconstruction proceeds on that assumption. What survives of the eastern ends of the outer bottom-planks in F1 suggests that when complete they would have matched the intact western ends and this supports the assumption based on study of the keel-planks. The only alternative to an equal-ended design which might find contemporary supporting evidence is that in F1 the western end was the bow and the eastern the stern, the latter perhaps finished off with some sort of transom, perhaps in the form of a vertical board inserted into slots in the bottom and side planks in the same fashion as was regularly employed in log boats of this and later periods. The weight of clues pointing to fore-and-aft symmetry and the convergence of the surviving parts of the outer bottom-planks convince me however that such treatment was unlikely.

To complete the restoration of the bottom-structure in F1, consideration must be given to the vestigial embellishments on the upper surface of the eastern half and to the evidence for repairs to damage presumably during the working life of the boat. The groups of projecting blocks on keel-plank and outer bottom-planks adjoining the scarf and again towards the eastern end (D9 and D13/14) can be reconstructed with confidence to form cleats to match those on the undamaged western half of the find. The pair of blocks (D10) and the single one (D12) between these groups appear to be the stumps respectively of paired blocks surrounding a slot of a size similar to the other two on F1, and incidentally also those on F2; while the single block can be seen to have a steep face towards the east and to be faired off at the other end,

consistent with a longer version of the chock or stop at the western end of the boat. By restoring the projections and eliminating the repairs it is possible to arrive at a reconstruction of an equal-ended bottom-structure in its original state, and this is shown in plan-view in Figure 5.13. It will be noted that the restored block (D12) is considerably further from the reconstructed eastern end than its intact counterpart (D4) is from the western. In our search for suitable stations for as many ribs as possible, Coates and I have introduced an additional block (D14) outboard of the most easterly group of cleat systems, that is matching the position of the western one. A winged cleat is also included beneath the reconstructed eastern end of the keel-plank.

Proceeding from the equal-ended bottom-structure as described so far, consideration can next be given to the contriving of the sides. With the two examples in F1 and F3 of the first of the side-planks, here termed the 'lowest side-strakes' (or SS1s), from which to work and both having been broken in antiquity, the first question that arises about these strakes is whether each was fashioned out of a single plank, which would be ideal from the structural point of view, or two or more planks, which would be much easier to make. After much debate, Coates and I have agreed on a two-plank strake with a joint rather over a quarter of the distance from one end. This would enable the maker to do the really difficult work of shaping the ends without too much concern about the overall length and then make final adjustments to the fit when cutting the joint where we have incorporated simple half-joints similar to those in the keel-planks in F1 and F2.

This done, the next question is how many more strakes there were on each side. There must have been one since the fittings and fastenings survived on the upper edge of the SS1s and along the edges of the keel-plank. The addition of only a single second side-strake (SS2) shaped to fill the whole of the available length and all the attachments along the SS1 and keel-plank would produce a boat which would float and carry a useful load. Freeboard amidships would be low; but some improvement against the effects of this could be obtained by adding a splash-screen, of hide perhaps, along the sides and inboard of the ends, as has been demonstrated in one of the models on display at Greenwich. Reference to the drawing in Figure 5.14 however shows that the presumably shaped ends of such strakes would be very wide and deep to occupy all the space available out to the tips of the keel-plank and thus calling for unusually large logs. Moreover there are signs in the spacing of the stitch-holes in the western end of the keel-plank in F1 that about the end of the SS1 (D3) the holes are unusually close together on each side of the plank and likewise 0.8 m forward where the transverse ridge crosses the plank (D2). This suggested to me in 1946 that the normal provision of stitches between the ends of a side-strake and the keel-plank is three (or four in a single case on the northern side) which would accommodate the ends of three side-strakes per side. I have never subsequently departed from this conviction and have been strengthened in it by the discovery of F4 which, always assuming it to belong to the typical Ferriby school of design, would be unduly and wastefully narrow if it were the sole additional strake. With SS2s of width similar to the surviving SS1 and third strakes (SS3s) of the width of F4, the result is a satisfactorily capacious and weatherly shell, and that has been adopted for the preferred design in the reconstruction.

Thought has been given to the arrangements of joints in each of the second and third side-strakes and the dispositions chosen (Figure 5.14) allow for separate, shaped end-pieces in each case, joined by as long a plank as can reasonably be accommodated, the latter being nearly flat apart from any protruding features left standing on the inner surfaces. This procedure would allow fitting and attachment with the minimal degree of bending and no twisting. The reconstruction

is also based on the upper edge of these planks being straight so that trimming to secure a fit with the bowed edge of the plank below could be confined to the lower edge only. Methods to obtain the curvature of the edges of planks to be bent into shape to form the shell of a boat are admirably set out in the late Eric McKee's booklet 'Clenched Lap or Clinker' (McKee 1972) and the reader should refer to that work for enlightenment or guidance.

A shell of such size and construction would not stand up to the stresses imposed on it afloat without a great deal more internal bracing than is provided by the cleat systems which are the only such structures for which direct evidence has survived. It has been necessary therefore to search for clues to a realistic system for adequate framing of the hull. Mention has already been made of the 1946 reconstruction in which three sets of ribs and thwarts were proposed using the slots on the keel-plank together with girth-lashings at each end through winged cleats whose function was as much to protect as to locate the rope or other material used. As the development of a complete reconstruction has proceeded, all these have been retained albeit in modified form; but other stations for ribs have been sought since three only, and those bunched near the middle of the boat, have been considered inadequate. Attention was then given to the blocks or chocks, two of which have been identified on the keel-plank of F1, the western one (D4) complete and the eastern (D12) somewhat damaged. There is no doubt that these were each deliberately shaped with a steep, flat surface facing outwards towards each end whereas inboard they were faired into the surface of the plank. The idea then emerged that they would serve just as well as slots for locations for ribs since the sides of the boat would be converging inwards at these positions so that a rib fitted there could not shift towards the narrowing space and would be prevented by the block from moving in the other direction. This scheme provided stations for two more ribs; but that

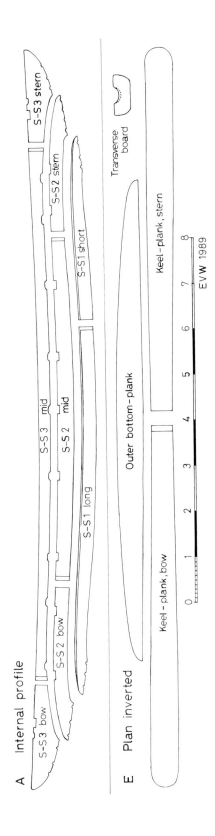

Figure 5.14 Diagram of separate planks composing hypothetical reconstruction based on F1, with estimates of dimensions of logs required to accommodate planks in reconstruction (in metres):

	SIDES			
Plank	*Length*	*Width in plan*	*Depth in profile*	
S–S3				
Middle	11.7	0.09 (all bent)	0.24	
Bow	2.3	0.40	0.80	
Stern	2.0	0.40	0.80	
S–S2				
Middle	7.5	0.20	0.36	
Bow	3.4	0.40	0.64	
Stern	3.0	0.40	0.64	
S–S1				
Long	8.1	0.36 (+ bending)	0.28	
Short	4.0	0.38 (all shaped)	0.26	

BOTTOM-STRUCTURE				
Plank	*Length*	*Width in plan*	*Depth in profile*	
Keel-plank				
Bow	8.0	0.60	0.75	
Stern	8.0	0.60	0.75	
OB–P (port and starboard)	10.6	0.60	0.20	
Inserted boards	0.88 (transverse)	0.09	0.40	

towards the eastern end is significantly further inboard than its counterpart to the west and it has been thought justifiable to add another block outboard of the easternmost group of cleat systems in a position similar to the surviving one at the eastern end. Thus we have stations for six ribs reasonably well distributed along the length of the hull and based on logical deductions from surviving features in five cases and in only one on conjecture.

The most serious stresses to which a shell of the form which emerges from the addition of three strakes to each side of the symmetrical bottom-structure would be subjected are those occurring when it is supported amidships but not at the ends. The effect of this would be to tend to straighten the bowed side-strakes and force the sides of the boat together. This could only be counteracted by the fitting of transverse timbers or thwarts fairly high in the 'box' of the shell. My original reconstruction of 1946 had them across the tops of the sides as is done for instance in the *madel paruwa* of Sri Lanka (Figure 9.3). Coates proposed most convincingly that they would be more effective structurally if placed across the tops of the SS2s and protruding through the side of the shell. Moreover in that position they would be at the most convenient height to act as benches for paddlers or rowers. The initial idea had been that thwarts would be combined with ribs to make up a complete frame; but this is of no great structural advantage and they might be located close to frames or in any other convenient distribution over the length of the hull provided the number is sufficient. This was the state of theorizing about the bracing of the reconstructed boat that Coates and I had reached in mid-1987 but we were still debating how ribs and thwarts might be attached effectively to the shell using such means as were thought to be available to the builders.

Late in that year we began for the first time to study F4 and I soon came to the conclusion that the vertical, oval hole through the inboard rail in such a plank would be ideally suited to anchor the trimmed top of a rib to the hull. Moreover the traces of wear and working on the face of the plank where such a rib would bear against it were consistent with the effects which might be expected from the flexing of the hull in use. The rounded cutout on the lower edge of F4 showed no trace of working or wear and again would be well adapted to provide clearance for a thwart passing out at right angles to the shell and keyed to the plank below. The first of these hypotheses seemed to us to conform with the design philosophy of the Ferriby boatbuilders as exemplified in the other finds and to be typical of the way in which they might solve the problem of fastening timber to timber in such a situation. The second hypothesis gave us independent assurance over the location of thwarts. We therefore adopted both these features, despite the difference of 5–900 years in age of the finds, and worked them into the reconstruction. Finally it was considered essential to secure the frames to the sides of the boat in addition to locating them on the keel-plank and at the top of the uppermost strake. From the evidence of F1 and F3, there are no traces of means of attachment to the SS1s and there remain only the SS2s on which such provision might be made. For this, therefore, we have postulated the shaping of slots between blocks, similar to those on the keel-plank but with the blocks or cleats somewhat longer and perforated for lashings of withies to hold ribs to strakes. When studying the relationship in F4 between the vertical hole assumed to be for a rib and the cutout for a thwart, it was found that cleats in the logical positions called for would be at a height convenient for a paddler's foot and some have been extended and other blocks provided for this purpose.

For ribs of the dimensions proposed it would plainly be impossible to procure grown crooks in a single piece bent in the right places to fit into the angles between bottom-structure and both sides. They would therefore have to be built up of two separate crooks and for

Figure 5.15 Inside of Portuguese *moliseiro* under construction to show alternate ribbing. (*Photo*: J. F. Coates.)

A   B

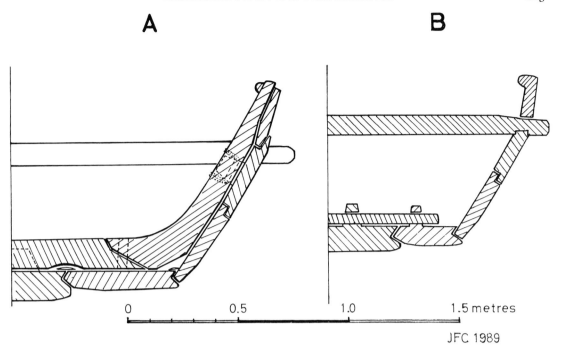

0   0.5   1.0   1.5 metres

JFC 1989

Figure 5.16 Half-sections of reconstructed boat to show rib attachment (A), thwart arrangement (B).

the purposes of our reconstruction we have followed the surviving traditional practice of joining one long to one short crook, the straight lower arm of the former running as a floor over most of the width of the bottom. This is well exemplified in the Portuguese *moliseiras* (Figure 5.16). The two would be joined using a simple scarf and pegged or, less probably, lashed together. Thwarts would be made from straight half-logs with the outer rounded side uppermost which with minor shaping would provide a good seat for the paddler's posterior as well as conforming with the shape of the cutout in F4. We have considered but discarded the alternative of ribbing by means of separate L-shaped crooks alternating from side to side of the hull as is not uncommon in early boatbuilding practice. This in our view would not conform with the interpretation of the existing slots and blocks as rib locations – and already all too few in number.

To complete the basic reconstruction, some

discussion is required of the girth-lashings. These clearly needed some internal framing against which the ends of the planks could be clenched together. At the western end of F1's keel-plank there is on the upper face (D2) the worn remnant of the transverse ridge in the same plane as a lashing through the cleat below. This would be aptly placed to prevent some form of frame in this position from slipping inboard whereas the convergence of the planks would prevent it shifting in the other direction. We have therefore utilized this to secure the bottom edge of a solid, inserted board somewhat after the manner used in logboats of the period. Similar provision would be necessary on the face of the uppermost strakes and this could be in the form of a continuous ridge or alternatively blocks after the fashion of those on the keel-plank. Finally it would be necessary to provide means of tightening the girth-lashing and for this a tourniquet device is proposed with a cutout in the top of the inserted board to allow

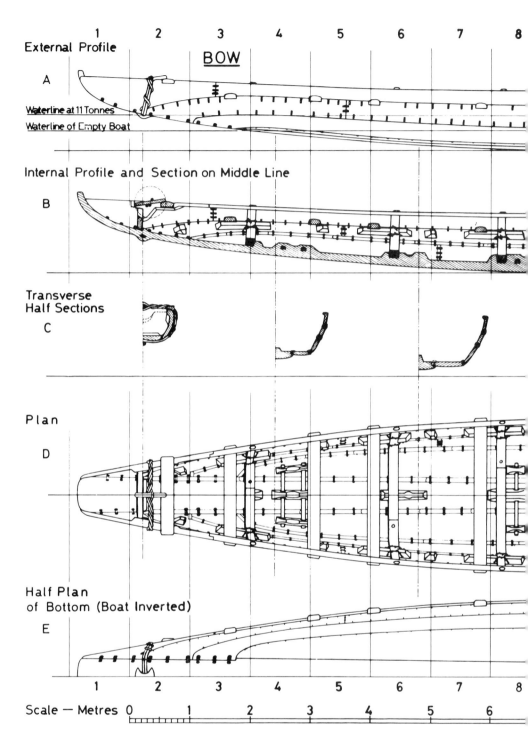

Figure 5.17 General arrangement drawings of hypothetical reconstruction of a complete boat (J. F. Coates).

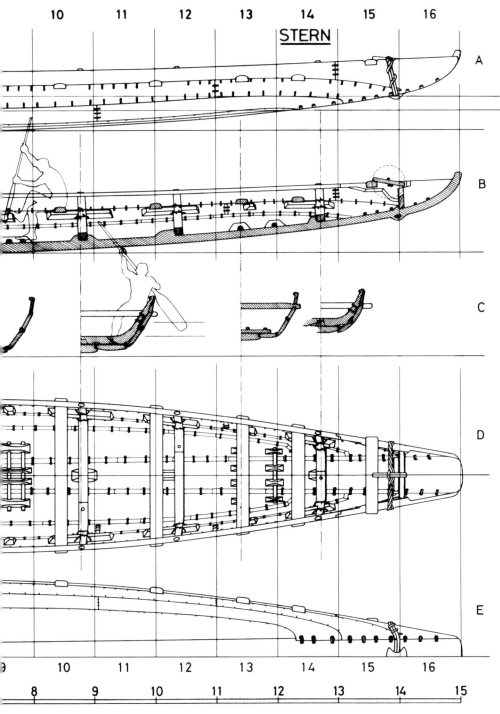

STERN

JFC 1988

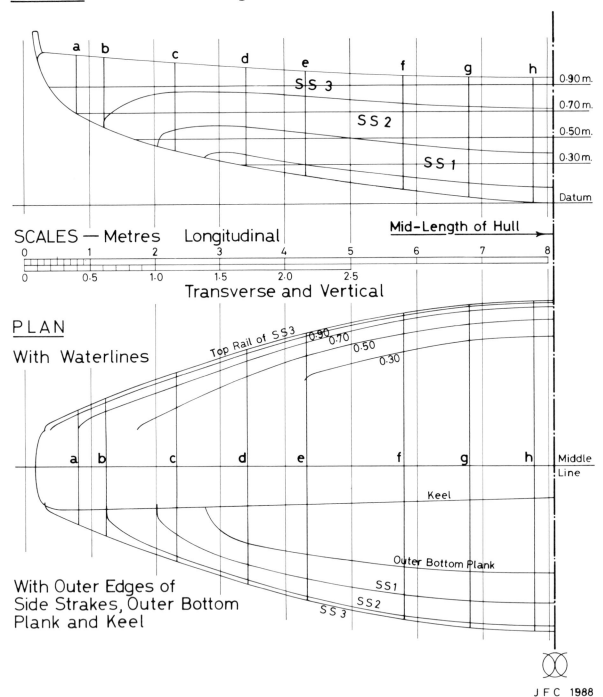

PROFILE — With Outer Edges of Side Strakes (SS)

SS3
SS2
SS1

0.90 m.
0.70 m.
0.50 m.
0.30 m.
Datum

a b c d e f g h

Mid-Length of Hull

SCALES — Metres   Longitudinal

0   1   2   3   4   5   6   7   8

0   0.5   1.0   1.5   2.0   2.5

Transverse and Vertical

PLAN

With Waterlines

Top Rail of SS3   0.90   0.70   0.50   0.30

a b c d e f g h   Middle Line

Keel

Outer Bottom Plank

SS1
SS2
SS3

With Outer Edges of
Side Strakes, Outer Bottom
Plank and Keel

J F C 1988

Figure 5.18a Lines and body plans for the hypothetical reconstruction (J. F. Coates).

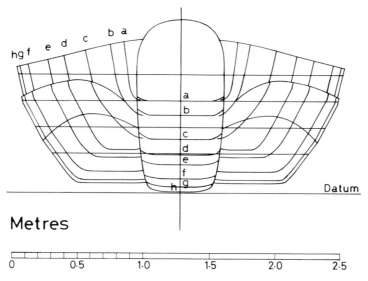

BODY PLAN — Reconstructed

a
b
c
d
e
f
g
h

hg f e d c b a

Datum

Metres

0   0.5   1.0   1.5   2.0   2.5

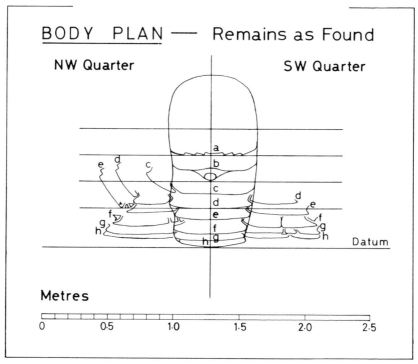

BODY PLAN — Remains as Found

NW Quarter   SW Quarter

a
b
c
d
e
f
h g

e d c

f
g
h

d e
f
g
h

Datum

Metres

0   0.5   1.0   1.5   2.0   2.5

Figure 5.18b Body plan derived from records of the remains as found (J. F. Coates).

rotation of the tightening bar through the rope or bunch of cords used for the lashing. Locking of the tightened lashing is arranged by the provision of a detachable thwart over the tops of the sides-strakes which would prevent the bar from rotating under the torsion of the twisted cords.

Some thought has been given to the need to protect the stitching along the floor of the boat from abrasion from the feet of passengers and especially of hoofed animals such as cattle and sheep. The integral features on the surface of the planks in the eastern half of F1 had been nearly obliterated whereas those in the western half were uniformly intact. The most obvious reason for this difference is that livestock were carried penned into the eastern half and in course of time their hoofs wore down the protuberances so that they were ineffectual, and some of the remnants were

then trimmed back. The stitches and sealing laths were however in pristine condition throughout and must therefore have been given protection. Panels of light hurdles have been introduced into the reconstruction to provide this. Similar needs are discussed and solutions proposed in the case of the Brigg 'Raft' (McGrail 1981a: 237 and Figures 4.1.4, 4.1.20).

All these proposals are brought together in the general arrangement drawings for the hypothetical reconstruction of a complete boat in Figure 5.17 and the utilitarian sketch in Figure 5.2. This is amplified by lines and body plan drawings in Figure 5.18a and it is the joint belief of Coates and myself that, from the available evidence, from deductions therefrom and from rational conjecture, these represent the most realistic design for one of these craft that can now be offered. Certain of

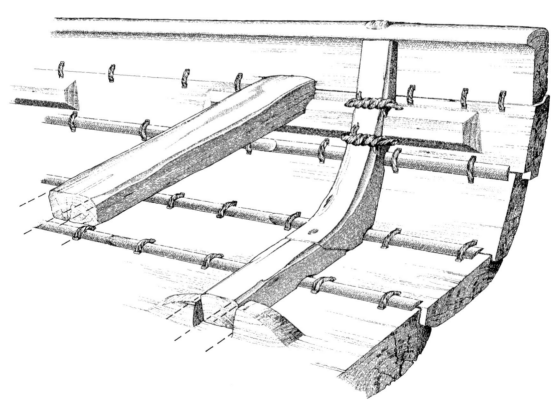

Figure 5.19 Perspective drawing showing reconstructed arrangements for ribs and thwarts (John Craig).

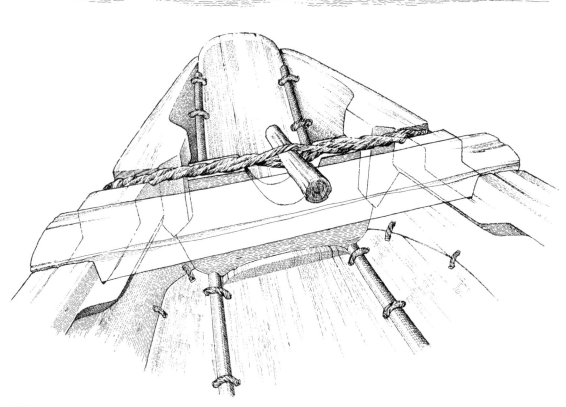

Figure 5.20 Perspective drawing of arrangements for the inserted board, girth-lashing and tourniquet (John Craig).

the more complex details are developed in perspective sketches based on these drawings (Figures 5.19, 5.20, and 5.21) and the finished boat is shown in a suitably reconstructed working situation in Figure 5.22.

The intricate design proposed in this reconstruction is of such fundamental significance for the archaeology of northern European boatbuilding that a summary of the evidence and arguments on which it is based may lead to a clearer appreciation of the reasoning behind it; this is set out here in tabulated form in Tables 5.1 and 5.2 (pp. 112–13).

Before leaving the subject of the reconstructed boat, the design proposed here being of satisfactory structure and capacity and, as will be seen, able to perform reasonably well if propelled by paddle, there are two questions

calling for discussion from the archaeological viewpoint: first the possible use of mast and sail; and second, the use of rowing as opposed to paddling. I tend to regard these as somewhat further removed into the realms of conjecture than the hypotheses embodied in the basic design and therefore to be considered separately.

For sails there is no surviving artefactual evidence in north-west Europe earlier than the Oseberg ship of c. 800 AD (McGrail 1987a) but there is clear inconographic evidence for a mast and yard in the gold boat model from Broighter, Co. Derry, Ireland dated to the first century BC, and literary evidence of the same age in the account of Strabo (*Geographicus* 4.195) and Caesar (*Bellum Gallicum* III.13) of the leather sails of the ships of the

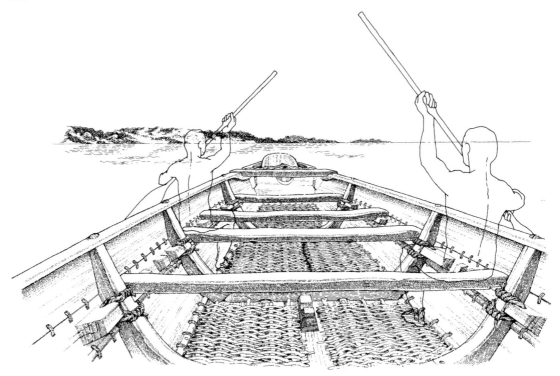

Figure 5.21 View of inside of reconstructed boat looking forward to show paddling positions and action (John Craig).

Veneti in modern Brittany. Less certain is the interpretation of a Norwegian rock carving of Bronze Age date as a boat with 'a very simple mast and sail' (Farrell 1979). The evidence for the earliest known use of mast and sail comes from a clay model of c. 3400 BC from Mesopotamia and a vase painting of c. 3100 BC from Egypt; while there are later representations on Minoan seals from c. 2000 BC (see McGrail 1987a: 225 for sources) and in the famous Thera frescoes (Casson 1975: Figure 2).

The earliest north-west European evidence for oars is a little gold boat model from Durrnberg, Germany, dated to c. 500 BC (McGrail 1987a: 21), and for the British Isles again the Broighter model, which had a full complement of oars as well as the mast and yard. Proposals for either sailing or rowing for a Ferriby boat of the mid second millennium BC would thus anticipate any parallel northern

European evidence by a number of centuries.

This said, and as will be considered under 'Performance', a simple mast and square sail would have greatly eased the task of propulsion of a Ferriby boat. The question whether there is any clue which might suggest that provision was made for the fitting of a mast can be answered by the fact that there is an otherwise inexplicable depression in the ridge (D6) which I have described as the 'saddle feature'. It was first recognized by Dr Ewan Corlett as a 'saddle' from a 1937 photograph and by analogy with similar features in Egyptian boats he interpreted it as designed to locate the forked foot of a pole. If such a pole were then secured to a thwart, by lashing or other means, and stayed by simple rigging lines from the gunwales, it would make an effective mast to carry a yard and a square sail as sketched in Figure 5.23.

The second conjecture concerning rowing

Figure 5.22 Reconstructed boat in live setting: in foreground passenger version with eighteen paddlers coming in to land in tidal creek; in middle distance a twelve-paddler version carrying herdsmen and livestock as proposed for F1 in its final state; South Ferriby shore in background (John Craig).

Table 5.1 Evidence and reasoning for features in reconstruction

Feature in reconstruction	Evidence or source
1 Equal-ended hull	Symmetry in disposition of protuberances along keel-plank in F1 and F2. Symmetry in plan of outer bottom-planks in F1. Production of planks for keel-plank in F1 and F2 from a single split trunk with thinner crown-ends towards scarf and thicker stump-ends outwards.
2 Three strakes each side	Provision and spacing of 6(7) stitch-holes in each side of keel-plank of F1 beyond the three used for attachment of SS1. Need for adequate freeboard in laden boat.
3 Joints in side-strakes	Disposition based on rational grounds to ease construction and ensure strength. Type of joint matches those found in keel-plank in F1 and F2.
4 Thwarts	Structural necessity. Preferred location at top of SS2s supported by cutout in lower edge of wash-strake (F4). Ethnographic parallels. Number variable according to crew needed for paddling; but six included in conjunction with ribs regarded as minimum for structural strength.
5 Ribs	Structural necessity. Three locations and dimensions suggested by slots on keel-plank in F1 and F2. Two more suggested by blocks in F1 (ends of cleats in F2) and a sixth added to fill space to the east of the remains found. Dimensions of ribs derived from dimensions of slots (similar in F2). Anchorage to sheer strake adopted from vertical hole through rail in F4. Crooks, one long and one short are conjectural based on practice in Portuguese *moliseira* with simple scarf. A single pin to hold them together, although without direct parallel in the remains found, is preferred to a withy-lashing which would be very difficult to attach when ribs in place.
6 Girth-lashings and inserted board	Structural need. Deduced from presence and shape of cleat under end of keel-plank. Transverse ridge on upper surface of keel-plank points to location of inserted board.
7 Propulsion by paddles	Availability of paddles in 2nd millenium BC well attested by find at Ferriby (undated), Canewdon Essex (Bronze Age) and much earlier (Mesolithic and Neolithic) in Britain and continental Europe (see Chapter 7). No evidence for oars in NW Europe earlier than c. 500 BC. Rowing potentially available for F4 (c. 500 BC).
8 Possibility of sailing	High degree of desirability to relieve paddlers; Suitability of hull for mainly downwind sailing. Identification of saddle feature and possibly more suitable alternative nearer middle of boat (depression in cleat) as apt for stepping mast.

Table 5.2 Dimensions of the reconstructed boat (in m)

Length overall	15.90
Maximum beam	2.52
Height of ends above underside of keel-plank amidships	1.32
Height of gunwale (measured as above)	0.98
Length along waterline when loaded to give 0.4 m freeboard amidships	13.75

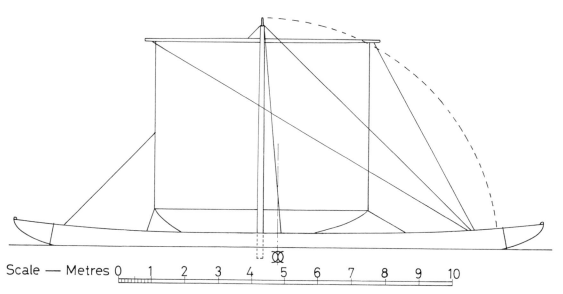

Figure 5.23 Hypothetical sailing rig (J. F. Coates).

as distinct from paddling would provide a great increase in the power exerted in propulsion. In the version based on F1, and therefore of mid second millennium date, paddles have been proposed and not oars; but it may not be entirely coincidental that in F4 the spacing between the thwart, whose position is deduced from the cutout, and a rib passing through the vertical hole through the rail is very close to that which would be required for a rower sitting on the thwart and pulling an oar against a fulcrum provided by an upward extension of the rib to form a thole. Perhaps by c. 500 BC rowing had superseded paddling as the preferred method of propulsion of Ferriby boats.

PERFORMANCE
(by J. F. Coates)

The main aspects of the performance of the proposed reconstruction may be considered under the headings of load-carrying capacity, stability, power and speed, seaworthiness and manoeuvrability together with their influence upon certain features of the reconstruction, or of possible variants.

The bare hull would weigh about 3.8 tonnes. Equipment such as paddles, poles, ropes and stone anchors would add about 0.2 tonnes which should be doubled if the boat had a mast and sail, making a total of rather more than 4 tonnes for the fully equipped boat, which would float with a draft of about 0.35 m and a freeboard amidships of just over 0.6 m. For a boat of this length a loaded freeboard of 0.4 m would be safe for normal estuarine or coastal navigation in moderate conditions. At that freeboard the boat would carry a load of crew and cargo of 6.7 tonnes with a draft of 0.58 m.

On occasions when good speed and endurance under paddle were needed, a full crew of twenty men (eighteen paddlers plus two) would have been aboard. Such a crew at 75 kg each including gear would weigh about 1.5 tonnes, leaving a load capacity of just over 5 tonnes for cargo or passengers. As a passenger carrier the reconstruction would have room for thirty people, weighing 2.3 tonnes, seated on the thwarts inboard of the paddlers and on their own baggage. Baggage capacity would have been limited more by volume than by weight.

Fully loaded, with a displacement of 11 tonnes, the metacentre would be 1.7 m above Datum (the plane tangential to the underside of the keel-plank amidships). The centre of gravity of the boat itself is about 0.6 m above Datum, while that of the crew, passengers, and baggage would be about 0.9 m above Datum, bringing the centre of gravity of the whole to about 0.8 m above Datum, so that the boat would be very stable with a metacentric height of about 0.9 m.

At 11 tonnes, the waterline would be 13.7 m long. The breadth at that waterline would be 2.3 m, only one-sixth of the waterline length, a ratio about half its value in the general run of cargo-carrying vessels and nearly as low as that in the faster types of Viking longships. Length and slenderness of hull have always been essential in muscle-powered craft of any appreciable performance and range not only to accommodate the necessary crew but also to avoid unnecessary resistance arising from making waves with the hull as it goes through the water. Length in boats has never come cheaply, so when needed to accommodate the propulsion power it is fairly safe to assume

that the largest practicable number of paddlers (or oarsmen as may be the case) will be fitted into the boat. In the proposed reconstruction three thwarts have been introduced into the longest spaces between the six frames and their associated thwarts, to raise the maximum number of paddlers from twelve to eighteen.

With eighteen paddlers the reconstruction may be expected to keep up about 6 knots for half an hour or so, on the assumption that each paddler could produce 90 watts of effective propulsive power for that length of time. The tidestream of the Humber river in the second millennium BC is assumed to have been about the same as it is today, 5 knots. If capable of 6 knots a boat could breast such a tide when steered at 60° off the direct course across the river and thus operate at any state of the tide subject to avoidance of sandbanks. With twelve paddlers the boat could be expected to achieve only 5.2 knots on the same assumptions, too small a margin over the tidestream to allow crossings to be made except around slack water at high tide. Hull length and the number of paddlers may thus be seen to have been quite critical in the effectiveness of this boat when acting as a ferry across the Humber.

It may be thought that as paddlers can work as closely spaced as 0.7 m, four more thwarts should have been fitted into the reconstruction to raise the maximum number of paddlers to twenty-six in order to exploit the length of hull fully. While such an arrangement would be feasible, its main advantage in performance would lie in raising the speed sustainable over long distances with the crew working in shifts rather than in higher speed for shorter periods, in which an increase of less than a knot would be obtained by adding eight paddlers to the crew. That small return for raising the power by more than 40 per cent reflects the fact that the required power varies with the cube of the speed to which has to be added the power also required by the wavemaking which would be significant for a hull of that waterline length at more than 6 knots. If built for speed by paddle over long distances, as for example for war or for a chieftain, the boat could well have been a variant fitted for twenty-six paddlers, and capable of carrying a force, including paddlers, of at least fifty armed men at a sustained speed which in calm conditions would be little short of 5 knots if they worked in shifts.

If boats of the Ferriby type were built primarily for carrying cargoes, they could be expected to have been built deeper and with more flare to their sides: they would also in all probability have been shorter. As speed under paddle would have been less important, paddlers would have been fewer and placed at the ends of the boat to keep the middle clear for cargo (but see p. 142 for the theory that wear and tear of fittings in the stern half of the boat might have been caused by the feet of hoofed livestock). Increased depth of hull and therefore freeboard, except when fully loaded, would make propulsion by oar instead of paddle a greater possibility.

There must have been coastal navigation round the southern North Sea during the second millennium BC and the proposed reconstruction may be considered seaworthy enough to have been regarded in the circumstances of that time as adequate for that purpose. However the reality of navigation at sea over any appreciable distances, even if only along coasts, calls the sole use of muscles for propulsion into serious question. All experiments in operating replicas of ancient oared ships at sea have served to emphasize the severe limitations of muscle power for propulsion as compared with sail over any but quite modest distances. It follows that notwithstanding the lack of incontrovertible evidence of sail in north-west Europe before the Broighter boat model of the first century BC, the use of sail in the preceding millennium should not be denied. Its overwhelming advantages could not have been obscure to seamen of the same society as the builders of the Ferriby boats. It therefore seems reason-

able to presume that if boats of the Ferriby tradition were taken to sea they might have been equipped with mast and sail. That possibility has been explored in the reconstruction.

The stability of the reconstruction is sufficient to enable a square sail of 30 to 40 sq m to be set on a mast 6 to 7 m high. It has been suggested that the forked heel of a mast could have been stepped in the 'saddle feature' (Figure 5.17, B6) on the keel-plank 2.5 m forward of the keel scar (Figure 5.17, B9), but that would be too far forward of the half-length of the waterline to sail in any but stern winds. There is a dip (Figure 5.17, B8) in a long cleat in the keel 0.6 m forward of the keel scarf which could have been the mast step, and a mast there would be better placed to enable the boat to be sailed across the wind. The flat-bottomed hull would however make much leeway in a beam wind unless fitted with some form of lee-board. Downwind performance under sail would be quite brisk, exceeding 7 knots in a 25-knot wind. Any real evidence about a Ferriby boat's possible performance under sail must however await trials with a full-scale reconstruction.

In considering seaworthiness and sailing, the consequences of swamping should not be neglected. The reconstruction may be expected to float when swamped with the thwarts amidships in or just above the water surface if the boat were empty. Stability, though reduced, would be positive owing to the thickness of the side-strakes of the hull, and the remaining freeboard should enable the boat to be bailed out in waves up to about 0.5 m high from trough to crest. The swamped condition of the boat when loaded depends critically upon the amount and density of the cargo remaining in the boat, but there should be a good chance of recovering from swamping in a fair proportion of the conditions in which such a boat is likely to have been at sea.

Owing to the rockered bottom, the manoeuvrability of a Ferriby boat would have been excellent. When paddled, the boat could have been steered conveniently by a paddle carried for that purpose. Running free, the boat could be expected to be directionally rather unstable and would veer to one side or the other if listing at the time. When sailed, the longer periods of heavier course-keeping corrections needed would call for something less tiring than a paddle, on the lines of a side rudder.

GROOVING OF THE KEEL-PLANK
(by E. V. Wright)

This feature (Figure 4.6), first observed in 1946, has always been something of a puzzle and various theories have been advanced to suggest its purpose. The grooves are cut so that the inner edges are deeper than the outer, giving an appearance reminiscent of overlapping, narrow planking. They are roughly symmetrical about the mid-line and converge towards the presumed bow of the boat. The treatment closest to the tip is not known since the underside was not examined between 1937 and 1946 by when much of the timber had been washed away (see p. 90). Nor is it possible to say whether similar grooving was carried out on the adjoining planks on either side of the keel-plank.

Two sorts of theory have been proposed for their purpose: ornamental or functional. Of the former, when the age of the Ferriby boats was still unknown, I suggested that they might be imitative of narrow, 'clinker' planking observed, admired, but not properly understood by the builders. This idea became untenable once a second millennium BC date had been established. My next suggestion was that they were a copy of the characteristic folds in the skin in the 'chin' area of the Balaenid whales, in which case a measure of sympathetic magic might have been intended in order to give the boats some of the seaworthiness of such great beasts which were clearly masters of their watery environment. The use of the 'oculus' on so many ancient and modern boats as an aid to navigation would be an obvious analogy.

Somewhere between the ornamental and the functional lies the suggestion that they were designed to improve performance through the water. The Maori of New Zealand developed a technique of special facetting with adze-strokes around the cutwater of their canoes which they held to increase speed by creating turbulence over that area of the skin. This later evolved into elaborate, decorative carving which in turn degenerated into painted copies of the carved patterns. It is generally thought that any such treatment in the Ferriby case would have had a negligible effect or indeed an adverse one since the resistance of a boat is increased by any additional source of turbulent flow past the hull, especially at or near the bow.

Two theories of a truly functional kind have been proposed: first, that by Trevor Green, that the grooves were designed to act as guides to hold in place cords strung over a bar passed through the cleat behind them and then wound together to form a stay running over the boat from bow to stern where they would be secured in similar fashion. This would be rigged over two or more props and tension applied by means of a tourniquet so as to achieve and maintain bending of the bottom-structure to the required curve (see p. 142). The second theory, strongly advocated by my colleague Ewan Corlett, is that they were provided to ease the task of unsticking the bows of the boat when as might often happen it was run hard onto a mud-bank, their effect being to break the suction which would be that much greater if the surface were left smooth.

Generally speaking I favour a functional purpose rather than an abstract or ornamental one, since primitive boat-builders are unlikely to go to great effort except for genuinely practical reasons. Trials alone will shed light on the mystery and perhaps suggest a quite different solution from those offered.

6

Materials and building

Having arrived at a preferred design of a complete boat and estimated its performance, the next stage is to consider how the actual parts found were made and how the reconstructed boat might have been built. There are few direct or relevant sources about boatbuilding methods and techniques used in the ancient world except those that can be derived from incomplete or obscure literary sources and pictorial or sculptured representations, as for instance in Egypt (Figure 6.1). There are however many situations where types of construction similar to those at Ferriby have been used in recent times and a declining number where they still are. Such ethnographic parallels can shed useful light on features and help to elucidate methods and sequences of working which might otherwise be obscure. There is obvious scope also for experiments to illuminate this field; some have already been done, and more are projected.

The subject matter will be treated under the headings: supply and preparation of materials; site-facilities and structures; tools; principles and sequence of construction; and finally repair and refitting in the light of the evidence of damage and wear provided by the finds themselves. I should however emphasize that some of the propositions which are put forward remain provisional. At the time of

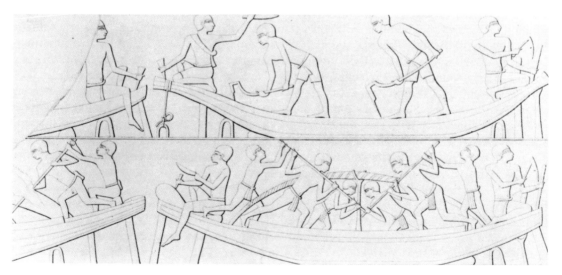

Figure 6.1 Egyptian boatbuilding c. 2000 BC. (*Photo*: British Museum.)

writing, study of the evidence and experimental work still continue, having received a welcome if only temporary boost in connection with a project, now unfortunately in abeyance, to build a full-size, working replica of a reconstructed Ferriby boat. It is self-evident that a hypothetical reconstruction can only be valid if the resulting design can actually be built by what are believed to be methods available in antiquity or by modern methods carefully chosen so as not to transcend the ancient ones. If such a project does go forward much will be learned and it is more than likely that ideas advanced now on a theoretical basis will be modified in the light of practical experience.

SUPPLY AND PREPARATION OF MATERIALS

Timber

First and foremost must come the selection and felling of oak trees for the planks and these can safely be presumed to have been both plentiful and large in woodland within reasonable distance of the building site. In the absence of any sizeable river nearby down which entire trunks might have been floated, it seems rational to assume that trunks were trimmed, split and roughed out for planks at the felling site in order to reduce the weight for carriage to a building site on the foreshore. Felling could only have been accomplished at that period with axes of flint, stone, or bronze (Figure 6.2c) with or without the aid of fire. It has been demonstrated that splitting of unseasoned or 'green' oak once felled can be done with wooden implements alone: wedges of seasoned oak and heavy wooden mauls (Figure 6.3). The half-logs can then be converted to single large planks or squared timbers by chopping the outer part away with axes or, if thinner planks are required, split radially and trimmed down to whatever thickness is desired. Where a long, flat plank is needed, radial splitting can be the most economical, given that the breadth needed is not too great. Where very broad planks are wanted and in particular planks with an array of upstanding protuberances left on the surface, they may have to be cut tangentially to the axis of the log and, in extreme cases, with only one plank extracted out of half a treetrunk, the waste then being very great (Figure 6.4).

When recording the timbers of boats 1 and 2 at Greenwich in 1946 I made some observations of the pattern of rays and growth rings at convenient breaks in the planks and these are illustrated in the section drawings in Figures 4.4 and 4.13. Additional evidence has been obtained in recent years from the surviving remains by Jennifer Hillam in her dendrochronological studies at Sheffield University (Hillam 1985). Together such data enable a reliable indication to be given of how planks of different sizes and configurations were extracted from trees and the minimum length and diameter of trees needed.

The availability of large trees has been clearly indicated by finds of other ancient craft from the same neighbourhood. A few examples may be helpful in providing comparative scale. A number of great logboats from the Bronze Age have been found in Britain, several in the Humber catchment area. The largest recorded is that from Brigg on the River Ancholme, only 18 km across the Humber from North Ferriby as the crow flies, dated to c. 1000 BC. This is 14.78 m long and 1.37 m wide at the transom-stern (Figure 6.5). The timber at the bow-end was affected by the emergence of the lowest branches from the trunk; but after allowance for the stump – and felling with bronze axes was unlikely to have been done at less than 1 m above ground level – this tree must have stood a clear 16 m high to the crown. The Hasholme logboat of c. 300 BC excavated from an extinct channel draining into the Humber only 9 km above North Ferriby was shorter than that from Brigg at c. 12.25 m excluding the extensions at the bow but of comparable width (1.40 m) at the transom (Figure 6.6). The planks in

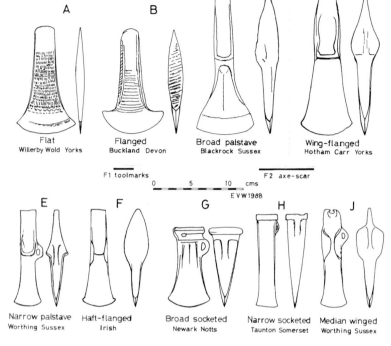

A
Flat
Willerby Wold Yorks

B
Flanged
Buckland Devon

C
Broad palstave
Blackrock Sussex

D
Wing-flanged
Hotham Carr Yorks

F1 toolmarks

F2 axe-scar

0   5   10 cms

EVW 1988

E
Narrow palstave
Worthing Sussex

F
Haft-flanged
Irish

G
Broad socketed
Newark Notts

H
Narrow socketed
Taunton Somerset

J
Median winged
Worthing Sussex

Figure 6.2a Bronze axe-heads.

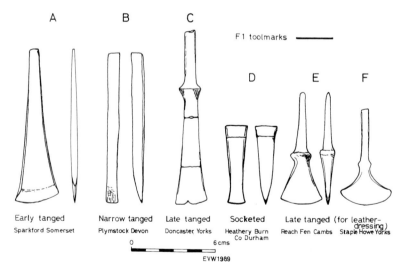

A
Early tanged
Sparkford Somerset

B
Narrow tanged
Plymstock Devon

C
Late tanged
Doncaster Yorks

F1 toolmarks

D
Socketed
Heathery Burn
Co Durham

E
Late tanged (for leather-dressing)
Reach Fen Cambs

F
Staple Howe Yorks

0   6 cms

EVW1989

Figure 6.2b Bronze chisels.

Figure 6.2c Bronze Age axes with replicas of shafts. (*Photo*: John Coles.)

the Brigg 'Raft' of c. 850 BC, the only other planked boat of the Bronze Age known from Britain, were estimated to have been made from trees of more than 12 m in height to the crown and 0.60–0.80 m in diameter (Hillam 1981). In mediaeval times, when oak was the most favoured timber for structural purposes, there are examples of the use of even longer trees than those from which the logboats were shaped. Perhaps the most spectacular of these were the eight matching vertical members in the octagonal lantern erected over the crossing in Ely Cathedral in the 1330s, each 'nearly 70 feet' (21.3 m) long (Purcell 1973). These must have been exceptional even then since it is recorded that in 1322 Alan of Walsingham, the sacristan, and Master Thomas the carpenter went as far afield as Bedfordshire to purchase suitable oak trees for the construction of a building which is one of the most spectacular feats of structural engineering in timber in mediaeval times. By comparison the trees specified later in the reconstructed boat are of quite modest dimensions even by modern standards and are clearly not of sizes to qualify as rare giants of the forest such as might be hard to find within reasonable distance from the boat site.

a

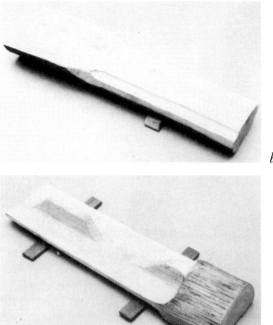

b

Figure 6.3 Splitting a log with wooden wedges (N. M. M. Greenwich).

c

Attention is directed first to the keel-plank since, from the way in which the timber was handled in the making of this, deductions can be drawn as to whether the boats were equal-ended or not. Hillam's studies of sections of the timber have demonstrated beyond reason-

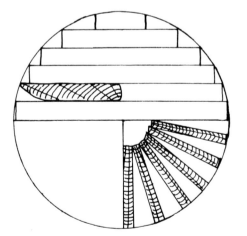

Figure 6.4 Diagram showing tangential and radial reduction of log to planks (N. M. M. Greenwich).

able doubt that the pairs of planks of which the keel-planks were composed in F1 and F2 were in each case derived from a single oak, split lengthwise (Hillam 1985). She also con-firmed my observation of 1946 that, whereas in F1 the planks were made from half-logs with the pith of the trunk downwards and the sapwood upwards, in F2 the southern of the two planks was made as in F1 but the northern plank was reversed with the pith side upwards and sapwood downwards (Figure 6.7). The implications of this phenomenon will be examined later. In F1, however, it seems most likely that the ends were equal with the upward curve and maximum breadth being shaped out of the stump-ends of the two half-logs and taking advantage of any extra thick-ness available from buttresses. It has been known since the first excavation of the western end of F1 in 1937 that the upcurved end at least had been carved to shape and not bent since the run of the grain was seen to be nearly horizontal right up to the tip (Figure 1.12).

Figure 6.5 The great logboat being transported from the excavations for the gasworks at Brigg in 1886 (*Illustrated London News*).

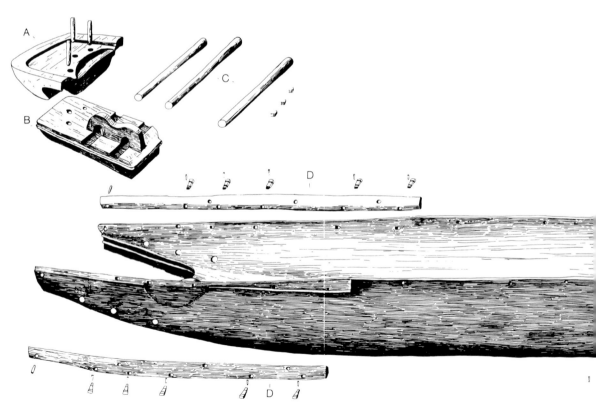

Figure 6.6 The components of the Hasholme logboat excavated in 1984: (*A*) upper bow, (*B*) lower bow, (*C*) transverse timbers with wedges, (*D*) washstrakes with treenails and keys, (*E*) repairs with

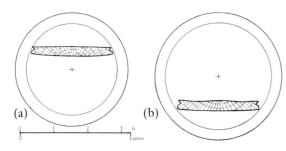

Figure 6.7 Sections of idealized logs related to the two components of the F2 keel-plank: (a) southern and (b) northern part.

The question then remains whether the rocker in the rest of the keel-plank was contrived by bending or shaping, or by a combination of the two.

Modern experiments with splitting unseasoned oak logs have shown that in the half-log there is a tendency for the timber to bow away from the plane of the pith (Richard Darrah: pers. comm). The phenomenon is strongly marked in logs up to c. 300 mm in diameter but it is thought that it would occur only marginally in logs of the much larger diameters used for the planks in a Ferriby boat. Be that as it may, the midships ends of the planks near the scarf could not possibly have been bent by weights or other mechanical means owing to the thickness and hence stiffness of the timber there and the difficulty of applying the requisite leverage. Artificial bending, if any, could have been confined only to the middle part of each plank. We are left then with the two options: entirely shaped, or part-shaped and part-bent. Theoretically it would be possible to shape a plank curved in the manner recorded for the nearly intact western half of F1's keel-plank from a half-log c. 8.5 m long and with diameters excluding sapwood of c. 1.5 m at the stump-end and c. 0.9 m at the crown. However, if it is accepted that the two planks came from the same tree, the trunk must have been nearly straight; therefore without recourse to bending this would result in the line of the

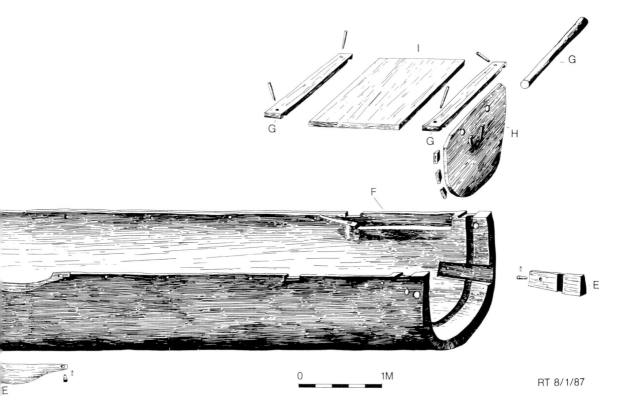

treenails, (*F*) shelves, (*G*) beam-ties with treenails, (*H*) transom with wedges, (*I*) steering platform or decking (NMM. Greenwich).

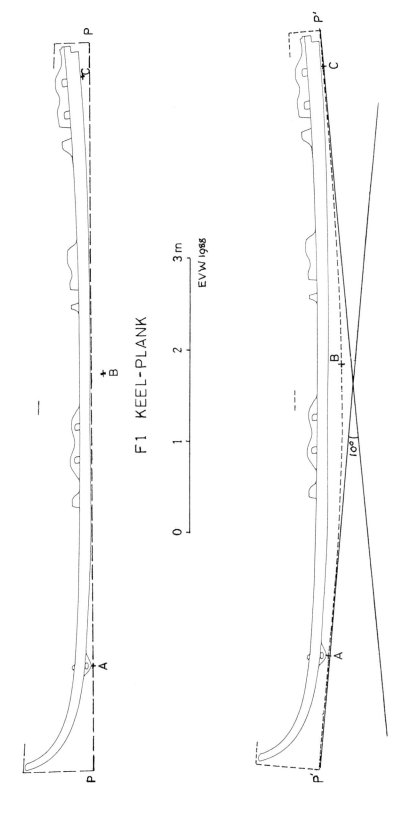

F1 KEEL-PLANK

0   1   2   3 m

EVW 1988

Figure 6.8 The case for bending the keel-plank in F1: A, B and C represent the observed positions of the pith (P – P) in relation to the plank. In 6.8a with the pith shown as straight, B and C do not coincide with the line P – P. In 6.8b with the plank curved, A, B and C coincide with the line of the pith, the degree of bending being 10° for eastern or western half.

pith lying only just below the bottom of the plank at its mid-length and some 0.07 m below it near the midship (eastern) end. My observations of 1946, however, show that the plane of the pith was c. 0.14 m below the middle and only c. 0.025 m below the bottom near amidships (Figure 6.8). Accommodation to these estimates calls for bending of the plank over about the middle half of its length through some 10° of angle. If this were done the required minimum diameter at the stump-end would fall to c. 1.4 m.

No sapwood has been observed in the edges of the keel-planks in either F1 or F2 so that it is not possible to estimate the maximum size of trees used. Figure 6.8 shows in diagrammatic form the minimum dimensions necessary in a half-log to accommodate the length, height, and breadth of the western half of F1's keel-plank assuming an ideal straight treetrunk with even taper from stump to crown. The other half-log would likewise accommodate the matching eastern plank. But Figure 2.17 shows that in fact the tree was not perfectly straight but that, as might be expected, it bent this way and that, and that the makers left their finished plank with wavy edges. These inequalities in the outline were then compensated for first by trimming the inner edges of the outer bottom-planks to an accurate fit with the keel-plank and in turn by shaping their outer edges to give a bilaterally symmetrical outline to the complete bottom-structure. The effect of this on the slightly protruding bottom of the keel-plank can be seen in the body plan in Figure 5.18b, where the mid-breadth of the plank diverges from the middle line of the boat.

The keel-plank in F2 was even broader than that in F1 and, as in F1, the two planks are taken to have been cut from a single split log. The dendrochronological evidence from dry sections indicates that this was of not less than 0.76 m diameter. Unfortunately, while the wood was still wet in 1946, I only recorded rays and growth rings for one section in each of the two planks and it is not therefore poss-ible to deduce the relationship of plank to half-log with the same confidence as in the case of F1 (western half) where I recorded them at three sections. Nevertheless on the analogy of F1, there would be no apparent problem in making the southern plank in F2 from a half-log of c. 1.4 m diameter at the stump and c. 1.1 m at the crown. With the northern plank, however, where the half-log was the other way up, problems arise not so much from the height or depth of timber available, where a diameter of c. 1.45 m would be adequate, but rather in the width needed since in this configuration the available timber narrows in breadth below the pith where of course the half-log is at its broadest (Figure 6.9); I have estimated that employing bending of c. 21°, that is up to twice the extent postulated in the case of F1, it should be just possible from a half-trunk of not less than 1.4 m diameter at the stump (excluding sapwood) and tapering to 1.1 m at the crown, to extract a plank of the dimensions and shape called for in the reconstruction. As will be seen from Figure 6.9, the line of the pith has to be above the upturned northern tip and then to intersect the 1946 estimate of its position at Section a–a. From there southwards bending is necessary in order to keep the plane of the pith above the top of the carved features on the upper side through to the scarf. This bending need be restricted only to the middle run of the plank as in the comparable case in F1. The problem and degree of bending would not in fact be eased by an increase in the diameter of the log since it is the positions of the pith in relation to the plank at the tip, at Section a–a and thereafter over the cleat systems towards the scarf, that effectively govern the need for bending. One can only speculate about the reasons for the production of the plank in the manner chosen, which can hardly have been other than deliberate bearing in mind the labour involved. Perhaps there was an imperfection in the timber on the outside of the log at the stump-end which was thereby avoided, since it is there that wood

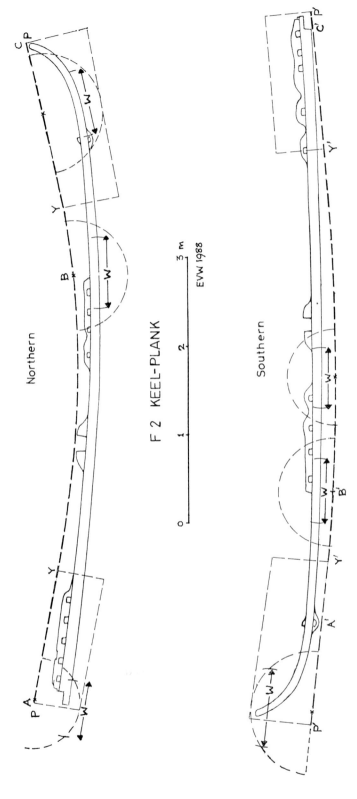

Northern

Southern

F 2 KEEL-PLANK

0   1   2   3 m

EVW 1988

Figure 6.9 Diagrams of the keel-plank in F2 showing how the two halves could be extracted from a single split tree-trunk, the northern with the pith upwards, and the southern downwards. It is assumed that bending is restricted to the lengths between Y–Y and Y^1–Y^1, shaping being done at each end. A/A^1, B/B^1, and C/C^1 represent the positions of the pith in relation to the planks recorded in 1946 and the curved lines P–P and P^1–P^1 are those required for bending to make these coincide with the lines of the pith: in the northern plank an angle of c. 21° and in the southern c. 10°. W indicates the width of plank at each station in relation to the section of log available as represented by the semicircle.

would be cut away below the upturned tip.

The paired outer bottom-planks in F1 were the longest single planks recorded in any of the three finds and with the damaged eastern ends restored would have been c. 10.5 m in length. Only two small fragments of the northern of these now survive at Greenwich; but in two of the sections measured in 1946 the pattern of rays and growth rings was recorded (Figure 4.4). These show that as in the case of the two planks which made up the keel-plank the outer bottom-planks were shaped with the plane of the pith below and the sapwood above. The same is true of the stealer inserted by way of repair in the outer edge of the southern of these two planks. The layout suggests that once again the pair of planks had been cut tangentially from a single split trunk. The position of the pith and width of the plank at Section h–h which is close to the middle indicate a diameter of more than 0.9 m there (Figure 6.10). My marks of the rays suggest that some sapwood may have been included at the inner edge and Hillam has identified sapwood in the comparable plank from F3. While not conclusive, the positions in relation to the log recorded at Sections O, E and H suggest that the curved profile of the plank was not achieved by shaping, but almost entirely by bending and, as can be seen from Figure 6.10, theoretically there is sufficient thickness of timber to obtain two planks from each half-log or four in all from one tree. This is feasible technically by splitting tangentially as recently demonstrated by Richard Darrah (1990) who has extracted five planks up to 40 cm wide from a quartered log of oak (Figure 6.10b). Trees of the necessary dimensions need not have been exceptional (Figure 5.14), and, although there would have been obvious advantages of economy in extracting the maximum number of usable planks from each one felled, what to our eyes today may seem extravagant use of timber would have been in keeping with the impression gained elsewhere in the finds.

Moving on to the next pair of planks, the

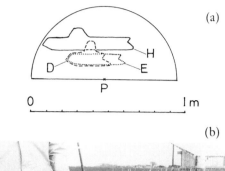

(a)

0   1 m

(b)

Figure 6.10a Diagram showing the position of the recorded sections in the northern outer bottom-plank in F1 in relation to that of the minimum sized half log required to accommodate them. The position of the pith (P) is derived from observations of rays and growth-rings made in 1946 in sections (*see* Figure 4.3c).

Figure 6.10b Reduction of a green oak-log to planks up to 40 cm wide by tangential splitting using wedges only. (*Experiment and photograph:* Richard Darrah.)

lowest side-strakes, we proceed beyond the recorded evidence and into the realms of hypothesis since the two examples found were both incomplete, having been broken across at some stage in their lives. The surviving intact end of each was, however, the most complex part, being skilfully shaped to fit into the space between the outer bottom-plank and the extension of the keel-plank, in the case of F1 with the internal hollow rounded and in F3 sharply angled. We cannot now prove positively whether these strakes were single planks or made up of two separate planks joined at about a quarter of the length from one end or two end-pieces with a plain length along the middle. It seems unlikely that the builders would arrange for the strake to be of two equal halves since the provision of a joint in the plane of the middle of the boat while not necessarily weakening the structure to an unacceptable degree would tend to increase the difficulty of achieving and maintaining the correct curvature in relation to the rockered bottom. The evidence from F3 is to my mind conclusive in this respect since the length of plank surviving in that find would bring the broken end close to the plane of the scarf in a boat of the same length as F1. If there had been a joint at the middle plane it would be most unlikely that the plank would break within 1 metre of it: rather it would come apart at the joint itself. I arrive at the preferred conclusion therefore that these lowest side-strakes were each made up of a long and a short plank, the shorter being all shaped and the unshaped part of the longer component bent in to meet the other at a joint at about a quarter of the length of the strake. Supporting evidence for this can be obtained from F3, where the shaped internal angle at the chine runs out c. 2.7 m from the tip so that an allowance of not less than 3 m for shaping at each end would therefore appear realistic. The recorded section 2.3 m from the tip and near to the broken end of the strake in F1 shows the plank was still slightly curved internally which would argue against significant bending in that plane and it would therefore appear likely that shaping extended for about 3 m in from each end as suggested for F3. The total length of strake required in the reconstruction of F1 is estimated as 12.3 m and this would allow for shaping of the outer 3 m of the longer plank with bending confined to 6 m up to the joint. A c. 9 m-long plank with shaping at one end does not demand any unusual size of log.

For the next two side-strakes – or one in the case of a 'two-strake' boat – to be cut each in one piece or made up of two, as in the lowest side-strake, might not only be stretching our conception of the powers of the boatbuilders and size of trees available beyond reasonable limits, but is also technically unnecessary since adequate strength can be provided with strakes of two or three planks provided the joints can be adequately shifted between adjacent planks. In the hypothetical reconstruction provision is therefore made for the second and third strakes to have been made each from a pair of shaped ends with a flat middle plank which would not demand drastic bending to match the curve of the plank below it (Figure 5.14). These could be derived from trees of more modest size than those postulated for the outer bottom-planks (see Figure 5.14). There is however evidence in F4 that curvature in plan-view was obtained at least in part by shaping from the solid log (Wright et al. 1989).

Considerable thought and some initial research has been devoted to the problems posed by the requirement of bending the bottom-structure to the determined profile and of accurate fitting of the plank-edges together with precise marking of the stitch-holes. A range of possible options is set out and discussed in Appendix 6.1 at the end of this chapter.

Use of piled rocks for weighting down the middle of a plank whose ends are supported as practised in China (Needham 1971, quoting Worcester) would involve problems of accommodating the very large weight necessary with such thick planks. The same would be true for people standing on them. Baking or steaming have long been and are still used to soften the walls of dugout bases for boats before they are expanded, for example in Bangladesh in modern times (Greenhill 1971: 112). Firing to a temperature sufficient to melt the lignin in the timber and achieve a considerable degree of bending has also been an accepted and widespread practice in recent frame-first construction where planking has to be curved to fit, especially round the bow and stern of a ship. The ingenious scheme to use tensioning ropes over the ends of the keel-plank has been proposed by Trevor Green, but has yet to be tested experimentally. Trimming plank-edges to the accuracy achieved in F1 and F3 must have called for repeated offering up of the components before the required fit was achieved and it is possible that the systems of transverse timbers through cleats may have come into play as an aid for this process. Only after final fitting could the stitch-holes be marked out and cut. Further investigations are planned to elucidate how these and other problems in the reconstruction might have been solved by the builders.

Other timber

The making of the sealing-laths of oak would seem to have involved skills similar to those of the shingle-maker in recent times, that is the production of long straight planks of narrow vee-section by splitting a log radially with wedges. The rough planks could then be trimmed down to the symmetrical cambered section of the laths at Ferriby. The average length of each main piece was 1.0 m and about 60 such laths would have been needed to cap the seams where they are known to have been used in F1, including in that case the repaired cracks. If the seams between side-strakes were also capped on the inside an additional c. 52 would be necessary in the three-strake case or c. 30 in the two-strake alternative.

The transverse timbers found in F1 were of ash and derived from radially split logs, as also were the oak timbers in F2. In neither case would the lengths, c. 0.9 to 1.2 m in F1 nor the quantity, 8 in F1 and 18 in F2, appear to present problems for the Ferriby craftsmen compared with the other fabricated components.

Withies

The availability of stocks of suitable yew branch for making withies presents problems of a different nature. First, as to quantity, the approximate numbers needed for three and two-strake boats would be as shown in Table 6.1.

Table 6.1 Stitches in reconstructed versions of F1

	Three-strake	Two-strake
Observed complete	108	108
Observed incomplete plus empty stitch-holes	85	85
Conjectural for restored parts	171	87
	364	280

Of these some 40 would be of the thicker size used to stitch the hood-ends of side-strakes to the keel-plank. The minimum length needed for each stitch is approximately 0.8 m. Practical experiment (Wright 1984) has shown that not all present-day yew branches are suitable and that the most satisfactory are the sucker-like branches growing up vertically and in deep shade from the sweeping boughs of large old trees. These do not occur frequently on modern park-grown trees and it is possible either that the boatbuilders had access to the now extinct fen variety of yew (Oliver Rackham 1982), or that normal yews performed differently in the more favourable climatic conditions then prevailing or even that some form of 'cultivation' such as pruning or, doubtfully, coppicing was used to induce suitable growth. It seems unlikely that purely casual gathering would produce enough to meet the demand for initial building and periodical restitching or repair.

Since my experiments of 1983–4, I have learned of an alternative method of contriving the withy fastening as used in Finland for the reconstruction of the Rääkkylä boat (Naskali 1986). In this case the twist is applied progressively as the spruce-root material is threaded through the holes to form continuous sewing. The twist is secured by wedging as the worker moves along the seam and more withy twisted and fibres separated only after the previous work is plugged. Such

Figure 6.11 John Cottrell, besom-broom-maker of Henley-on-Thames, winding a withy of yew branch.

have been large and its collection a considerable task. *Neckera complanata* alone was identified in a sample from F2 and the mosses were presumably chosen for their specially suitable properties. In F3 the additional use of a caulking-rope of the long-fibred common hair moss, *Polytrichum commune* (Figure 6.14) again implies access to ample supplies of raw material from nearby bogs and then skill in spinning yarn and laying cord. The minimum length needed for caulking the seams of the bottom-structure of F3 reconstructed on lines similar to F1 would be of the order of 50 m including the seams between the outer bottom-planks and lowest side-strakes. It is not known from either F1 or F3 whether or how the seams between the side-strakes were caulked.

Rope, cordage

We know for a fact that the builders were masters of the art of stitching with withies of yew and that fragments of withies of other species are of common occurrence in the deposits (Figure 6.15). We also know, from the example described in Chapter 7, that a length of laid withy material was made and can be presumed from the intimate association to be contemporary with cord of hair moss typical of that used for caulking in F3. In addition we have the evidence of rope-laying capability in the caulking cord itself, again at the time of the building of F3. A short length of similar cord was found during the 1946 excavations near to F2. Rope made of hair moss has not been tested for strength; but the fibres are typically over 0.2 m in length and can be presumed to yield cord of useful strength so that it need not have been used solely in a passive way for caulking seams.

a method could undoubtedly have been used in the Ferriby situation and would have avoided the demanding preparatory twisting of a complete length of yew branch (Figure 6.11). I commend it for both trial and use in any exercise of replica building (Figure 6.12).

Caulking

The final major needs for materials were the mosses for caulking, *Neckera complanata* and *Eurhynchium striatum* in mixed masses in F1, reported to be common woodland species today and presumably even more freely available in the native woodland in ancient times (Figure 6.13). The quantity required would

The only applications of binding material postulated in the reconstruction in Chapter 5 and not actually observed in the remains are: the attachments between the ribs and the second side-strakes for which yew-withies would be entirely satisfactory; and the more

Figure 6.12 Esko Laulajainen, boatbuilder of Padasjoki in southern Finland, sewing a seam in the replica of the Rääkkylä boat, using fir root. (*Photo*: Eero Naskali.)

A

B

Figure 6.13 The mosses *Neckera complanata* (A) and *Eurhynchium striatum* (B) used for waterproofing the seams in F1, F2, and F3.

Figure 6.14 The common hair moss (*Polytrichum commune*) whose fibres were made into cord used additionally for waterproofing the seam in F3.

demanding ropes or bundles of cords for the girth-lashings. The amount of such cord or other material is limited by what could be threaded through the hole in the winged cleat which has a cross-section area estimated at c. 30cm^2 which could accommodate say two strands each of 4 cm diameter or 12.5 cm girth. The lashing would also spend most if its working life saturated by water and would not serve its purpose effectively if it stretched unduly when wet. It is thought worthwhile to speculate on possible candidates for the material in question.

Animal hide comes to mind as a possibility, but in general is thought to fail the test of resisting stretch when saturated with water. Its inadequacies are attested by the fact that for this reason the Eskimos use sinew rather than strips of hide for stitching their kayaks and umiaks (Adney and Chapelle 1964: 192). In later times, and indeed until quite recently, use was made of elk-skin ropes in Norway and of pigskin thongs worked into multi-stranded

Figure 6.15 Withy material from the Ferriby site. (*Photo*: Q. E. Wright.)

rope 'for the tiller-ropes of very large sailing ships in the last century' (Arne-Emil Christensen pers. comm.), an example from the frigate *King Sverre* being preserved in the Oslo Maritime Museum. In the north, thongs and ropes made from the skin of aquatic mammals have a long history: whale, seal, and especially walrus being prized (Clark 1952: 83–4), the last for ships' ropes in particular. Animal skin cannot therefore be ruled out entirely in the Ferriby case and traces of it would not be expected to survive in the conditions prevailing in the shore deposits.

Cords and ropes made from vegetable fibres appear more promising than thongs of hide, and there are several possible materials. Long-fibred moss is obviously one which could prove to have the necessary strength and resistance to stretching. Others are bark-fibre (bast) or nettle fibre used for net-making as early as Mesolithic times (Clark 1952: 45), and bast is favoured in experiment over hair moss for the cords used to make the impressed decorations on beakers (Clark 1952: 297). Bast too was used for the sewn fastenings of the Hjortspring boat (Rosenberg 1937). Flax if available would probably be the most satisfactory material for cordage for girth-lashings in terms of strength, durability and stretch-resistance. The use of its stalks for fibres rather than its seeds for food or oil goes back to Neolithic times in the Alpine area but evidence for its appearance in ancient situations in Britain is less certain, although seed impressions have been recorded in Bronze Age pottery (Clark 1952: 233–4).

To sum up, therefore, rope made from animal hide is thought unlikely whereas several possible vegetable fibres are known to have been available by the time the boats were built, of which hair moss, bast and flax appear the most promising, with some preference for the last of these on grounds of its quality and performance in marine situations (Morrison and Coates 1986). Hemp was not known in north-west Europe at least until Roman times (Godwin 1967).

BOATBUILDING SITE AND FACILITIES

The obvious prime requirement for the boat-building site is a firm strand close to the waterside and above high-water mark. Experience in recent times in Europe and at present in places where wooden boats are still constructed by traditional methods suggests that nothing more elaborate than this is needed. There are indications, admittedly somewhat tenuous, that in the North Ferriby case there might have been small channels or gullies in which boats could be floated at mid to high tide and this too would be consistent with the writer's own observations of a boat-working site at Chittagong in Bangladesh (Figure 6.16). It seems probable too that at North Ferriby problems of rising water levels required counter-measures in the form of trackways and the provision of 'hards' to prevent loss of potentially reusable planks or parts of boats as in the structure of parallel poles on which F3 had been laid (Figure 3.5). Traces were also recorded in 1946 of some sort of structure near and under the southern end of F2 (Figures 2.12 and 2.13).

Otherwise, means to support planks would be essential during the fine-trimming stage and thereafter for marking and cutting stitch-holes. As will be seen, the stitching procedure undoubtedly required access to both sides of seams and so some form of trestles would be needed on which the boat could be supported during construction, along the lines used by the Chittagong boatbuilders (Figure 6.17). When boats were launched or beached and refloated before and after refitting and repairs, they would have to be hauled up and down the strand and this would be made easier with the help of a capstan of the kind described in Chapter 7.

TOOLS

Some toolmarks have been recorded and it is possible to infer the dimensions of the

Figure 6.16 The boatbuilding and working area near the fish market at Chittagong, Bangladesh in 1963. (*Photo*: M. S. Anwar.)

Figure 6.17 Dugout base of *Khalidar* boat in Chittagong raised on trestles and expanded. (*Photo*: M. S. Anwar.)

implement used in two cases. In both of these the evidence of plaster casts taken when the wood was still wet is, unfortunately, no longer available owing to their disappearance since they were deposited at NMM in 1947. They are, first, a group of scars at the bottom of the midships and other slots in F1; and second, the best of several axe marks in the hollow between cleats just north of the scarf in F2.

The first are 25 mm wide and up to c. 55 mm in length (Figure 2.18). In modern terms they resemble the scars which would be left by either a narrow square-ended adze or a joiner's chisel. Their peculiarity in a Bronze Age context is that they are rectilinear, since most bronze cutting tools have a curved rather than straight edge. Only a few of the many bronze axe-heads known from Britain have the single, bevelled edge appropriate to hafting transversely, adze-fashion and I am not aware of any as narrow as 25 mm. Of the chisels the great majority also have the curved cutting edge typical of the axes. Axe-heads could also have been mounted on straight shafts to produce the tool known to boat-builders as a 'slice' (McGrail 1977). The range of Bronze Age chisels is shown in Figure 6.2b. Regrettably therefore it is not easy to identify a known bronze tool with the characteristics necessary to produce the marks observed in F1. It must not be overlooked however that flint tools continued in use in the Bronze Age and even later and were presumably both cheaper and more readily replaceable than bronze in areas such as the Humber shore where flint of high quality in the form of glacial erratics could be had for the collecting. Well-made axes or adze-heads of flint and as narrow as 25 mm are known and some have nearly straight edges. It is conceivable there-fore that, in the absence of suitable metal tools, flint ones formed part of the boatbuilder's kit.

The mark on F2 (Figure 2.19) was 75 mm wide and c. 12 mm deep with the impression of a curved cutting edge sharpened with the double bevel of an axe. The typology of axe-heads through the British Bronze Age is well attested from hoards and burial deposits: pro-gressing from the earliest 'flat' axes through 'flanged' forms to the 'palstaves', the various winged types, and finally the 'socketed' type (Figure 6.2a). Dating of the sequence is not yet very precise owing to the scarcity of finds from sealed, datable deposits. It can be said however that socketed axes do not exceed 60 mm in width and only a few of the many palstaves 65 mm, and then mainly the earlier forms. In the generally accepted dating range for the sequence, socketed axes are in any case too late for the Middle Bronze Age Ferriby boats. The notably broad flat and flanged axe-heads are altogether too early for our period and the matching type must be sought among those characteristic of the Middle Bronze Age (Smith 1959). These include palstaves, 'half-flanged' and 'wing-flanged' forms of which only a few are as broad as the mark on F2. Distribution of wing-flanged axes is densest in Yorkshire and north-east England where palstaves are plentiful also. The assemblage which appears most relevant is that in the Hotham Carr hoard (Burgess 1968) from which the broadest of the wing-flanged axes has been selected for illustration in Figure 6.2a, Hotham Carr being a short 14 km inland from North Ferriby. I have included the pal-stave from the Blackrock, Brighton hoard although it is of a predominantly southern type, because it is of almost exactly the same breadth as the mark on F2 but also because it has the comparatively rare feature of single-bevel sharpening making it suitable for shaving a flat surface.

The surface finish of the planks was remarkably smooth and without any local roughness or faceting such as might be left by crude or blunt tools, whether axe or adze. After the 1946-7 operations we reported (Wright and Wright 1947) the possibility that signs of lengthwise streaking on the surface of F2 might be the vestiges of adze/axe finishing, but subsequent to that observation I have identified that the area in question was that which had been exposed and roughly cleaned in the second excavation of November 1940, so the marks might have resulted from that intervention and not be ancient at all. The record should therefore be discounted. In general however, and the more so since there are few identified Bronze Age adzes, it is not I believe necessary to postulate the use of a highly refined adze to achieve such a finish since work of very high quality can be done with a well-sharpened axe with a single bevel provided the user has the requisite skill. Skilled axing could likewise have produced the shaping of the grooves in the edges of the planks. I have often been asked whether fire might have been used in the production of planks or perforations for stitches, and it has always been my opinion that it was not. The one area of charring observed was on the surface of the southern plank of F2 and it stood out so prominently (Figure 4.17) that any similar traces could scarcely have been missed. Indeed I do not think it necessary to look beyond splitting with wedges and thereafter skilful application of the presumably available cutting tools to achieve both the shapes and finish observed in the finds. The one critical area of the planks where the shape imposes constraints on the sort of tool needed is the inside of the ends of the side-strakes where from the evidence of F1 and F3 two different styles have been used: in F1 smoothly rounded and in F3 cut out to a distinct angle. In the latter case the work could very possibly be done with an axe-mounted blade since the degree of curvature is nowhere extreme. In the former case, however, axing out the double curvature might present problems which would be expected to be reduced if an adze or slice were employed (McGrail 1977).

The next group of features from which inferences can be drawn concerning tools are the stitch-holes. As described earlier they are of four sorts: the square holes, turning in their length through 90°, which were used for the majority of the stitching of the bottom of the hull; the oval holes going straight through the

thickness of the planks for the repair of cracks in F1; the larger oval holes used for the stitching of the hoods of the side-strakes to the ends of the keel-planks in F1, F2, and F3; and the square but straight holes in the outer edge of the lowest side-strakes in F1 and F3. Within each of these categories dimensions were uniform, as shown in Table 6.2.

Table 6.2 Dimensions of stitch-holes

	length (mm)	width (mm)
(a) Squared, bottom structure	25	25
(b) Oval, repairs in bottom-structure	30	20
(c) Oval, keel-plank extension(s)	45	25
(d) Squared, outer edge of lowest side-strake	25	25

It can be said with certainty that those in category (a) were worked from each end since it would be physically impossible to cut them from one end only. It is likely in fact that all holes were done in this manner with the possible exception of those bored for the repair of cracks where access to the outside might have been restricted unless the structure was completely dismantled for refitting and restitching. There is no reason why a rotary drill should not have been used for starting all holes; but the squared holes would certainly have been finished with an axe or form of chisel. Drilling seems unlikely for any stage of making the squared inboard holes in the seams of the bottom-structure, turning as they do with a curved path to come out in the edges of the planks. As to size of tool used for cutting the squared holes, the one that left its scars in the slot on F1 as described earlier would have been apt also for the squaring of holes as well as for cutting the little ramps observed on F3.

Drilling could well have been the main means of making both sizes of oval holes. Even with modern hand-held carpenter's tools it

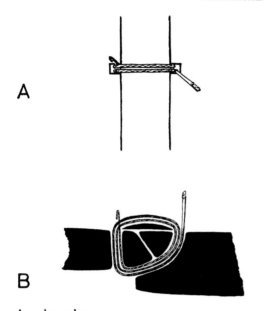

A

B

A. In plan

B. In section

Figure 6.18 Diagrammatic view of the run of a withy stitch. *Note*: thin end hooked back to form a lock and untwisted free end yielding offcut.

needs much skill to achieve perfectly circular holes owing to slight rocking of the brace or auger (Clarke R.S. pers. comm.). Controlled production of oval holes could be contrived by deliberate rocking of the drill. If worked from both sides the effect would be to make holes of oval section near the surfaces but contracting to circular in the middle. These could then be enlarged with a gouge to be of more or less even oval section throughout. I discount the possibility that these holes were originally round and became oval due to shrinkage (McGrail 1978) since they were undoubtedly oval in both F1 and F2 when first exposed and oval would accommodate the stitching of withies better than would round holes.

The boatbuilders' reasons for switching between the squared and oval holes observed in the finds are difficult to fathom. The pattern is not quite consistent, witness the provision of three squared and only one oval hole on

the hood-end of the lowest side-strake in F3; but this is the only exception recorded. The run of withies through the squared holes in the bottom-structure appears to be as shown in Figure 6.18 with accommodation for three thicknesses of withy and some waterproofing and wedging material in the inboard hole, assuming that the free end was turned back into the outboard hole to lock the stitch.

The preparation of stitching material would appear to call for no specialized cutting tools and otherwise only those needed for tightening stitches and knocking in wedges or caulking material all of which could have been of wood, as witness the supposed stitch-tightening tool described in Chapter 7.

METHOD AND SEQUENCE OF CONSTRUCTION

Perhaps the most graphic account of the building of a sewn boat is that of Timothy Severin in his book *The Sinbad Voyage* (Severin 1980) in which he describes the complete sequence of construction of his replica of an Omani *bhoom*, the *Sohar*, from assembly of materials to launching for the voyage to China. It is to be hoped that modern ethnographers will not miss the opportunity to record in similar detail the construction of other surviving large sewn boats.

I envisage that the first stage of construction of a Ferriby boat was the assembly including the bending, followed by detailed finishing and stitching up of the bottom-structure. In a new boat this would be composed of four planks: the two that make up the keel-plank, joined amidships by a box-scarf; and the outer bottom-planks on each side. Possible techniques for achieving the rocker in this assembly were referred to earlier (see also Appx 6.1).

During experiments in stitching with a short test-piece representative of the seam between keel-plank and outer bottom-plank at about Section G-G in F1 (Figure 6.19), I had considerable difficulty in keeping the two planks in the desired relative positions while

Figure 6.19 Full-scale replica of short length of planks and sealing lath used for trial of stitching method.

threading and tightening stitches, and deduced from this experience that the procedure would have been greatly eased with planks of the full length or if the planks could have been held in the correct register as would have been the case if they were keyed together by the transverse timbers running through the holes in the cleats.

Once trimmed to fit, with the outer planks bedded closely into the vee-groove in the edge of the keel-plank, the way would be clear to mark out and then cut the stitch-holes. The planks would then have to be separated to make it possible to cut the holes in the edges of the keel-plank since access would perforce be needed to the edge itself deep in the recess of the groove. While it would be just possible to cut the holes through the edge of the outer

bottom-plank if it were laid up against the keel-plank, it would still be necessary to cut from both top and bottom of the hole. It is likely therefore that both inner and outer holes would be cut into the planks when they were separated. The planks could then be brought together for the final time for stitching, again using the transverse timbers as guides, not only to secure the correct alignment in plan but also to hold them in position in the vertical plane.

All these steps would be facilitated with the planks assembled on a structure of simple trestles although this does not become essential until stitching begins. In experiments with the test-piece it was soon found that with only two hands it was very difficult when using pre-twisted withies to thread the withy back through the opposing hole while at the same time maintaining the twist, relaxation of which results in weakening of the stitch. With planks of the full width it would be physically impossible for one worker to reach round to the underside while keeping a grip on the withy above. If pre-twisted withies were used, stitching must therefore have been carried out by pairs of workers and the 'outside man' would have to be able to reach the seam from below. I think it likely that two workers would also have been needed using the modern Finnish method. So the task could not be performed without the structure being raised clear of the ground. Severin describes similar teamwork in the building of the *Sohar*, his stitching men operating in pairs each consisting of an 'inside' and an 'outside' man (Severin 1980). When considering the caulking and sealing of the seams, there are alternative possible sequences. Bearing in mind the thickness and rigidity of the planks and the hardness of the wood, a very exact fit cannot be expected and a purpose of the thick masses of moss used for caulking would be to take up minor irregularities. Another problem is the comparative stiffness of the withies themselves which would need to be pulled very tight indeed to follow the shortest path round the angles in the holes. I have therefore toyed with the idea that stitching was done first and the moss caulking then rammed into the seam and the capping laths knocked in under the stitches to complete the joint, each step progressively tightening the stitches. It would however have been very difficult not to say impossible in the case of F3 to locate the caulking rope in the vee of the grooved edge after stitching and I now incline therefore to the view that the sequence was to insert both caulking moss, plus rope in the case of F3, as well as the sealing laths before stitching. In the Ferriby case it can be presumed that the caulking moss would have been inserted dry so that it would swell when immersed in water.

Work on the experimental model has facilitated the development of a plausible hypoth-

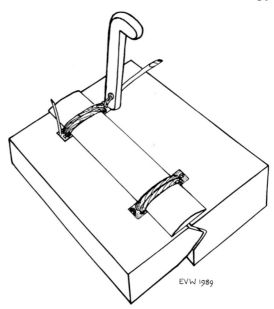

Figure 6.20 Perspective sketch illustrating stitching process.

esis for the actual stitching procedure. Withies wound from branches of c. 1 m in length would naturally taper from butt to tip and preparation would leave each end less pliable than the main middle part, since the thicker end is held under the foot of the worker and the thinner in the hands (Figure 6.11). After preparation withies of birch or hazel can be kept coiled into loops for storage without relaxing the twist of the fibres (Hoeg 1977), so it is possible to envisage the accumulation of a stock of withies sufficient to stitch a complete boat. The thinner end would be used as the leader and the withy be threaded for two and a half turns through the holes so as to leave both ends projecting inside the boat. A wooden tool as described in chapter 7 was found by experiment to be ideally suited for gripping the thicker end of a withy in such a way as not to lose the twist during the threading process. When threading was completed a second similar tool could be attached to the projecting thinner end and both could then be worked simultaneously to lever the stitch tight (Figure 6.20). Calculations of the friction of wood on wood in such a situation have been made by Coates (Wright 1984) and these demonstrate that lubrication with tallow or fat would greatly ease the task of tightening. The data are shown in Table 6.3.

Table 6.3 Friction between wooden surfaces

Wood on wood	Approx. coefficient of friction
Both dry	0.5
Damp with water	0.7
Lubricated with tallow or lard	0.2

From these Coates calculated that the pull required for stitching dry would be approximately 6.7 times greater than for stitches lubricated with tallow or lard and proportionately greater still if both were damp with water. This factor would apply to a single turn only and would go up to 43 times greater for a double turn; in both cases it is assumed that pull is applied to each end of the withy, suggesting that to tighten the stitch by pulling from one end only would not be a practical proposition.

The locking of the stitches has unfortunately not been adequately investigated, but some information is recorded. Examination of one stitch in the 1970s by R. Varrell, then of the Department of Ships at the National Maritime Museum, showed one end of the withy doubled back on itself through 180°; it would appear that this was the thinner end, which after tightening could be cut off short and bent over to be reinserted in the hole to lock that end of the stitch. The thicker end would still be protruding in the shape of an untwisted piece similar to the offcut described in Chapter 7. After final tightening from this end it could be bent over and a wedge pounded in to lock the stitch and waterproof the hole. A sample of such filling from F1 was examined by Allison and Godwin in 1947 without positive identification of the macerated wood of which it consisted (in Wright and Wright 1947: App. B). More may yet be learned from study of the stitching of F3 in which the tightening process would have been further eased by the cutting of the ramps on the inner side of the stitch-holes so as to give a straighter direction of pull than would be the case if it were done at right angles to the plank.

With the bottom-structure completed, it would become possible to shape and fit the side-strakes. While the fitting and stitching would be feasible with the bottom-structure lowered to the ground, the need to maintain the longitudinal curvature makes it most unlikely that the boat would have been moved at this stage; in any case access to the outer edges for stitching would be easier if it were left raised on trestles. Detailed finishing of the edging would still require repeated offering up and trimming before the necessary fit was achieved, including of course the hollowing out of the shaped hood-ends of the planks. Experiments with simple card models suggests that, except for the shaped ends, the fit of the strakes to mate with the curved edges of the outer bottom-planks could be achieved by bending only and without resorting to twisting, which would have been very difficult with such thick planks. The need for twisting to fill the spaces where the side-strakes were joined to the extensions of the keel-plank beyond the ends of the outer bottom-planks is of course avoided by shaping out of the solid. The shaped ends of the lowest side-strakes would be stitched to the bottom-structure first and the straight part of the longer member then levered or pulled into place, with final trimming at the joint left till last so as to achieve an exact fit. The two separate shaped ends of the second side-strake could then be trimmed and attached and the more or less flat middle planks trimmed and bent in to fit between them. Thus far the planks would probably be held out to the proper section of the boat by temporary shores across the bottom.

The adoption of the two features from F4

into the reconstruction requires that the next stage was the insertion of the ribs and attachment of the thwarts, both being secured to the second side-strakes and with the tops of the ribs trimmed down to oval section and protruding upwards. Only then could the third or sheer-strakes be marked out and finished with vertical perforations through the rails at the appropriate stations to fit on to the rib-ends. The separate end-pieces of the sheer-strakes having been fitted, stitched up and secured by the girth-lashings, the final stage of construction would have been to fit the long middle planks over the rib-ends and stitch them to the second side-strakes to complete the boat.

It is probable that only then could any temporary means by which the bottom was bent be relaxed, that job then being transferred to the side-planking and frames acting in concert. The whole structure, in assuming its self-strained condition, would hog (i.e. dropping of the ends of the hull) a little but thereafter be taut. The resulting built-in loads in the stitches would afford some protection from their working under the influence of the varying loads imposed upon the boat in service. This state of self-strain would be at its most severe upon the first completion of a boat with newly wrought components, because heavily stressed timber relaxes with time. The bending stress in the rails of the top side-strakes due to keeping the curvature in the newly bent bottom would however be only a tenth of the stress arising when the fully loaded boat was on the crest of a steep wave.

The strength of the hull, when loaded by waves or when supported only amidships when left high and dry by the tide, is adequate, the tensile strength in the rails amidships being about 4 Newtons/mm^2 after relaxation of the stresses arising from bending the plank to the plan shape of the hull. The stitching between the side-strakes can be expected to be the main cause of hull-hogging through allowing one side-plank to slip upon the next, but this will be resisted if the thwarts are fitted tightly since they act as keys where they pass through the seam between the second and top side-strakes.

In this and the preceding chapter the aim has been to provide sufficient information to enable a model-maker to build an accurate scale model or a shipwright to build a full-sized working version. I hope to live long enough to see this done and our theories put to the test of sea trials.

REPAIRS AND REFITTING

As a postscript to the account of ways of building such boats, some inferences can be drawn from the remains on how they stood up to actual working. The useful life of the boats cannot be reliably estimated in the climate and conditions prevailing in Britain before 1250 BC. Information can, however, be gained from the finds to indicate one serious weakness in the structure and the measures taken to repair the resultant damage. The weakness can be identified from the fact that all three examples of outer bottom-planks have suffered fractures of a similar kind in the form of long, lengthwise cracks. Of the two in F1, that in the northern plank had been stitched up throughout its length, the seam being caulked and capped with the customary sealing-laths. In the southern outer bottom-plank of F1 nearly 5 m had been cut out and replaced with a new plank, that is with a vee-groove into which the bevelled edge of the new piece fitted. The crack extended west for c. 1.5 m beyond and alongside the end of the area cut out and had been stitched up in the same manner as the long crack in the northern plank. Since it would be impossible to turn the path of the stitch-holes twice within the thickness of the planks, they were drilled straight through to the outside, the stitches thus being exposed to abrasion on grounding. The only way of avoiding this would have been to drill straight holes from above at an oblique angle to meet towards the lower inside edges of the crack, as is done to produce the buried stitching of the Cheops funerary boat (Lipke 1984: Figure 48); but this course evidently did not occur to the Ferriby builders. The long splinter at the western end of the fragment of the outer bottom-plank represented in F3 is evidence of a fracture similar to those in F1, suggesting that this may have been a recurring problem. A possible cause of this trouble could have been a tendency for parts of the plank-keel of the rockered but otherwise flat bottom to rise, imposing some twist upon the outer bottom-plank.

The other indications from which inferences can be drawn concerning construction are the marked differences between the surviving features on the two halves of the bottom-structure of F1: those of the western half being uniformly intact and virtually unworn, while those on the eastern half were all broken or worn down, some being reduced to mere vestiges (Figure 1.21). Was this perhaps the result of carrying domestic animals only in the aft part of the boat? In that case the upstanding features on the floor would be vulnerable to repeated damage from the feet of cattle, sheep, or other hoofed animals, the stitching on the other hand being protected as far as possible by hurdle-panels. By the time these features had been rendered ineffective by wear and tear they would in any case have become unnecessary, as suggested later. As described above (pp. 67 and 72), in all the situations in F1 and F2 where the cleats survive more or less undamaged the run of stitching is interrupted, whereas they continue at the normal intervals past the remnants of the two sets in the eastern half of F1. In the case of modern sewn boats of comparable size, complete dismantling and restitching are carried out at regular intervals.

Assuming that the Ferriby boats required similar regular restitching it can be expected that the main objective would have been to prolong the useful life of the planks to the limit and that this would continue even though the cleat systems had ceased to be of any use

through wear, damage, or the assumption of permanent curvature of the bottom by relaxation. Where they were still usable, as on the western half, they were presumably fitted with fresh transverse timbers of ash; where they were not, additional pairs of stitch-holes would have to be cut and stitching alone employed to secure the planks, support perhaps for the proposition made earlier that the prime function of the cleat systems was as aids in the initial construction and that they were no longer so necessary in refastening a boat whose planks had assumed permanent curvature.

APPENDIX 6.1

Bending planks

As described earlier, the fact that the planks of the bottom-structure were bent to shape, as well as in part at least carved from the solid timber, has been established beyond argument. How this might have been done is more debatable and a number of possible options have been considered. The feature is of such fundamental importance in the building of the boat and the behaviour of the hull structure that it justifies more than cursory treatment. First, some of the possible options are outlined in brief and then their respective merits are discussed.

Group 1, in which the bottom-structure is assembled with planks shaped but not pre-bent and then subjected to bending as a complete entity:

1A. The ends are supported and weights applied to the middle.
1B. The structure is inverted, the middle supported and the ends borne down by weighting and/or other means.
1C. The structure is supported on trestles and a tensioning stay of rope(s) rigged over the ends of the keel-plank. This is then tightened as required by a tour-

niquet, the desired curvature being obtained by means of props between the stay and the top of the structure.

Group 2, in which permanent bending is applied to the two parts of the keel-plank independently of each other and the outer bottom-planks then added:

2A. The ends of each plank are supported and weights applied to the middle.

2B. As in 2A, but with the planks inverted, the middles supported, and the ends borne down by weighting and/or other means.

2C. The two components laid back to back *either* with the ends suitably separated to give the required curve and the middles pulled together by a tourniquet or other mechanical means *or* with the middles clamped together before driving wedges between the ends to obtain the curve.

Note 1: Firing or steaming could be used in the case of 2A, 2B and 2C to achieve permanent distortion.

Note 2: There would have been less need to pre-bend the longer outer bottom-planks: they could be weighted down to register with the edges of the keel-plank and the vee-shaped seams could then be trimmed to fit before keying the planks together by means of the transverse timber and cleats.

Discussion

First it should be said that bending under strain in the bottom-structure, as opposed to a state in which the timber is completely relaxed, is a desirable feature as it would cause the structure of the boat to be self-strained as a whole and so keep stitches tight and less prone to working, thereby giving rise to leakage.

Some thought has been given to the weights which might be required to bend the very thick planks and in general it appears that it would be difficult to find room on the surface areas available for sufficient stacked rocks or for standing people to meet the need.

Without practical tests it is also thought that bending of the entire bottom-structure would present very considerable problems owing to its size and weight. It could only be effected in a controlled manner by use of the device of the suggested tensioning-stay but with the significant risk of breaking off the tips of the keel-plank where end-grain is involved.

At the time of writing the most attractive options seem to be those in Group 2, with 2C as perhaps the most promising. In this group the permanently bent keel-plank would act as a guide for the sprung outer bottom-planks and a satisfactory measure of strain be retained in the complete structure. This might also account for the charred area on the *upper* surface of one of the components of F2 at approximately half of its original length, since with the two planks clamped together bottom-to-bottom it would be their upper surfaces which would be exposed to firing (Figures 4.17 and 6.9).

7

Other artefacts from the site

It is appropriate to introduce this chapter with some remarks on the most recognizable features of the post-glacial deposits on the North Ferriby foreshore as sources for a wide range of artefacts. The boulder clay and overlying greenish, sandy, weathering layer charged with frost-fractured flint need not concern us, both being barren deposits of the Ice Age. The variation in thickness of the succeeding peat bed between the hollows and ridges in the boulder clay can be confusing since over the ridges, including that immediately to the west of the boat site, it is almost entirely absent. The peat reaches its maximum development to a thickness of 1.07 m in the hollow to the west of this ridge (Figure 8.1); but in the area of the boat site it is rarely more than 0.30 m thick; in certain places the upper layer shows signs of erosion before deposition of the overlying grey estuarine clay, whereas elsewhere the transition from one to the other is gradual. The peat layer is not only typically dark brown in colour but also has a solid texture which can be crumbled or broken but is never plastic. It is therefore virtually impossible after its formation for an artefact to become embedded in it from the outside, and by extension it can be assumed with certainty that an object found protruding from it arrived where it did during the accumulation of decaying vegetable matter from which the peat developed. These conditions do not necessarily apply in the case ·of the estuarine clay and any other similar

sediments which succeeded it. It is a practical possibility that artefacts of hard and heavy materials can sink in such deposits, unlikely that they can rise, but possible that they can be moved sideways and be redeposited. The likelihood of such movement from the original place of deposition may be less in the case of waterlogged wooden objects but is not entirely removed. It is necessary therefore to emphasize the principle that proximity of artefacts to each other either vertically or horizontally is no absolute guarantee of association. Nevertheless in the conditions prevailing in the 1930s and 1940s and occasionally later the bank was so clean of recently deposited silt that with regular observation it has been possible to say with confidence whether or not an artefact or other object could be associated with the clay surrounding it and only been revealed by new erosion. Such conclusions were in certain cases reinforced if the consistency of wooden objects was unusually soft. What cannot be guaranteed is that the clays represent a single phase of deposition. Ideally it would have been desirable to obtain radiocarbon dates for all major artefacts, but two of the larger ones were lost in World War II. Direct dating has so far covered only the boats and adjoining structures. In fact all the radiocarbon-dated wooden artefacts from the estuarine clay together with the single metal object and all but two of the potsherds (ascribed to the Early Iron Age) can be assigned to the Bronze Age. My presumption therefore is that undated wooden objects from this deposit are also of Bronze Age date unless there are grounds for suspecting otherwise, as in the case of F4 which was deposited in a filled channel cutting into and potentially later than the main deposit.

The artefacts tend to fall into two categories: those that can be interpreted as having some connection with the building or operation of boats; and those of a more general nature. It is a fact that the horizontal distribution of the former shows a clustering of finds in the immediate area around the boats (Figure 4.1) and I do not think that this is entirely attributable to more intensive searching of this particular area than of the remainder of the exposure. Over the years the whole strand has been examined regularly and it is unlikely that artefacts at a distance from the boat site would altogether have escaped the eye. The tally of finds from areas of peat or clay separated from the main boat site is five sherds of pottery, a group of struck flakes of flint from a restricted layer of the peat, and a

number of wooden objects including F4 from what are taken to be sediments intrusive into the estuarine clay to the west. The search has also yielded several finds of small metal objects of mediaeval date among shingle on the surface. Thus it is, I think, fair to claim that the relative frequency of finds from the estuarine clay near the boats is a genuine reflection of their density rather than the result of accident of discovery.

Each of the wooden objects is treated separately in the text that follows, in certain cases at some length. This underlines the fact that although less spectacular than the boat-finds, they are of kinds rarely recorded or are in some cases unique. Moreover, as interpreted and collectively, they amplify the picture of the waterside environment surrounding the boats themselves.

1 Patch or 'tingle' Figures 7.1 and 7.2 (Wright 1978: 190)

This small plank from the estuarine clay 30 m to the north-east of F1 was found in 1946 with

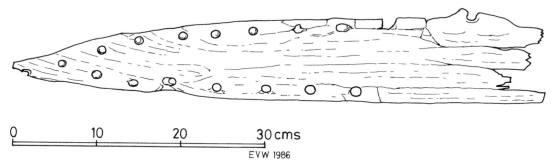

Figure 7.1 Drawing of the patch or 'tingle' made within two hours of its excavation on 19 September 1946.

Figure 7.2 The 'tingle' photographed to show surface-finish.

one end exposed and the remainder securely buried in estuarine clay.

Material   Identified as oak (*Quercus*).

Dimensions

Length surviving: 0.62 m
Original length (estimated): c. 0.8 m
Maximum width: 0.11 m
Average thickness: 0.015 m

Description   An incomplete object, tapered at one end and, to judge from parallels, originally also at the other to give a symmetrical plan. Inset 10–15 mm from the edges are circular holes evenly spaced at 38–51 mm intervals and of 8–9 mm diameter. The broken end was so much fragmented that it was not possible to determine whether the line of holes continued beyond those positively recorded.

Interpretation and attribution   Identified on discovery as a patch or 'tingle' for repairing a hole or short crack in a boat. Two similar examples were recorded in position on the Brigg logboat found in 1886, one of which was plain, as with this example, and the other

furnished with lengthwise perforated cleats which were slotted through the crack and secured on the inside of the shell by transverse pegs (Figure 7.3). In the Brigg case the holes round the edges were for stitching the patch to the hull, the material for this not being identified. Subsequently another example has been brought to notice on the logboat from Oakmere in Cheshire (McGrail 1978: 248), being fastened to the hull by trenails, the holes being of c. 9 mm diameter as in the Ferriby specimen.

Dating   Not directly dated. The Brigg logboat has been dated to the beginning of the first millenium BC on the strength of a single radio-carbon determination (Q-78, 834 BC ± 100). The Oakmere logboat has yet to be dated. Attribution to the Bronze Age for the Ferriby patch would therefore be consistent with the limited evidence of parallels.

Conservation and present state   The patch when found was very soft especially at the exposed and damaged end but was successfully excavated and transferred to a flat board for removal. It was drawn within an

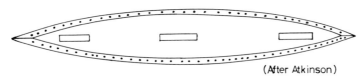

(After Atkinson)

A Brigg Logboat

(After Sheppard)

B Ferriby

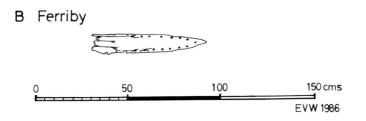

0   50   100   150 cms

EVW 1986

Figure 7.3   (*a*) Two views of the cleated tingle used for a repair on the Brigg Logboat with (*b*) the Ferriby tingle to the same scale for comparison.

hour or two of discovery, and then immersed in glycerine. It was deposited with the remains of F1 and F2 at NMM Greenwich in 1946, where it survives in fair condition after being subjected to further treatment to achieve stability.

2 Forked timber Figures 7.4, 7.5 and 7.6 (Wright 1986)

A natural, grown fork of timber from the estuarine clay found in 1939, c. 23 m WNW of the position of F1, the end of the shorter arm exposed at the surface and the remainder covered by the clay.

Material By observation, the wood had the normal characteristics of oak.

Dimensions

Length – longer arm: 1.84 m
        shorter arm: 1.28 m
Thickness of arms: 0.11 to 0.13 m

Description The arms had been very roughly squared and the root rounded. Both arms were pierced by 50 mm square mortices, the complete straight arm having three equally spaced 0.46 m apart. The incomplete curved arm showed only one hole intact with traces of a second towards the broken tip. The end hole of the straight arm contained the broken end of what was either an oak batten of square section or a tenon. At right angles to the axes

Figure 7.5 The forked timber found in 1939: end view.

of the mortices in the arms the root of the fork was bored with a large oval hole, 0.12 m on the long and 0.09 m on the short axis.

Interpretation Shown photographs of the object at Cambridge in 1947, J. A. Hutton suggested that it might be the base of a sledge of the sort commonly used in Africa and elsewhere for transporting such materials as firewood, the mortice holes being provided to take the ends of vertical posts to secure the load and the large hole at the root for a tow-rope. Soon afterwards however Grahame Clark

Figure 7.4 The forked timber found in 1939: side view.

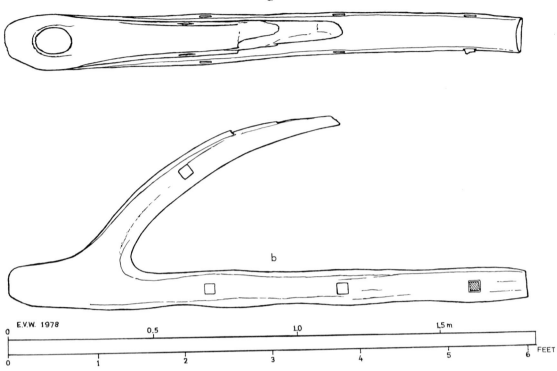

Figure 7.6 The forked timber: measured drawings worked up from 1939 photographs.

offered the counter-suggestion that it was designed to stand on edge and was one of two side frames of a beach-windlass of which primitive examples were known into historic times from Fennoscandia. This seemed the more likely interpretation since a sledge could be expected to be symmetrical about the lengthwise axis whereas our object had one arm straight and the other curved. As in the Fennoscandian parallels, the mortices would be to accommodate the ends of cross-battens or tenons protruding from planks joining the pair of frames to each other. The large hole at the root would be ideally placed to take a stout stake to secure such a machine to the bank. The method of mounting a horizontal drum between the upper arms as in the Fennoscandian example could not be reconstructed with any confidence since the end of the curved arm was missing; nor would it have been possible to provide fixed, long bars to

exert powerful leverage for the winding of such a drum. Another unresolved problem was the effect of the pull being exerted 0.67 m above the base, which would require the back of the apparatus to be held down by some form of anchorage to the ground. Nevertheless the 1947 reconstruction (Figure 7.7) stood without challenge until 1979.

It was then that S. McGrail observed in a reproduction of a late nineteenth-century watercolour of a beach scene at Etretat on the French Channel coast (Figure 7.8) an accurate portrayal of a massively constructed beach capstan used for pulling fishing boats ashore, and drew it to my attention to emphasize that such devices survived into modern times. The similarity of this apparatus to the reconstruction of the Ferriby object, however, was striking in respect to the framework; but in the French case the pillar was mounted vertically in true capstan fashion. The effect-

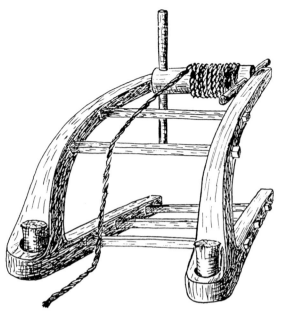

Figure 7.7 Hypothetical reconstruction of forked timber as a side-frame of a windlass, 1947.

iveness of such an arrangement was obviously far greater than in the case of a windlass with its drum horizontal, since the pull could be near to ground level, there would be no problems in providing satisfactory bearings for a pillar set in transverse boards fixed between the side-frames, and there would be no limit to the length of bars which could be used since they would rotate in a plane above the level of the top of the framework. Figures 7.9a, b, and c show the Ferriby object incorporated in a reconstruction of such an apparatus. For the sake of simplicity bindings have been omitted, although to judge by the nineteenth-century example they would almost certainly have been necessary to hold such a structure together and in the Ferriby case would presumably have been of withies. Such a capstan would have greatly eased the task of beaching boats as large and heavy as those from Ferriby.

Figure 7.8 Watercolour of beach scene at Etretat, France with massive beach capstan used for hauling boats. (*Photo*: NMM, Greenwich.)

ELEVATION

PLAN

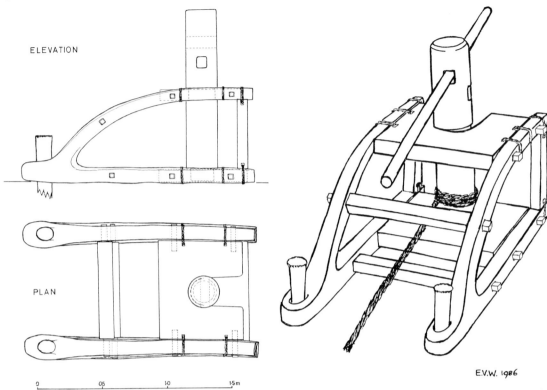

0   05   10   15 m

EVW 1986

E.V.W. 1986

Figure 7.9a Forked timber: reconstructed as frame in beach capstan.

Figure 7.9b Forked timber: perspective view of scale-model capstan.

Parallels No ancient parallels are known. In modern or recent examples side-frames seem normally to have been constructed of two timbers joined at the 'root'. Recent enquiry suggests that beach capstans broadly of this type have been in common use round the coasts of Europe in recent times and a typical example from Gismerøya near Mandal in Norway and now in the National Maritime Museum at Oslo is illustrated in Figure 7.10.

History of find After lifting, the timber was deposited in Hull Museum and stored without attempt at conservation. It was lost in the fire of 1943. Records taken were limited to four photographs and the measured length along the lower arm of 1.84 m. The information to prepare the measured line drawings (Figure 7.6) and the reconstruction sketches (Figures

EVW 1986

Figure 7.9c Forked timber: 'exploded' view of components of capstan.

7.7 and 7.9) was derived from the photographs. No direct dating was done and the attribution rests solely on the presumption that the wooden artefacts from the estuarine clay are broadly contemporary with each other.

Figure 7.10 Similar modern beach capstan from Gismeroya near Mandal, S. Norway, now in the Oslo Maritime Museum. (*Photo*: Norsk Sjøfartsmuseum, Oslo.)

Comment This could be a unique find if of the Bronze Age, and if the interpretation and attribution of date are correct could represent part of one of the earliest known machines in which mechanical advantage is obtained on such a scale. Technically, the principles are no different from those of the bow-drill, which presumably has a very long pedigree, and there is no reason to suppose that such devices were other than commonplace in antiquity but have failed to survive or be discovered.

3 and 4 Paddles (Wright 1978: 193)

Discovery, excavation and subsequent history

The first example was found early in 1939 in the estuarine clay 15 m north-east of F1 with one corner of the tip exposed and eroded and the remainder buried. It was cleared, lifted and removed to our home where it was immediately washed and recorded; the outline drawing traced round the original and the sections being done on cartridge paper (Figure 7.11). Figure 7.12 is the best that can be made of the photographs. Recognizing the fragility of the object, the next step was to have an accurate replica made while it was still wet. This was done by G. K. Beulah and the product given to Hull Museums, a copy of this replica being made in 1947 and lodged at the National Maritime Museum. The find itself was then the subject of an experiment in conservation through the courtesy of G. S. Wade, whose firm had facilities for pressure-

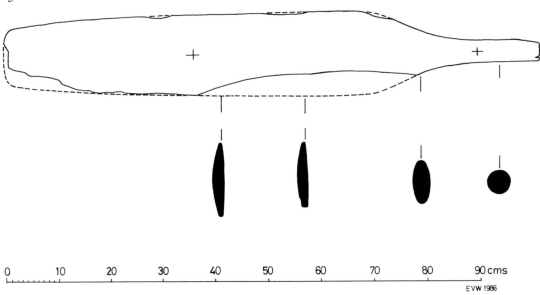

Figure 7.11 Drawing of paddle blade made immediately after excavation in 1939. (Redrawn 1986.)

Figure 7.12 Paddle blade photographed on day of excavation.

impregnation of wood with preservatives such as creosote. The attempt was unsuccessful and the much contorted, dried fragments which resulted were returned to Hull Museum where they were lost in the fire of 1943.

A second fragment was found during the excavations of 1946, again from the estuarine clay a few metres west of F2. It was soaked in glycerine and in 1947 with other finds deposited at the National Maritime Museum, Greenwich, receiving no further treatment. It was just possible for the writer to identify what was left of it when examining the remnants of stored material in the 1970s.

Material   The wood from which the first had been made was not identified beyond the fact that on superficial examination it bore no resemblance to oak. The remains of the second were positively identified as ash (*Fraxinus*). The writer's observation of both objects when freshly excavated suggests that they were made from the same species of wood and the presumption therefore is that the first was also made from ash.

Dimensions

No. 3

Surviving length: c. 1.0 m
Length of blade: 0.85 m
Breadth of blade (max.): 0.15 m
Thickness of blade (max.): 0.023 m
Diameter of shaft: 0.044 m

Estimated area of blade restored including
'cutout': 1,100 sq cm

No. 4
Approx. length: 0.15 m
Diameter of shaft: similar to No. 3

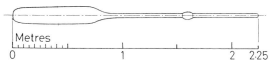

Figure 7.13 Paddle blade reconstructed incorporating a shaft similar to that of the Canewdon, Essex paddle (J. F. Coates).

Description The first find consisted of a nearly complete blade and some 0.2 m of the lower part of the shaft. The shape of the tip could be recovered from the fact that the edge was intact around one corner. In addition to minor damage to the very thin edges, a piece c. 0.42 m long at one shoulder of the blade gave the appearance of having been trimmed out by shaving rather than broken away before discovery. In section, one face was nearly flat and the other cambered.

Restoration and interpretation With the blemishes in the edge replaced and the tip restored to match the surviving corner, the blade emerges as an elegantly shaped object, subject only to the debatable question of the cutout at one shoulder. There are three possible solutions to this phenomenon: that it was originally made this way; or that the edge suffered damage in use and was tidied up to prevent cracks extending; or that the piece was cut out by deliberate intent, for instance to enable the user to work the paddle as close as possible to the side of the hull of a boat. The crudity of the finish contrasts with the careful shaping of the rest and I therefore discount the idea that it was original. Of the remaining two options, I think the more likely is that its purpose was to tidy up the edge to contain further damage. For this reason I have shown the restored paddle with the cutout filled in to give a symmetrical shape (Figure 7.13). In the absence of the complete shaft, interpretation of the object must take into account three possibilities: oar; paddle; or specialized steering oar or paddle. Information on the dimensions of ancient oars is scanty; but the relationship between blade area and shaft thickness as reconstructed for classical Greek triremes, illustrated in Morrison and

Williams's *Greek Oared Ships* (1968) and based on the many iconographic representations from archaic times onwards, suggests that the shaft in the Ferriby case would have needed to be at least twice as thick as it was to match so large a blade. This is confirmed by the actual examples of oars which equipped the Cheops Ship where small and short rounded blades were fastened to substantial shafts. By the same token a steering oar, paddle, or sweep would necessarily need to be made strong enough to withstand the forces exerted by the leverage of a long shaft. I think therefore that there is very little doubt that our Ferriby finds were parts of ordinary paddles.

Reconstruction Assuming that the original blade was symmetrical and with the cutout portion restored, there remains to be determined what length of shaft would be suitable to complete the paddle. Here I originally turned to the ethnographic parallel of the Maori of New Zealand who used paddles to propel their large and heavy war and ceremonial canoes. Selecting from the large collection of paddles in the Auckland Museum, I found that in terms of blade area and shaft thickness the Ferriby paddle conformed readily with the Maori *hoe* (Figure 7.14). Most of the *hoe* have a pointed tip; but Figure 7.14 also shows an uncommon form with blunt tip approaching more nearly the spade-shape of the Ferriby paddle. The length of shaft is governed by the attitude of the paddler and the type of grip employed. In the Maori case the upper hand of the user grasps round the end which is usually finished with a decorative terminal boss.

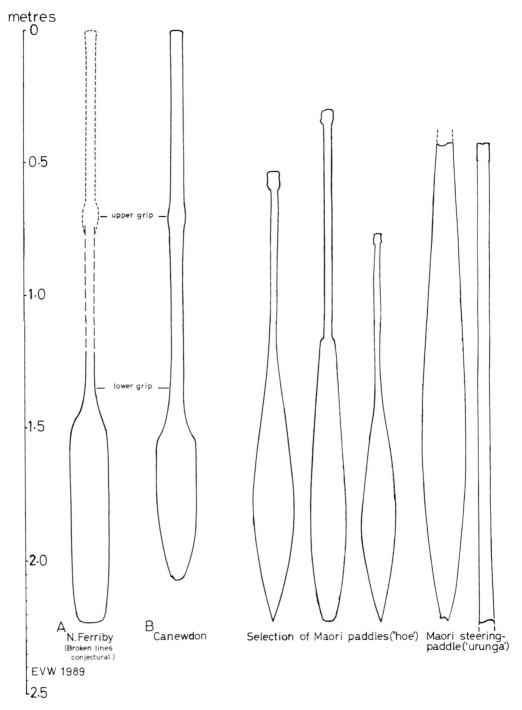

metres

upper grip —

lower grip —

A
N.Ferriby
(Broken lines
conjectural)

B
Canewdon

Selection of Maori paddles ('hoe')   Maori steering-
paddle ('urunga')

EVW 1989

Figure 7.14 Reconstructed Ferriby paddle, (A) compared with Canewdon paddle (B) and a selection of modern Maori paddles in the Auckland, New Zealand Museum.

In 1983 however a complete paddle was found at Canewdon near Burnham-on-Crouch, Essex (Heal 1989) and has been dated by radio-carbon assay to 950 ± 70 BC (BM 2339) that is within the limits of the Late Bronze Age (Figure 7.14b). The blade is quite unlike the North Ferriby paddle in outline and is of smaller area. Most interestingly a novel upper grip is provided c.1.56 m from the tip in the form of a bulge in the shaft, above which the shaft continues at the same diameter as the lower part to give a total length for the paddle of 2.02 m. This suggests one type of shaft with which the North Ferriby paddle might conform. The familiar modern paddle usually has a broadened flat terminal shaped integrally with the shaft over which the upper hand is clasped. An alternative is an attached T-piece which serves the same purpose. These last incidentally give better control of the angle of the blade, for example when feathering the stroke. In the Canewdon case the length of shaft is not critical since it can project any distance beyond the grip of the upper hand. In the latter, however, the length has to be suited to the length of the arms of the user. I should expect the Ferriby paddle to have been not less than 1.75 m long, if with a straight shaft as first described, or c.1.5 m if fitted with a T-piece or its integral equivalent, these estimates incidentally having been made before the Canewdon paddle had been found.

Dating No direct evidence for date is available and the assumption of a Bronze Age date is based on the occurrence in the estuarine clay of that period.

Parallels Prehistoric paddles from Europe are recorded from the Mesolithic era onwards, for example Starr Carr (Clark 1954) and Denmark (Rieck and Crumlin-Pedersen 1988); and Neolithic examples are known from Denmark, Finland, and Switzerland. The earliest paddles are not always identifiable beyond dispute as such and some may indeed have been primitive digging implements. The Canewdon example is significant not only for its provenance and positive dating to the Bronze Age; but also for the lenticular outline of its blade and the form of grip provided.

5 Pistol-shaped tool. Figures 7.15a and b (Wright 1978: 195)

Discovery, excavation and subsequent history

This object was found towards the close of the 1946 excavations and shortly before the lifting of F1, buried in the estuarine clay just to the west of F2. It was immersed in glycerine within hours of removal and delivered with the other wooden material to Greenwich early in 1947. A sketch was made at the time but cannot now be traced. The badly decayed remnants of it were identified among the stored material in the reserve collections.

Material By observation, the wood was identified as oak.

Dimensions Not measured; but approximate length 0.025 m, other dimensions proportionately as in sketch in Figure 7.15.

Description L-shaped artefact with the end of the longer arm bored with a round hole c. 13 mm in diameter. The shorter arm had a rounded finish, shaped as if to fit the hand.

Interpretation From its appearance and proximity to one of the boats those present at the time of discovery all agreed with C. W. Phillips's spontaneous pronouncement that its purpose was concerned with the stitching process (he referred to it as a 'bodkin'). I have not diverged from this view since; and in experimental work with withies have found a replica to be excellently adapted for pulling and levering up the protruding end of a withy stitch while at the same time maintaining the twist which is essential if the strength and flexibility of such material is to be preserved. Further reflections on its use are introduced in Chapter 6.

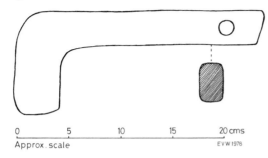

Figure 7.15a Wooden tool found during the 1946 excavations near to F2 and interpreted as designed for tightening withy stitches.

eastern end of F2 during the excavations of 1963, the loop, some of it very much degraded, was traced for a length of c.1 m. It was lifted and bagged for subsequent study in Hull Museums. When uncontaminated material associated with F3 was sought for radio-carbon assay, we agreed to sacrifice this object, which produced the anomalous radio-carbon date referred to later.

Material   Withies of hazel (*Corylus*) and yew (*Taxus*).

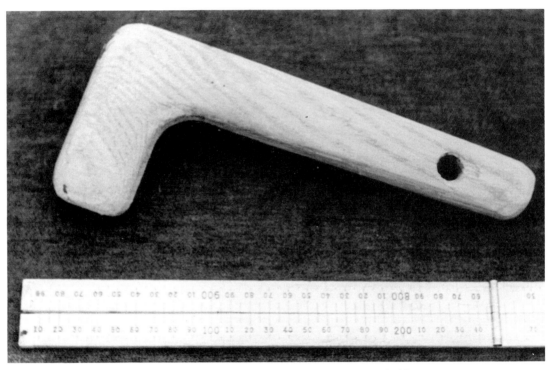

Figure 7.15b   Replica used for experiments in stitching.

Dating   Not directly dated; but found in estuarine clay of presumed Bronze Age date.

6 Loop of twisted and knotted withy
Figures 7.16 and 7.17 (Wright 1978: 195–7)

Discovery, excavation and subsequent history

Exposed in estuarine clay c.2 m east of the

Dimensions   C.1 m length of withy of c.15 mm diameter, or c.25 mm when laid together.

Description   As can be seen from Figure 7.17, the object is a complex of laid withy including a well formed knot or lock entangled with pieces of moss cord.

Interpretation   The association of withy and

Figure 7.16 Complex of withy material mixed with moss-cord found during excavation of F3. (*Photo:* Hull Museums.)

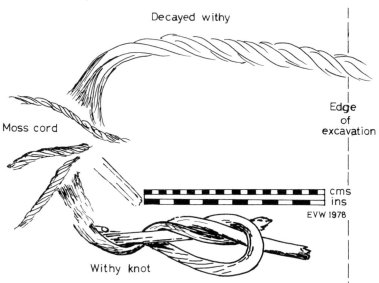

Decayed withy

Moss cord

Withy knot

Edge
of
excavation

cms
ins
EVW 1978

Figure 7.17 Withy material and moss cord (Figure 7.16) drawn in simplified form.

cord of the kind used extensively for caulking in F3 argues strongly in favour of association and therefore contemporaneity with the boat-fragment. By appropriate manipulation prepared withies can be laid into rope and joined to produce lengths longer than can be derived from a single branch. In the absence of traces of any binding material other than withy in association with the boats, except for the moss rope used for caulking, withy rope must be among the choices for any lashings longer than stitches hypothesized in reconstructions, for example girth-lashings at each end of the boat. It is possible therefore that this object was part of such a feature.

Age Radio-carbon assay gave an extra-ordinary date (Q-836, 12,950 BP ± 240). Neither of the trees identified in the sample could have existed in the harsh late-glacial climate prevailing at that time and it must therefore be concluded either that there had been accidental mixing of samples or ancient blendings of materials or that this was a 'wild' radio-carbon assay, as can occasionally occur.

7 Offcut of yew-withy Figures 7.18a and b; 7.19 (Wright 1984)

Discovery, excavation and subsequent history

On a visit in 1977, the end of what appeared to be a piece of typical yew stitch was seen projecting from undisturbed estuarine clay in the bottom of the western extension of the trench up which F3 had been hauled in 1963. On removal and cleaning it was seen to be unusual in that the fibres were twisted and separated only at one end, the rest being untwisted and the butt showing clean-cut toolmarks. It has been deposited at the National Maritime Museum, Greenwich.

Material Branch of yew (*Taxus*).

Dimensions
Length: 250 mm
Max. thickness: 13.5 mm
Min. thickness: 12.5 mm

Description A length of peeled yew branch with c.50 mm of the thinner end having the fibres separated and twisted. Slight stress-

Figure 7.18a Offcut of yew-withy discarded after completion of stitch. (*Photo:* NMM, Greenwich).

Figure 7.18b Butt end of offcut showing toolmarks. (*Photo:* NMM, Greenwich)

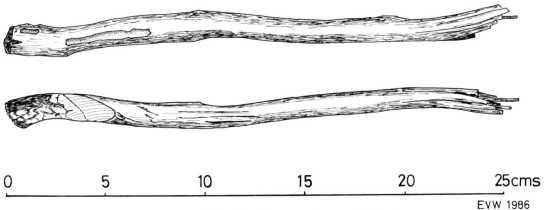

0   5   10   15   20   25cms

EVW 1986

Figure 7.19 Line drawing showing detail of offcut.

cracks are visible 100 mm from the thicker end. At the butt there are two intersecting toolmarks showing clean cuts in the fine-grained wood to about half the thickness of the branch, the remainder appearing to have been torn away.

Interpretation Study of and practical experiment with withy-making of yew and other traditional materials leaves me in no doubt that this is a waste offcut such as would be left by a worker making the stitches in a boat of Ferriby-type. The normal practice in winding a withy preparatory to its use for binding is to hold the thicker end of the chosen branch to the ground with the foot and wind the thinner end with the hands to twist and separate the fibres (Figure 6.11). It is most easily done with the leaves and bark still in place leaving peeling until the final stage. This results in all but the part held under the foot being cracked, twisted, and pliant; and such an uncracked part of the withy would be left protruding from the plank after a stitch was completed and then be trimmed off and discarded. The same result would occur if the alternative method were employed of twisting the binding progressively during the threading process, as in modern Fennoscandian practice.

Age Not directly dated, but available for any future minimally destructive dating process. Its situation in undisturbed estuarine clay at the same horizon as F3 suggests the likelihood of a Bronze Age attribution consistent with the relationship to the stitching technique of the boat.

8 Axe-chips Figure 7.20

Discovery, excavation and subsequent history

On a visit to the site in 1977, a quantity of small chips of oak were observed at the bottom of the southern end of what remained of the trench from the 1946 excavation of F2. They were left in place for possible future detailed investigation but when this did not prove practicable those still in position were collected on a later visit. The matrix was typical estuarine clay and the horizon slightly lower than the lowest level of F2. Similar chips have been collected near the eastern end of the exposure of the estuarine clay. All the material has been deposited at the National Maritime Museum, Greenwich.

Material Oak (*Quercus*).

Dimensions Range of widths across cuts: 45 mm (max.), 30 mm (min.).

Figure 7.20 Axe chips of oak from
the F2 excavation trench.

Description   The chips are uniformly short
and broad, typical of the waste to be expected
from axing rather than the longer and thinner
shavings produced by adzing or slicing
timber.

Comment   Little can be deduced from these
other than that woodworking must have been
taking place at and near the remains of the
boats, F2 in particular.

9 Structures

Over the years a number of structures of
roundwood have been observed in the vicinity
of the boats and some have been investigated.
Those most relevant are:

(a) *Arrangement of short posts near F2 and
short pole beneath it*

Figures 2.12a and b show the nature of
this 'structure' of roundwood posts of up
to 70 mm in diameter. These were close
to F2 and in the plinth under the boat-
fragment and c.1.0 m from the southern

limit located in 1940. They were exposed
during the excavation of F2 in 1946 and
a sample of the timber was recovered,
delivered to Cambridge, but not identified. No further investigation was undertaken. It is possible that they were the
remnant of some sort of 'trestle' used to
support the planks during dismantling.

(b) *'Hard' under F3*

Figure 3.5 shows the array of poles and
other timbers on which F3 was found to
be lying. The majority were of roundwood
60–120 mm in diameter and 2.33–4.66 m
long. Of these one was sampled for radio-
carbon determination (Q715 3120 ±
105BP) and identified as alder (*Alnus*).
Among them was a much worn timber of
oak.

The structure appears to qualify as a 'hard'
within McGrail's definition (McGrail 1983)
and to have been deliberately spread to
provide a firm platform under the damaged
and dismantled fragment of boat.

(c) *Structure to north of F2*

An indefinite structure of short lengths of roundwood of oak (*Quercus*) and birch (*Betula*) with a few vertical sticks with worked points was excavated by the National Maritime Museum in 1978–80 (McGrail 1983) (Figure 3.8). Samples from the vertical sticks yielded the following radio-carbon dates:

HAR – 2759: 3150 ± 80 BP (c.1200 Cal. BC)
HAR – 3682: 3540 ± 100 BP (c.1590 Cal. BC)
HAR – 4204: 3240 ± 90 BP (c.1470 Cal. BC)

The pattern of finds was thought to have been consistent with these being the vestigial remains of horizontal wickerwork held in place by short vertical stakes, comparable with a number of better preserved examples observed over the years by the author at North Ferriby (Figures 7.23 and 7.24) and a mile upstream at Melton. McGrail interprets the structure as either a 'hard' (see 9(b)) or 'a causeway giving dryshod access to the lower foreshore where boats were beached'.

(d) *Melton*

While of less direct relevance, mention is included of work on the similar structures at Melton. The author's unpublished notes on some of these (Wright 1977) have been lodged with Hull Museums and the National Maritime Museum, Greenwich. In general the structures (Figure 7.21) are stouter, more elaborate, and better prepared than those at North Ferriby and they include one short stretch composed of cleft planks of oak (Figure 7.22). One of the best preserved of these was exca-

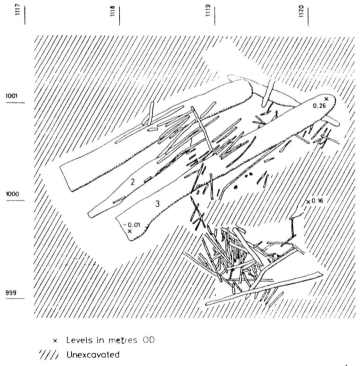

× Levels in metres OD
//// Unexcavated

0 _____ 1m

Figure 7.21 Wooden structure excavated by D. R. Crowther at Melton, also the subject of radiocarbon determinations.
(D. R. Crowther.)

Figure 7.22 Structure of cleft oak timbers, Melton 1946.

vated and photographed c. 1935 (Figure 1.8) and was erroneously recorded as located at Ferriby. Photographs of it have been used to illustrate the type of structure found at both sites and this oppor-tunity is taken to correct the error in locality. More recently a pilot survey and excavation were undertaken under the direction of D. R. Crowther, Keeper of Archaeology at Hull Museums and Art

Figure 7.23 Typical structure of roundwood, N. Ferriby. (*Photo*: Q. E. Wright.)

Figure 7.24 Typical withy material, N. Ferriby. (*Photo*: Q. E. Wright.)

Non-organic artefacts

The metal, stone and ceramic finds are described in Appendix 7.1. Whilst generally supportive of the view that the contents of the peat are of late Neolithic or the earliest Bronze Age and those of the estuarine clay of the middle or later Bronze Age, the distribution is not such that any definite conclusions can be drawn about the reason for their presence. It is perhaps noteworthy that the collapsed remains of the most complete pot were found where the peat and estuarine clay deposits were thinning out nearly to extinction over a ridge in the boulder clay, indicating drier ground than in the immediate vicinity of the boats and other artefacts.

In concluding this chapter which completes the record of finds from the site, I assert my confident belief that the whole assemblage represents the sort of debris which might be expected to accumulate around a site where boats were built, repaired, and operated, perhaps over a long period. Without more precise evidence of dating than is at present available it is impossible to say how long such a period might be. There must always remain a possibility that some at least of the finds may have strayed in from outside the period for which direct indications of date exist. In the next chapter, this evidence will be examined together with that for establishing the environment on the bank of the estuary in ancient times.

APPENDIX 7.1

Artefacts other than wood

Galleries, and samples from the structure excavated gave radio-carbon dates as follows:
HAR – 6367: (*? Pinus*) 2910 ± 90 BP (c. 960 Cal. BC)
HAR – 6368: (*Corylus/Alnus*) 2990 ± 70 BP (c. 1040 Cal. BC)

The initial phase has been published (Crowther 1987) and further work is planned for the site which may result in a clearer interpretation of the purpose of such structures.

Where identification is possible the wooden artefacts from the Ferriby site can in the main be interpreted as related in some way to the construction or operation of boats. In addition to these there is a small accumulation of finds of other materials from both the estuarine clay in which the boats were submerged and from the underlying peat. Some can be dated but

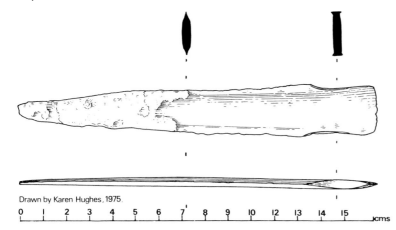

Drawn by Karen Hughes, 1975.

0 1 2 3 4 5 6 7 8 9 10 12 13 14 15   cms

Figure 7.25 Bronze knife blade from N. Ferriby, 1939 (Karen Hughes).

only within broad limits, thereby yielding indications, if nothing more precise, of the age of the deposits. All have been or are about to be published and are here catalogued with only brief descriptions.

Metal

A single, tanged, bronze knife blade (Figure 7.25) made from the broken tip of a rapier of Lisburn-type (Burgess Group IV). Found in the estuarine clay c.75 m north-east of F1 by E. V. Wright in 1939. Datable within the range 1000–500 BC (Longworth, in Wright 1978: 201).

Pottery

1 Rim-sherd of Late Neolithic Grooved Ware (Figure 7.26a). Found in the outlier of peat 400 m east of the boat site by E. V. Wright in 1946. Grooved Ware occurs from c.2500–2000 BC (see Table 8.6) (Longworth in Wright 1978: 201).

2 Bucket urn of typical Bronze Age type (Figure 7.26b). Found in estuarine clay c.175 m north-east of F1 by E. V. Wright in 1946 (Longworth in Wright 1978: 201).

3 Wall-sherd of fabric similar to 2 (Figure 7.26c). Found in estuarine clay c.150 m east of F1 by E. V. Wright in 1947.

4 Base of a vessel smaller than 2 (Figure 7.26d) and of similar but heavier make. Found in estuarine clay 50 m north-west of F2 by E. V. Wright in 1947 (Wright and Wright 1947: Figure 16.3).

5 Rim-sherd of shouldered bowl or jar with narrow everted rim (Figure 7.27a), flint-tempered fabric, paralleled at Castle Hill, Scarborough and Stonea, Essex. Found by E. V. Wright in estuarine clay c.200 m west of F2 in possible infill of ancient tidal channel, in 1986. Dated to first half of first millennium BC. (Rigby, in Wright *et al.* 1989).

6 Rim-sherd of shouldered jar with deep tapered rim (Figure 7.27b) fabric tempered with broken erratic stone, a technique occurring in Yorkshire and Humberside from the Late Bronze Age. Found by V. S. Heal 1983 in estuarine clay near 5. A date in the first half of the first millennium BC is also likely (Rigby, in Wright *et al.* 1989).

Baked clay

Part of a (?) sinker (Figure 7.28), found close to the surface of F2 during excavation in 1946. The large hole and light weight argue against it being a loom weight, of which a variety of shapes were made in prehistoric times. The situation in a maritime context suggests the

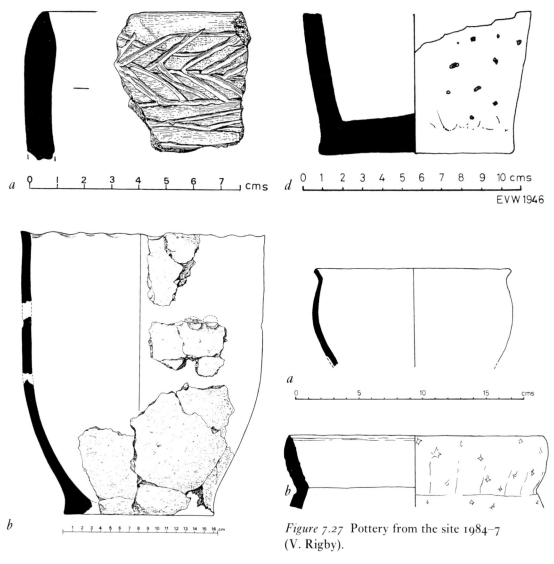

a

d

EVW 1946

b

a

b

Figure 7.27 Pottery from the site 1984–7 (V. Rigby).

c

Figure 7.26 Pottery from the area adjoining the boats, 1946 (Karen Hughes).

possibility that it was a sinker for weighting the edge of a net (Wright and Wright 1947: Wright 1976).

Flint

The peat has yielded a number of struck flakes, none of any significance, and a single well-made implement interpreted as a borer (Figure 1.9). The last was found by C. W. Wright in 1936 south of the position of F1. (Wright 1976: Pl. 2A).

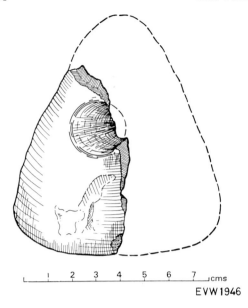

2 3 4 5 6 7 ⌐cms

EVW 1946

Figure 7.28 Part of baked clay sinker from surface
of F2, 1946.

The knife blade and pottery items 1–3, 5, and
6 are deposited in Hull Museum. Pottery item
4 and the baked clay (?) sinker cannot now be
traced. The flint borer was destroyed in the
Hull Museum fire of 1942.

The sherd of Grooved Ware apart, the
general impression of age conveyed by the
small collection of pottery is that they are later
than the earlier dates for the boats; but only
the sinker was found in association with any
of them. They do however support Buckland
and Beal's (1989) view that the deposition
of the estuarine clay took place over a span
covering much of the Bronze Age.

8

Environment, dating and archaeological background

There are three methods available for determining the age of artefacts such as those from Ferriby: dating by comparison or association with other objects or deposits of known age; direct dating by radio-carbon determination; and absolute dating by dendrochronology. The first of these, as has already been emphasized, cannot be relied upon fully owing to the ever-present possibility that objects found in a water-laid deposit could have been sorted or otherwise shifted horizontally or vertically before discovery. The second remains imprecise owing to the considerable range of variation inherent in the process and, in the Ferriby case, the still relatively small (albeit growing) number of determinations at present available. Only the third gives promise of complete reliability and here again the quantity of evidence is low, the quality is less than perfect where timber had deteriorated before examination and, in particular at the time of writing, the long awaited curves taking the table of measured growth rings for north-eastern England back into the the second millennium BC have not yet been linked together. Connections may be made within a few years but, until they are, comparisons are alone possible with floating chronologies whose absolute age can be estimated only within broad limits. Evidence for the age of artefacts and that for reconstruction of the ancient environment are interrelated and consideration of the latter is undertaken first to demonstrate the geological, topographical,

and climatic background for the periods before, during, and after the deposition of the boats at the site. Discussion of the dating evidence follows and this leads on to examination of the relevant archaeological framework for the period during which the design of such boats evolved and the fully developed examples which we have were in use.

ENVIRONMENT

The results of the most recent studies of the palaeo-environment at Ferriby are published in Buckland et al. 1990 and a brief summary of their work is all that is necessary in the present context. Mention has already been made in general terms of the sequence of the deposits on the foreshore and this is now given more precisely in Table 8.1, reproduced from their paper.

The greatest thickness in the post-glacial beds was observed c.150 m west of the boat site (Wright and Wright 1933) where there is a filled channel or runnel in the boulder clay (Skipsea till) (Figure 8.1). Traces of the other runnel referred to by Buckland and Beal are not now easy to detect but were most obvious in the area of F2 until 1979 (Figures 8.2a–c). In 1946 F1 was found to be lying directly on the 'weathered top' of the boulder clay (Figure 8.3) possibly at the bottom of a similar runnel. Whether these were existing gullies used or even improved by the boatmen or were the result of turbulence and consequent erosion

Table 8.1 Section through deposits exposed at low water at Section B. North Ferriby, September 1978

0 – 0.36 m	Dark olive grey (Munsell no. 5Y 3/2) poorly sorted clay-silt with some sand and scattered unidentifiable plant debris; occasional gasteropods and bivalves occur in the deposit, some of the latter in life positions.
0.36 – 0.78 m	Very woody detrital peat with complete tree trunks and some *in situ* stools. Dark reddish brown (5 Yr 2.5/2) darkening on exposure to air.
0.78 – 1.02 m	Silty dark olive grey (5Y 3/2) clay with some organic debris, fine chalk and broken flint towards the base. Weathered top of:
> 1.02 m	Dark greyish brown (10 YR 4/2) clay with chalk and other erratics (till).

Note: To the east of this locality, the peat is cut out and the clay-silts rest directly on the underlying till. It seems probable that this reflects a runnel up which the boats had been dragged or in which they had been moored.

set up by the presence of the substantial water-logged timbers themselves is open to debate. The relationship between the boats and the surrounding deposits is shown in Figure 8.4, which is the result of records made from 1975 onwards when the site had been considerably disturbed by excavation and natural erosion. The highest point of F1, the western tip of the keel-plank, was surveyed in 1946 at −1.36 m OD (i.e. 1.36 m *below* Ordnance Datum) and it has been estimated that between 1937 and that date some 0.30 m had been removed vertically by erosion. The southern, seaward end of F2 at the same date lay at −2.11 m OD. The level of the bed of poles under F3 in 1963 was measured at −1.0 m OD. Although they show F2, F1, and F3 in that order at successively higher levels

Figure 8.1 Section of post-glacial deposits showing maximum development (c. 2 m thickness) in a runnel c. 100 m west of F2.

in the deposit, it is unlikely that there is any significant difference between them owing to the potential effects of current action in formation of the runnels.

The question has been asked whether the remains of the boats might have drifted from the position where they were operated to that in which they were found. I think that this is unlikely since in the first instance timber in the bottom of boats could be expected to have become largely waterlogged during their working life and therefore to have lost its buoyancy so that in the absence of sides the structures would have sunk to the bottom. Studies in the movement of logs along the northern coasts of Siberia and Russia to beaches on Svalbard have demonstrated that according to species they sink within a maximum of two years after immersion and could only have reached their destination if they had been frozen into ice-floes (Haggblom 1982). Furthermore in the case of F2 and even more so F3, not only would the detached parts almost certainly have become separated from each other, but the two finds could hardly have found their way by accident on to the wooden structures on which they lay. The survival of comparatively delicate fittings on F1 is also inconsistent with random drifting to its resting place. The signs of deliberate dismantling and the presence of axe chippings alongside and under F2 referred to in Chapters 4 and 7 also point to work having taken place at the find-spot.

The recent studies of indicators of the immediate environment cover first the insect fauna, the exoskeletons of beetles being of special significance as they are notably sensitive to habitat and the salinity of their surroundings; second, the seeds and fragments of plants which provide similar evidence; and third, the pollen content which gives even more information including that of the tree cover in the hinterland. I cannot better the conclusions drawn by Buckland and his co-authors:

The examination of several lines of palaeo-ecological evidence allows the reconstruction of a fairly detailed picture of the Ferriby boats' environment. They had been abandoned on saline mudflats below contemporary high tide level, beyond the zone of any extensively vegetated salt marsh. On stratigraphic grounds, noted by Wright and Churchill (1965), it seems probable that the boats lay in shallow creeks or runnels in the foreshore, although, unlike the Brigg situation (McGrail, 1981a), the palaeo-environmental evidence did not provide further support for this conclusion. The intertidal mudflats were backed by estuarine vegetation, giving way to wet, oak–alder carrlands beyond. Although both the archaeology and palaeoecology provide evidence for the activities of man, both in the presence of domestic stock and the palynological record of his impact upon the wider landscape, the immediate area was still essentially wooded, with lime, elm and pine still forming a part of the forest canopy. The more recent impact of man upon the Humber has removed such gradual intergrades between habitats from its landscapes and several of the invertebrates only survive as disjunct fragments of former communities in temporary refuges from development and pollution; the only record of the natural landscapes of the Humber lies in its sediments and these are worthy of more detailed investigation.

Discussion of the environment cannot exclude the question of climate. Following the Atlantic period extending from the later Mesolithic and earlier Neolithic when the climate over northern Europe was measurably warmer than at the present time, the Subboreal period after c.3000 BC shows a gradual if fluctuating decline until c.1250 BC after which there is evidence for a very marked deterioration in conditions affecting both population and agricultural patterns. Certainly during the earlier part of the estimated

(a)

(b)

Figure 8.2 (and see overleaf) Eroded remains of the F2 (a, b and c) and F3 (d and e) excavation trenches in 1977 with indications that the boat fragments lay submerged in tidal runnels.

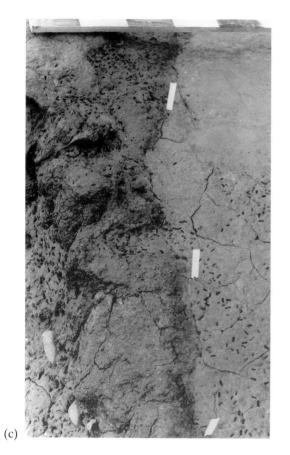

(c)

(d)

(e)

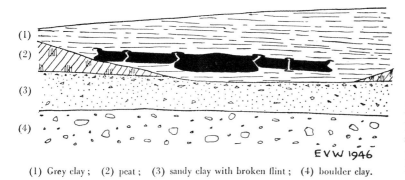

EVW 1946

Figure 8.3 Section of deposits under F1 showing absence of peat, indicative of presence of a runnel or possible effects of tidal scour.

(1) Grey clay ;   (2) peat ;   (3) sandy clay with broken flint ;   (4) boulder clay.

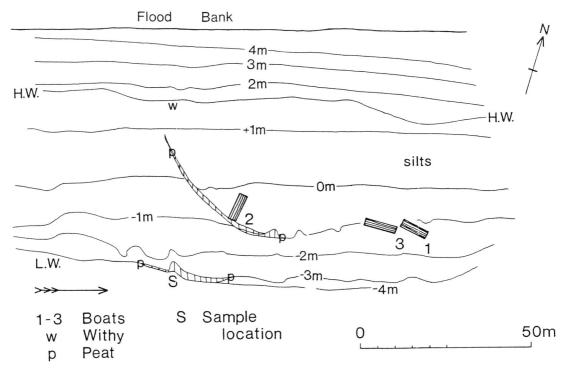

Figure 8.4 Diagrammatic presentation of levels of boat finds in relation to the post-glacial deposits as reconstructed in 1984 (P. C. Buckland).

span for the construction and operation of Ferriby-type boats on the Humber, the climate can be envisaged as somewhat more genial than that with which we are now familiar and they cannot therefore be associated specifically with the colder, wetter conditions of the last quarter of the second millennium BC in the sense that these might have stimulated an impulse for greater maritime activity. The situation was probably the reverse with favourable climate encouraging commercial traffic through enhanced demand.

DATING

Dating of the sequence represented in the deposits relies on comparison with other similar deposits within the region and direct dating of any objects contained within them. The former are not yet particularly helpful although there are two radio-carbon dates for the top of the peat some 25 km inland at Thorne (Q481 3160 ± 115 BP and Q482 2931 ± 115 BP) which suggest that the deposition there was rather later than the similar episode downstream at Ferriby. Artefactual evidence is at least indicative of a Late Neolithic or Earliest Bronze Age date for the peat 'outlier' to the east of the main deposit at Ferriby in the find of a single sherd of Grooved Ware (Figure 7.26a) typical of the period. The single bronze object (Figure 7.25) and all but two of the pottery fragments (Figure 7.26b–d) from the estuarine clay are consistent with Bronze Age dating for that episode or series of episodes involved in its formation. The other two sherds (Figure 7.27a–b) are thought to be somewhat later and may be associated with the infill of the

channel running through the estuarine clay already mentioned in connection with F4. Indeed most of the evidence for dating the deposits comes from the direct dates obtained for the boat remains themselves.

Interpretation of radio-carbon ages calls for caution, especially when the list is short and the product of several laboratories; and, before valid comparisons can be made, radio-carbon years must be converted to their calendar equivalents by calibration, which can in turn yield multiple results. Where reference is made here to radio-carbon years these are expressed as 'BP' or 'before present'.

The uncertainty of the ages is shown by the use of the plus or minus sign (±) to indicate that there is a 68 per cent statistical probability that the true age in radio-carbon years lies within the limits of a single standard deviation (1 SD or σ). If the standard deviation of the activity is doubled (2 SD or 2 σ) this probability rises to 95 per cent and in most of my arguments this is the method used. Where ages have been converted by calibration to calendar years they are shown as Cal. BP or Cal. BC.

Table 8.2 Radio-carbon dates for North Ferriby

Laboratory number	Description of sample	Radio-carbon age BP	uncertainty ±
HAR–8972	F4 timber	2390	60
BM–58	Fragment of sealing lath collected in 1953 from a point over the position where Boat 3 was found 10 years later	2700	150
Q–715	12-year old alder (*Alnus*) branch directly beneath Boat 3, collected 1963	3120	105
Q–1217	Yew (*Taxus*) stitches from boat 1 collected from material at NMM, Greenwich in 1973	3312	100
Q–1197	Oak (*Quercus*) from main planking of Boat 1. Collected from material at NMM, Greenwich in 1973	3380	100
Q–837(a)	Yew (*Taxus*) stitches and slat from underneath Boat 2 collected 1941	3393	210
Q–837(b)	Duplicate oxidation of sample Q–837(a) (a second 'run' of the same material designed to reduce the standard deviation)	3506	110
HAR–2759	Samples of sticks from structures in area adjoining boats, excavated by ARC, Greenwich in 1978–80	3150	110
HAR–3682		3540	100
HAR–4204		3420	90

Table 8.3 Additional radio-carbon determinations for the boats

Laboratory number	Description of sample	Radio-carbon age BP	Uncertainty ±
Q3147	F3 Yew withy ⎫ *	2945	40
Q3145	F3 Yew withy ⎭	2975	45
Q3043	F1 Yew withy ⎫ *	2980	55
Q3124	F1 Yew withy ⎭	3020	40
Q3044	F2 Top of cleat ⎫ *	3095	40
Q3023	F2 Top of cleat ⎭	3120	45
Q3212	F4 timber	2350	40

* Each pair of determinations has been made using separate parts of the same samples.

Until very recently the list of radio-carbon dates for North Ferriby material was as shown in Table 8.2.

While this chapter was at a late stage of revision more evidence became available from Dr V.R. Switsur at the Cambridge radio-carbon laboratory and the preliminary implications of this have been taken into account to provide as up to date a view as possible of the estimated age of the North Ferriby boats. Although the conclusions which follow are reliable at the time of writing, they should not be regarded as final until the data have been fully assessed and published in the technical media (Switsur and Wright, 1989). They are as set out in Table 8.3.

Some other radio-carbon ages for comparative material which have a bearing on the Ferriby picture are given in Table 8.4.

Since 1975, and before the appearance of F4 on the scene, the generally accepted theory has been that, using 2SD, the ages for the first three boat-finds overlapped at c.3330 BP in radio-carbon years, calibrated approximately by the methods then available to c.1500 Cal. BC in calendar years (McGrail and Switsur 1975: 193). The discovery and dating of F4 and recent advances in the technique of

Table 8.4 Radio-carbon dates for comparison

Laboratory number	Description of sample	Radio-carbon age BP	± (1SD)
HAR 6394 ⎫ HAR 6395 ⎬ HAR 6441 ⎭	Hasholme logboat sapwood ⎫⎬ pooled ⎭	2375	75
Q78	Brigg logboat	2784	100
Q79	Short Ferry logboat	2796	100
Q80	Appleby logboat	3050	80
Q1261	Brigg 'Raft' hazel post	2560	50
Q1256	Brigg 'Raft' hazel lath	2605	50
Q1255	Brigg 'Raft' hazel lath	2655	50
Q1258	Brigg 'Raft' moss-caulking	2670	75
BM 2339	Canewdon, Essex paddle	2900	70
HAR 6367 ⎫ HAR 6368 ⎭	Sticks from Melton structures	2910	90
		2990	70
BIRM 336	Thorne Waste oak	3080	90

calibration with the new Cambridge determinations have prompted a review of this conclusion with the result that previously held views have had to be modified. The need for this is accentuated by the fact that the quality of the new determinations has been enhanced by Switsur's improved methods of sample preparation to remove contaminants such as preservative chemicals. Greater precision of technique has also had the beneficial effect of substantially reducing the quoted uncertainty in the ages.

For ease of comparison the calibrated dates equivalent to the radio-carbon ages given in Tables 8.2, 8.3 and 8.4 are displayed diagrammatically in Figure 8.5 and can be interpreted quite simply. As a first step it is clear that the dating ranges for F1 and F2 overlap over the period 1385–1310 Cal. BC. In addition the tree-trunks from which their keel-planks were hewn have been shown on dendrochronological examination to match and therefore to be contemporary (Hillam 1985). Thus the combination of radio-carbon and tree-ring dating leaves little doubt that they are of broadly the same age despite indications from the earlier radio-carbon assays that F2 could have been considerably older than F1. The next question for consideration is whether F3 should still be regarded as contemporary with the other two. As can be seen from Figure 8.5, its age could overlap with that of the other two at c.1300 Cal. BC; but there remains the likelihood that it is contemporary with the debris lying immediately over it in the estuarine clay from which the sample for BM58 was obtained and for which an earliest date is c.1260 Cal. BC. Moreover the tree-ring curves for F3 do not match with those for F1 and F2 and there are several distinct differences in details of construction in F3: notably, the absence of cleat systems; the sharp internal angle in the shaped end of S-S1 contrasted with the rounded section in F1; and the use of luting-cord of hair moss not recorded in either of the others. The new dates therefore suggest a date range for F3

where it overlaps with the earlier part of that for the BM58 sample from 1260–1050 Cal. BC. Even if F3 is separated from F1 and F2, the ages for all three overlap with the date obtained by radio-carbon assay for some oaks from Thorne Waste for which there is a 250 year long 'floating chronology' and with which that for F3 has been matched (Hillam pers. comm.). Such an interpretation for F3 denies the possibility that F4 was contemporary with the BM58 sample at the latter end of its range and effectively demolishes any argument on dating grounds alone that F4 could have been related to material unquestionably of the same make as F1, F2, and F3.

To sum up, current estimates for the dates of the Ferriby boats would appear to be as set out in Table 8.5.

Table 8.5 Estimated dates for the North Ferriby boat-finds

	Cal. BC
F4	*either* c.800 *or* c.400
F1, F2, and F3	c.1300

F3 may eventually be found to be later than F1 and F2 by as much as 250 years.

Further refinement of the radio-carbon dating evidence with or without additional determinations may modify these estimates or narrow down the degree of uncertainty in the figures. It is likely however that greater precision will eventually come from developments in the dating of the tree-ring sequences for north-east England so that absolute dates can be attributed to the timber from which the boats were built.

ARCHAEOLOGICAL BACKGROUND

Even if they could all be positively associated with each other, the objects other than the rarely paralleled wooden artefacts are not very helpful for the clarification of the archaeological context of the boat-finds. Although

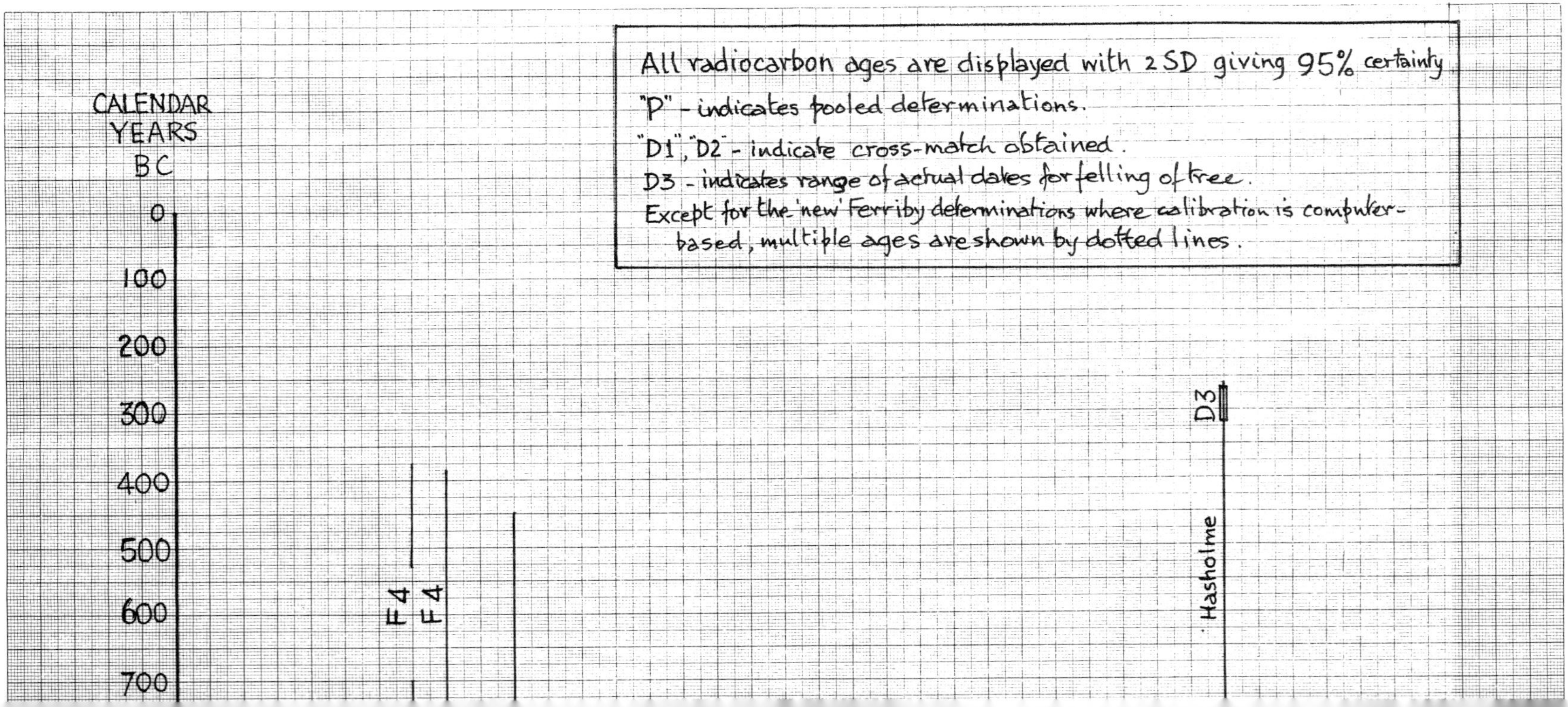

All radiocarbon ages are displayed with 2 SD giving 95% certainty

"P" - indicates pooled determinations.

"D1", "D2" - indicate cross-match obtained.

D3 - indicates range of actual dates for felling of tree.

Except for the new 'Ferriby' determinations where calibration is computer-based, multiple ages are shown by dotted lines.

CALENDAR YEARS BC

0
100
200
300
400
500
600
700

D3

Hasholme

F4

F4

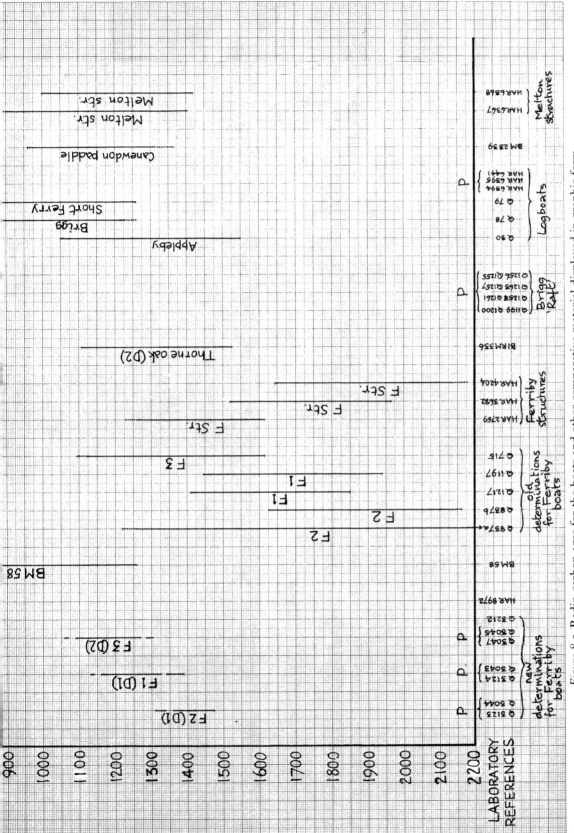

Figure 8.5 Radio-carbon ages for the boats and other comparative material displayed in graphic form.

broadly typical of the Middle and Late Bronze Age they are neither readily attributable to a specific culture nor closely datable. It becomes necessary therefore to rely on the evidence for the age of the boats themselves from a date before c.1300 BC and onwards and then to relate that to the archaeological chronology for the period. In recent years there has been a growing trend among archaeologists, however reluctantly, to abandon the old 'Three Age' system of Stone, Bronze, and Iron Ages with their long-established subdivisions; but as far as the metal-using periods are concerned no concise and generally accepted alternative for Hawkes's 'Scheme for the British Bronze Age' (Hawkes 1960) has yet emerged, although the accumulation of dating evidence has produced some changes in the chronology assigned to his scheme. The most comprehensive attempts to establish a clear, dated framework for the early metal-using cultures in the British Isles have been those of Burgess, and as more dating evidence has emerged even he has been obliged to withdraw and modify his most positive published essay in that direction (Burgess 1980 and 1986). He has however responded to my plea for help by supplying me with a framework which represents his latest thinking and this is given in Table 8.6.

Taking the simplest view, it will be seen that Ferriby boats were already in a fully developed state by c.1300 BC during the first phase of the British Middle Bronze Age, or Montelius MIIA in northern Europe; and, depending on which of the alternative models for dating is adopted, may have continued in use through the rest of the Middle Bronze Age or beyond to the end of the Late Bronze Age (British LBA3 or Montelius M VI for northern Europe) if F4 is included. They must however have been the product of an ancestry stretching back for many years before the date of F1 and F2 since by no stretch of the imagination could a design of such complexity have been reached by a single process of invention. Such an ancestry, of whatever duration and geographical spread,

must therefore in the English context be related to 'Early' rather than 'Middle' Bronze Age cultures. While not denying the possibility that the phenomenon revealed at Ferriby of three major boat-fragments of similar construction, together with another fragment and boat-related debris which may or may not be associated with them, could have been the result of a temporary incursion of an exotic kind, I think this to be remote. The impression I have gained is rather that they were the traces left by a local boat-using community of long standing whose prime sphere of operation was the tidal estuary and the main rivers draining into it. This view is strengthened by the possibility that the time span covered by the finds may have been of more than a millennium's duration rather than briefly about 1400–1300 BC. Such activity could have been stimulated by the arrival in the estuary of a boat or boats of novel type or just as well by the arrival of a single boat-builder experienced in their design and construction. Equally tenable is the proposition that demands imposed by topography and economic growth in the area generated pressures to provide an improved service for the transport of people and merchandise, in which case the development could have been of mainly local origin and of very long duration. Between these extremes of wholly exotic or largely indigenous development a whole range of hypotheses could be advanced which would carry equal weight.

Forty years ago it was still customary to ascribe to immigrant settlers or 'invaders' such significant introductions into Britain as the practices of agriculture, the making of pottery, and the techniques of metallurgy, these in the millennia following the separation by rising sea levels of the British isles from mainland Europe from c.7500 BC (McGrail 1989). Nowadays, however, the appearance even of revolutionary changes such as those is thought to be the result of cultural contacts and exchange of artefacts, products or ideas rather than movement of populations. In the

Table 8.6 Chronological table for the Bronze Age in Britain

DATE CAL BC	BRITAIN			MAINLAND EUROPE	
	METAL	PHASES, BURIALS ETC.	THREE AGES (Developed from Hawkes 1960)	ATLANTIC FRANCE (Burgess)	NORTHERN EUROPE (After Montelius)
2500	CASTLETOWN-ROCHE ?	NEWGRANGE-STONEHENGE I Grooved Ware and Peterborough wares begin First Beakers	LATE NEOLITHIC	CHALCOLITHIC Late megalithic tombs Beakers	LATE NEOLITHIC
2400	KNOCKNAGUE-MOEL-ARTHUR	MOUNT PLEASANT Henges Stone Circles etc Early Beakers	CHALCOLITHIC 1		
2300	FRANKFORD		CHALCOLITHIC 2		
2200		DISLOCATION			
2100	MIGDALE-KILLAHA-ODDINGTON	Late Neolithic wares end STONEHENGE II & III	EARLY BRONZE AGE 1 (EBA 1)	BRONZE ANCIEN I (BA I)	
2000	AYLESFORD-	FARGO Early Food Vessels and Urns			
1900	MILECROSS	Step 5,6 Beakers	EBA 2	Breton tumuli BA II	M I A
1800	BUSH BARROW-WILLERBY WOLD	BUSH BARROW WESSEX I Last Beakers			
1700		Last Food Vessels			M I B Sogel
1600	ARRETON-INCH ISLAND	ALDBOURNE-EDMONDSHAM WESSEX II	EBA 3		
1500					
1400	ACTON PARK I ACTON PARK II		MIDDLE BRONZE AGE 1 (MBA1)	BRONZE MOYEN I (BM I) Treboul	M II A Wohlde-Ilsmoor
1300	TAUNTON-BISHOPSLAND	KNIGHTON HEATH Deverel-Rimbury and equivalents	MBA 2	BM II Portrieux Baux-St-Croix Mont-St-Aignan	M II B,c Froik-Ostenfeld
1200	PENARD I	COLLAPSE		BRONZE FINAL I (B F I) Rosnoën	M III
1100	APPLEBY PENARD II	ANGLE DITCH-RAMSHILL	MBA 3	BF II a	
1000	FFYNHONNAU			BF II b	M IV
900	WILBURTON-WALLINGTON	STABILISATION RUNNYMEDE-MUCKING	LATE BRONZE AGE 1 (LBA 1)	BF III a St Brieuc-des-Iffs Caix	
800	EWART PARK I Isle of Harty EWART PARK II Heathery Burn CARP'S TONGUE		LBA 2a LBA 2b	BF III b CARP'S TONGUE Prairie-de-Mauves Vénat	M V
700	LLYN FAWR (Hallstatt C)	STAPLE HOWE	LBA 3	HALLSTATT ANCIEN	M VI
600					
500	(Hallstatt D) EARLY IRON AGE			HALLSTATT FINAL	EARLY IRON AGE
400		LA TÈNE (in Yorkshire)			Colin Burgess 1988

British case it is even argued that this sort of process occurred with the introduction of agriculture to the original hunting and gathering communities of Mesolithic times. What is beyond dispute is that after separation from the mainland such contacts must necessarily have involved boats capable of making the sea passages. It is perhaps noteworthy that in his Mount Pleasant phase from c.2400–2100 BC, during which copper and later bronze-working and Beaker pottery appear on the British scene, Burgess has suggested (1980) that the earliest traffic into Ireland may have stemmed from Italy to Iberia and then via the Atlantic coasts whereas that into southern and eastern lowland England shows a greater affinity in terms of artefacts with Central Europe and the lower Rhine-basin. This hints at seafaring across the eastern part of the Channel and by coasting around the southern North Sea at this period.

Even earlier sea-voyaging must have been involved in the contacts which took place in Neolithic times to account for the grain crops, and perhaps livestock too, of the emergent farming communities, the first dated evidence for which occurs in Northern Ireland, necessitating crossing not only of the Channel but of the Irish Sea, colonization by sea having already taken place by c. 7000 BC. There is a school of thought of which the late Paul Johnstone was one of the leading advocates (Johnstone 1980) which holds that the hide-boat was the vessel *par excellence* of the Neolithic period. If the successors of these craft into historic and modern times such as the Irish curraghs are anything to go by, such boats would have been capable of making the sea passages involved together with a useful load including livestock. Though there is no reason to question a Neolithic or even much earlier origin for hideboats – and there have been recent suggestions (Figure 8.5) of dates back into Late Paleolithic times for these (Ellmers 1984) – they were not the only type of boat made. The earliest logboat dated so far is that from Pesse in the Netherlands (if it

is a boat and not a trough) of 6315 BC ± 275 (Grn 486) (McGrail 1978) and there is a growing list of Danish finds of the seventh and sixth millennia BC of logboats and paddles, some elaborately decorated (Rieck and Crumlin-Pedersen 1988). For lack of radio-carbon determinations there is no British example earlier than the find from Locharbriggs, Dumfriesshire of 1804 BC ± 125 (SRR–326). No doubt hideboats and logboats existed contemporaneously, as they have done in recent historical times. There is however no record from any Neolithic context in northern Europe of a boat constructed from planks. Although the seagoing qualities of hideboats are well enough attested, the merits of log-boats even without stabilizers in the form of outriggers or logs attached to the sides for added buoyancy cannot be discounted, especially if travelling in company as I have seen them from an ocean liner off the west-ernmost tip of Africa (Figure 8.7). Overseas exchanges between the islands of the British archipelago and with the mainland could therefore well have been carried on, if at times precariously, by wooden boats of much less elaborate construction than, for example, versions of plank-built boats of Ferriby-type well before the second millennium BC. The existence of fast, capacious and weatherly boats at and before c.1300 BC does not therefore necessarily imply that traffic between Britain and the mainland was especially favoured at that period, but it could certainly have been easier than at times when only logboats were available. With Ferriby-type boats of timber and well made hide-boats of the curragh type, conditions certainly existed for any and all of the maritime interchange attested by the archaeological record in the second millennium BC. Either would have been suitable for the carriage of the only two Bronze Age cargoes so far identified in British waters, those from Langdon Bay near Dover and Salcombe in Devon and both dated to c.1200–1000 BC (Burgess 1980: 157).

When considering whether the origins of

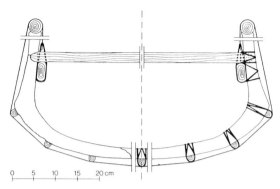

0 5 10 15 20 cm

Figure 8.6 Hypothetical reconstruction of frame of a hide-boat incorporating antler crook of Later Paleolithic age (D. Ellmers).

so advanced a form of boat as those from Ferriby might have been local or foreign to the Humber catchment, one needs to examine the sort of social and economic environment which might be favourable for their development. Stability and prosperity over a period of centuries appear to be the prerequisite not least because boatbuilders the world over are notably conservative in their ways – witness the survival even today throughout the tropical belt of craft of the most ancient lineage. Such conditions prevailed in southern and

eastern England in the Early and Middle Bronze Ages with indications of economic growth and expanding population, until the nearly catastrophic downturn in the last two centuries of the second millennium BC generally thought to be caused by a sharp deterioration in the climate which forced a much reduced population off the marginal lands cultivated previously (Burgess 1986).

I have long been of the view that there are a number of features in the Ferriby boats which are unlikely to have been capable of production to such uniform standards of dimension and finish without metal tools, the most notable examples being the squared stitch-holes and the shaped ends of the sidestrakes. While the rectilinear scars so clearly displayed in the slots in F1 remain something of an enigma, the best preserved axe mark, that on F2, can with some confidence be identified with some of the wider Middle Bronze Age blades. With bronze increasingly becoming available for utilitarian as well as prestige purposes after the Early Bronze Age, conditions again favour the development of complex and accurately made wooden structures. It appears therefore that, without

Figure 8.7 Two of a group of unstabilized logboats fishing out of sight of land, photographed by the author from the RMS *Durban Castle* off Cape Verde, the western tip of Africa, in 1948.

pressing the argument too far, there is a fair correspondence between the evidence for date and what is known of the tools which might then have been used by a boatbuilder.

The archaeological evidence for the local scene calls for little comment since for the relevant periods there are ample signs of widespread and dense settlement. This is attested to a greater extent by funerary monuments than by habitations, but in recent years more of the latter have been reported (e.g. Manby 1974). As with the rest of England in the first three quarters of the second millennium BC, the pattern is one of social stability, more conservative perhaps than in southern and south-eastern areas, but no less prosperous if the barrows and earthworks of the Chalk Wolds to north and south of the Humber are anything to go by. Indeed before the depredations of modern agriculture these presented a scene to rival that of the uplands of Wessex. In the heyday of pioneers such as Greenwell (1877) and Mortimer (1905) the array of tumuli visible on the Yorkshire Wolds must have been spectacular and remained so well into the 1950s. Settlement continued through to the Late Bronze Age, especially in the low-lying areas of Holderness between the River Hull and the sea (Varley 1968), and timber structures of the same period have been identified at Melton just upstream of the Ferriby site (Crowther 1987). The first indications of significant change in the established pattern of social stability occur with the appearance of settlements of the latest Bronze Age typified by those at Staple Howe (see Table 8.6) (Brewster 1963) and Scarborough Castle (Smith 1928); but nothing of a revolutionary kind can be inferred before the fourth century BC when there was an incursion of people associated with the La Tène cultures of northern France (Stead 1965). What can be seen therefore from the third to the middle of the first millennium BC is evidence pointing to a population large enough and an economy prosperous enough to generate demand sufficient to encourage the development and operation of a sophisticated service of water transport in the waterways and especially over the major water barrier of the Humber estuary.

In conclusion, while it is impossible to make any pronouncement in favour of either a local or an exotic origin, it would be surprising indeed if once they were available in the Humber estuary boats of such a kind were not also used throughout the waterways feeding into the southern North Sea. I think that the examples that we have from Ferriby and the presumably allied type from Brigg point to building, operation, and development in the Humber area over a span of several centuries at the very least. Only more finds will determine how, where, and when they originated.

9

Conclusion

In the preceding pages I have aimed to set out all the relevant information now available about the boats and other finds; to give an assessment of their age and a picture of their surroundings; and to offer a reasoned hypothesis for the design of a complete boat. From the last, deductions have been made about how it might have performed and how it was built. In this final chapter I shall discuss the possible purpose of the site and role of the boats found there and conclude with some reflections on their place in the record of early boatbuilding and design. In both respects it is worth reiterating the cautionary words already written about the uncertainty of associations between artefacts even from so homogeneous a deposit as that at North Ferriby; about the conjectural elements in the reconstruction which can only be resolved with more finds and from experiment leading to the construction of a full-scale replica; and about the effects of the regrettably small sample worldwide of actual boats of the period with which ours can be compared.

To deal first with the terrain, Buckland's (1989) investigations have established that the surface of the solid ground in the immediate vicinity, consisting of firm boulder-clay or till, was undulating with shallow ridges and valleys trending inland from the tidal zone. As the base-level rose to that approximating to the present range, with accumulation of silt against the shore, the ridges could be expected to provide firmer going and more suitable

sites than the valleys for handling beached boats. Reference to Figure 8.4 shows that the boat site lies on the eastern flank of just such a minor ridge, with the deepest of the nearby valleys beyond this to the west. Moreover the distribution of finds, particularly of wooden artefacts which can be related to boats, appears to be clustered around the immediate area of the boats themselves (Figure 4.1). What we have, therefore, is a site favourable for boat-working and an accumulation of the debris typical of such activity coinciding in that stretch of the shore. The most apt modern example of such a situation that I have seen was that on the waterside near the fish market at Chittagong in Bangladesh (Figure 6.16), where sewn boats could be seen in various stages of construction from the roughly trimmed logboat base to complete boats either moored in small channels or out of the water for refitting or repair (Figure 6.17). *Mutatis mutandis*, I visualize a similar range of activities being undertaken on the site at North Ferriby when it was in use. No particular order or organization would be required by way of facilities for slipping boats as they could have been floated ashore at high spring tides or where necessary hauled out above high water with the aid of a capstan like that described in Chapter 7, and raised as necessary by means of rollers on to trestles to provide access to the bottoms. Building *ab initio* would take place in similar fashion and use could be made of any tidal channels in the vicinity for sheltered moorings.

Figure 9.1 The river-bank immediately above the boat site c. 1900 with the drying sheds of the brickyard on the right. *(Photo*: H. V. Wright, the author's father.)

Most primitive boat-working sites have the users' living quarters on the nearest available dry ground above the reach of the tide. There are no records of any finds to indicate the presence of a settlement in the area of the nineteenth-century brick-clay workings (Figure 9.1) behind the flood-bank immediately inland of the boat site. The depth of the flooded pits visible until the 1940s (Figure 9.2) suggests that the clay-silt was extracted down to the level of the underlying bed of peat and it is unlikely therefore that any traces of pottery or other durable artefacts would have entirely escaped the eyes of the diggers, stimulated as they used to be by cash inducements on offer from collectors such as Canon Greenwell who was active at the time. If there was a nearby settlement, it might have lain to

the north-east of the boats in an area which to my knowledge has never been excavated and the level of which has been raised in recent years following its use as a rubbish-tip. It is perhaps indicative that three out of the six finds of pottery from the clay-silt, including the collapsed remains of the large and fragile 'bucket urn', have been found well up the bank from the existing water's edge. Unfortunately the older deposits in this area are only rarely exposed when the mantle of shingle and recent silt piled against the flood-bank is cleared away by gales, and it has therefore been less regularly searched than the rest of the exposure. Settlement nearby or not, it would appear to be an acceptable proposition that over a long period large boats were operated from the foreshore at or near to

Figure 9.2 The brick-ponds in 1939 before landfill and levelling.

where the abandoned fragments were found, and that they were likely to have been repaired and refitted there as well. There is no positive evidence for or against their having been actually built on the spot.

Rational presumptions can be made about the uses to which the boats were put, the most obvious one being as ferries across the estuary, the high ground on both sides of the Humber being a vital channel for overland communication from prehistoric until modern times. It is equally likely that they were used as well for transport up and down the estuary and the tidal reaches of the rivers draining into it. Loads which can be envisaged would include livestock as well as people, produce as well as manufactures and raw materials of which pottery, bronze, and flint or stone would be realistic possibilities. Another conceivable use might be for fishing: boats of much the same size and similar construction are still used off the coasts of Sri Lanka for

seine-netting. In general, capacious and seaworthy boats could scarcely have wanted for passengers or cargo throughout prehistory from Neolithic times onwards in a system such as the Humber estuary and its tributary rivers.

Rather more debatable is the question whether boats of the Ferriby type were capable of open-sea navigation. Most of those consulted in the past seemed to think not; but Coates's estimates of the performance of the boat as now reconstructed suggest otherwise. Furthermore the archaeological evidence indicates beyond doubt that sea crossings between the British islands and with the mainland of Europe were made from the Early Neolithic era onwards; nor need they have been confined to the notably weatherly hideboats thought to have been available from very early times. Boats of not dissimilar construction such as the *madel paruwa* of Sri Lanka (Figure 9.3) and the *masula* 'surf-boats'

Figure 9.3 A *madel paruwa*, Sri Lanka 1963.

Figure 9.4 A *masula* surfboat, Mahabalipuram, Madras 1963.

of the coasts of south-east India (Figure 9.4) are still launched from open beaches to venture out into the Indian Ocean (Kentley 1985 and Kentley and Gunaratne 1987). There the boatmen plainly choose their weather with care and it may be more predictable than that of the North Sea today. It is generally agreed that the climate in Britain before the last quarter of the second millennium BC was more genial than at present and it is possible to envisage a summer season suitable for sea-voyaging and a close season when it would be too hazardous, as so graphically described in the account of St Paul's voyage to Rome when the captain set out only reluctantly from Crete 'when the season was already too late for sailing' and they ended up shipwrecked on Malta (Acts 27:9). The very careful attention given to protection of the stitching under the bottom-structure in the Ferriby boats suggests that running them ashore was a routine procedure so that they could have been beached at night or whenever the weather turned unfavourable. Support is therefore growing in favour of the proposition that in experienced hands they could have been capable of coasting voyages around the North Sea, but not necessarily in all weathers. The new reconstruction put forward in Chapter 5 gives an idea of better seaworthiness than did some of my previous essays: but the truth will only be obtained from a programme of controlled sea trials with a replica.

It has been said that boatbuilding represents one of the highest of technical achievements by early man and the Ferriby assemblage unquestionably supports such a contention. In the quality and intricacy of their design and finish they are outstanding examples of inventiveness and craftsmanship. At every turn one finds remarkable ingenuity in solving problems within the limits imposed by the materials and tools available. In developing the reconstruction from the actual finds, there are few features for which a rational purpose cannot be advanced without departing from the techniques observed or introducing anachronisms. We have been at pains to avoid gilding the lily!

To modern eyes some of the expedients apparent in the design may seem grotesque as well as extravagant of materials, and the absence of any recognizable descendants suggests that, as alternative techniques reached Britain in the second half of the first millennium BC from Gaul, then Rome, and later the northern Germanic world, what had become the archaic methods of the Ferriby builders disappeared with little or no trace. This would be easier to detect if a wider sample than that from the Humber were available; but unfortunately in the area most likely to yield it, the coasts of the Low Countries, North Germany, and Denmark, Bronze Age levels lie submerged under either several metres of water or an equal depth of sediments so that opportunities for discovering parallels are restricted. We have been fortunate that the deposits at Ferriby were laid down within approximately the same tidal range as today's. Would that there were many similar situations around the coasts and waterways bordering on the southern North Sea.

Any attempt to fit them into a framework for the evolution of boatbuilding comes up against the fact that so little is known for certain through actual finds. As the Danish marine archaeologist Ole Crumlin-Pedersen said to me recently: 'If it had not been for your finds at Ferriby, that of the Brigg "Raft" and of the Hjortspring canoe [of third century BC from the island of Als in Denmark], we should still believe that the inhabitants of North West Europe before Roman times had only log-boats.' He might perhaps have added hide-boats such as curraghs and coracles for which the artefactual evidence is minimal, the fact of their existence being derived from literary sources; but his point was well made. It can therefore be fairly claimed that the half-century of work described in this book has opened up the existence of a wholly new field of boatbuilding achievement by Bronze Age people, the full extent of which in time and

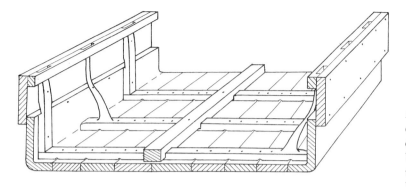

Figure 9.5 Reconstruction drawing of the second century AD Romano-Celtic barge, Zwammerdam 2, from the Netherlands (IPP: B. Donker).

space has still to be explored. No prototype is known from which these boats might have sprung; but the shaped ends of the side-strakes are reminiscent of logboat practice though of more sophisticated form than any British examples whether earlier or later than c.1300 BC. The flat bottom and shoe-shaped bow and stern on the other hand call to mind the more obvious raft-derivation of the Brigg 'Raft' and some of the northern European riverboats of later times. In spite of careful study of the growing list of boat-finds of pre-Roman type from central and western Europe, I have been unable to identify any which strike the eye immediately as resembling the Ferriby boats in general conception. There are, however, individual features and devices of construction identifiable in certain of the boats found in the Rhine basin and the Swiss lakes dating from just before and during the Roman period which are reminiscent of Ferriby practice, the most striking being the Zwammerdam 2 parallel for the device for securing the ribs to the sheer-strakes deduced from F4 (Figure 9.5).

Perhaps the most unusual feature when my brother and I began to investigate F1 was the use of stitching to fasten the planks, and it remains so to those unfamiliar with ancient and modern parallels for the practice. Also startling was the system of 'tongue-and-groove' shaping of the plank-edges. As more and more information is collected from archaeological and ethnographical sources,

however, it has become apparent that, before the availability of plentiful copper and bronze for tools capable of accurate cutting of mortices and later of cheap metal for nails or rivets, forms of sewing with continuous cord and stitching with individually separate stitches were the rule rather than the exception. Sewing or lashing was evidently and freely used in Ancient Egypt, most notably in the Cheops boat (Figures 9.6 and 9.7) and is illustrated in a number of bas-reliefs of boats and ships, the techniques persisting into modern times in the upper Nile and the African lakes. Literary references in Greek and Latin authors to sewing, coupled in some cases with mortice and tenon joints between plank-edges, have long been recognized; but there are growing numbers of finds of actual examples around the Mediterranean such as the Bon Porté (Pomey 1981) and Giglio (Bound 1985) wrecks, the latter perhaps Etruscan and of sixth century BC date, and the boats from Nin (Brusic and Domjan 1985) on the Adriatic and Ljubljana inland as late as the first to third century AD (Figures 9.8 and 9.11). The earliest clinker-built boats from Scandinavia were sewn and the practice has continued in historic times through Fennoscandia to northern Russia and Siberia. Some of the closest parallels for stitching as opposed to sewing come from that area, the most usual material being tree-root, of spruce in particular. Sewing was and is equally common in Asian waters where until the nine-

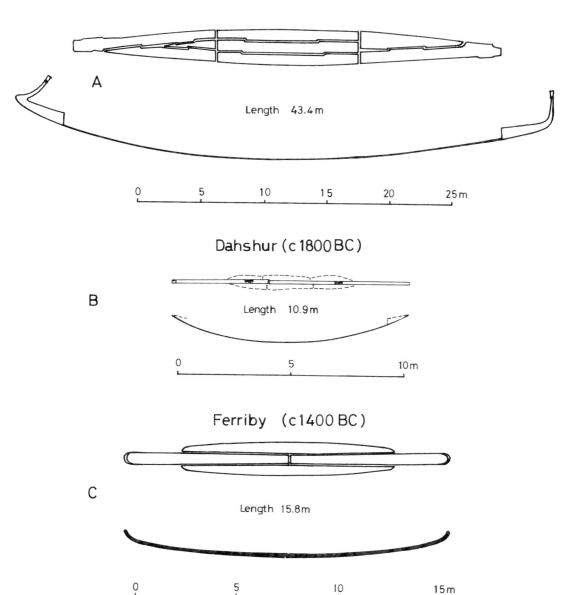

Cheops (c 2600 BC)

A

Length 43.4m

0   5   10   15   20   25m

Dahshur (c 1800 BC)

B

Length 10.9m

0   5   10m

Ferriby (c 1400 BC)

C

Length 15.8m

0   5   10   15m

Figure 9.6 Bottom-structure of the Ferriby boats compared with those of the Cheops and Dahshur boats from Egypt.

teenth century the sewn *bhoom* was the standard trading vessel between the Arabian coast to India and even China. They were first described by a European in the writings of Marco Polo and have been reproduced with great accuracy by Tim Severin in his *Sohar* which made the passage from Oman to China in 1980–1 (Severin 1980). Sewn boats of a wide variety are still built around the coasts of the Indian Ocean, Indonesia and north to

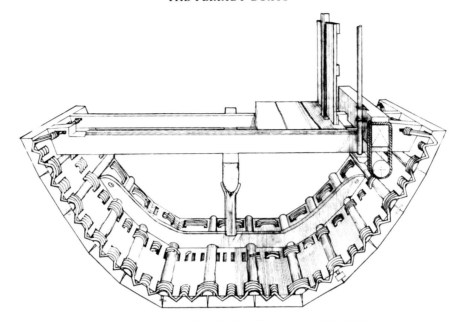

Figure 9.7 Stitching method in the Cheops boat (Paul Lipke).

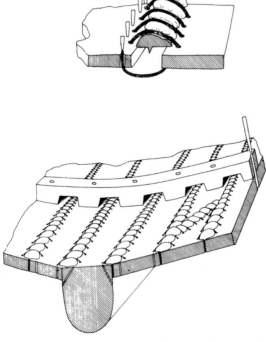

Figure 9.8 Stitching of the Nin boat, Jugoslavia (Brusic).

the Philippines, and in the western Pacific. One interesting observation by the writer of a modern trend was the change by the builders of the *madel paruwa* in Sri Lanka from cords of coconut fibre (coir) in 1963 to synthetic material by 1975, the construction of the boats being otherwise unaltered (Figure 9.9). There would appear to be no great significance between the different practices of continuous sewing and separate stitching as a method of fastening planks. Examples of stitching seem to be rarer, perhaps because sewing was found to be the more efficient and therefore adopted where suitable cord was obtainable. In this connection it is noteworthy that in the Brigg 'Raft' (Figure 9.11) cord made from split willow-canes was used (McGrail 1981a). Stitches of yew-withy are as far as I know unique to the Ferriby group and may well have been favoured because although difficult to handle it was unusually strong and durable.

The majority of recorded sewn and stitched boats require luting or caulking and many also employ some means of capping the seams

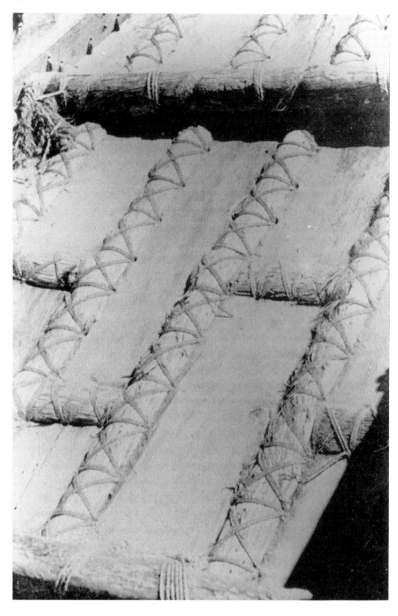

Figure 9.9 Sewing of the bottom planking in a *madel paruwa*.

either with wooden laths or battens or bundles of fibre, the latter feature combining retention of the caulking in place in the seam with the provision of a curved rather than angular path for the stitches or cord so as to ease tightening and avoid breakage over sharp corners. Moss as such for caulking is not without early parallels, as for instance around the inserted transom-board in the Brigg logboat or in the

seams in a number of examples such as the Brigg 'Raft'. The caulking-cord combined with wadded moss in F3 appears to be an unusual feature without early parallels although a similar combination is used in the Bevaix and Yverdon boats of first century AD date from Lake Neuchâtel in Switzerland, but in those cases caulked and capped from the outside (Arnold 1978: Figure 38). The whole

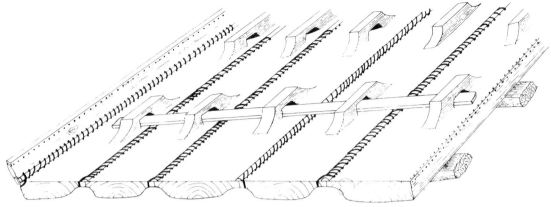

Figure 9.10   Sewing and cleat-systems in the Brigg 'Raft' (McGrail).

subject of caulking in ancient boats calls for research, with special reference to the use of moss for the purpose in Romano-Celtic vessels.

After the first observation in 1937 of the method of rebating or 'rabbitting' the edges of the planks in the bottom-structure and when even the widely knowledgeable James Hornell could recall only a single ethnographical parallel for the practice and that not a close one (Figure 1.17), several variations were revealed in the remains of F1 so that altogether five distinct methods can be identi-

fied or six if the repaired cracks are included (Figures 4.8a–f). Each appears to be contrived to provide the most effective joint possible in a given situation and the combination is not only unique in ancient or modern boat-building but emphasizes the thought and ingenuity which has gone into the boat's development.

Other details such as the use of upstanding blocks and cleats left proud of the surface as the planks were shaped exhibit similar evidence of very careful planning by the builders. Though patently wasteful of timber, this is a

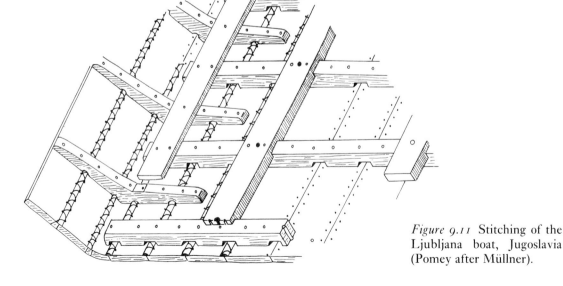

Figure 9.11 Stitching of the Ljubljana boat, Jugoslavia (Pomey after Müllner).

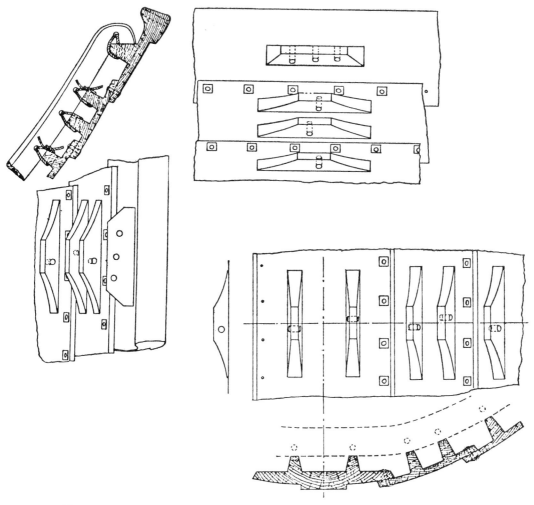

Figure 9.12 Lashing of frames to integral cleats in the Nydam ship (Akerlund).

natural enough procedure for the provision of attachments or abutments when there was no other readily available means of securing fittings to planks or other timbers. It has been widely used in north-west Europe, as for instance in the arrangement for securing ribs to planks (Figure 9.12) in the northern shell-first tradition with its thin 'clinker' planking from the Nydam ship of the fourth century AD (Åkerlund 1963) to the lower part of the Gokstad Viking ship of the eighth century (Brøgger and Shetelig 1971). The only close parallel to the use of transverse timbers passed through perforated cleats is in the Brigg 'Raft' with ten such systems, where they were an even more prominent feature than in Ferriby 1 with eight, though fewer than in Ferriby 2 with eighteen. The only comparable ancient examples of a similar feature are the cleated patch used to waterproof a split in the Brigg logboat, cross-pins being fitted on the inside to hold it in place, and the rather less obvious method of attaching the 'lower bow-piece' to the main dugout shell in the Hasholme logboat (Figure 9.13) (Millett and McGrail 1987).

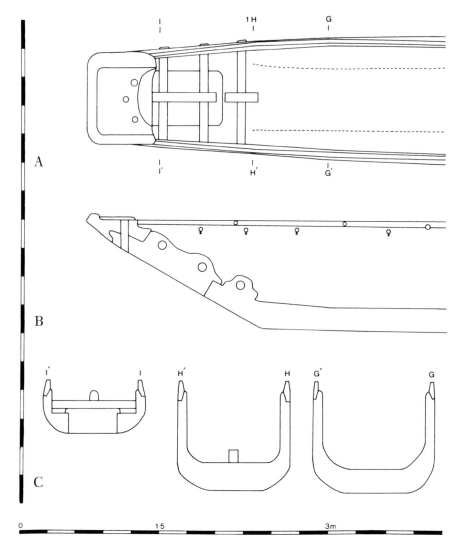

Figure 9.13 The attachment of the prow-piece in the Hasholme logboat by means of cleats and pins. *A* plan, *B* lengthwise section and *C* transverse sections (see also Figure 6.6) (NMM, Greenwich).

It is possible to go on searching indefinitely for possible kinship for features recorded in the Ferriby boats but in general it can be said that few details are entirely without parallel in boatbuilding practice at some period somewhere in the world. What is unique in time and place as far as is known from finds to date is the actual combination of methods employed. This technological isolation is shared with the Brigg 'Raft' found nearby and, further away and without any suggestion of kinship whatsoever, by the completely unparalleled Hjortspring canoe cited earlier (p. 19). In the state of present knowledge, the relative isolation of such finds and the exploitation of locally available materials in each case point towards origins by independent regional invention rather than any widespread diffusion of techniques around the ancient world.

EPILOGUE

The principal achievements of more than fifty years of work on the North Ferriby project are essentially three in number. Foremost is the identification of a hitherto unknown school of boatbuilding practice, the possible ramifications of which in terms of origin, duration, and geographical distribution remain obscure. Second is the demonstration of a remarkable level of technical competence by people of the north-west European Bronze Age several centuries if not a millennium earlier than anything of the kind has been conceived as within their capability. Third is the recognition of a realistic candidate in addition to hideboats or logboats for the carriage of cross-channel and coastal traffic from the Middle Bronze Age down to the prehistoric Iron Age before it can be presumed that any vessel of comparable capability became available.

While these gains may justly be claimed on the credit side, it must also be admitted that the programme has been dogged with misfortunes over the recovery and conservation of the remains of the boats themselves. Happily, as can be seen from this account, little of the essential information has been lost, the only real problem being to convey adequately the astonishing intricacy and craftsmanship revealed when the finds were first exposed. The difficulty is underlined by the fact that in the years since they were first published several authors have introduced deliberate crudity into copies of my earlier reconstructions, thus conveying a wrong impression of the skills of the boatbuilders of the period. I trust that the contents of this book will counteract any such tendency. I also hope that its publication will lead on to the construction of a full-sized working replica and that theories can be tested in practice so as to reveal the true skills of the Bronze Age people of North Ferriby as shipwrights and seamen.

Glossary

Words and phrases used in this book are in the main normal descriptive terminology, in some cases ones which have been found apt for features unique to the Ferriby boats. Technical boat-building terms have largely been resisted as they are often modernisms inappropriate to our ancient craft. More extensive glossaries may be found in Sean McGrail's *Ancient Boats in North West Europe* (London, Longman 1987) and Eric McKee's *Clenched Lap or Clinker* (National Maritime Museum, Greenwich 1972).

Bevel A surface which has been angled to make a fit with another.

Bilge The curved surface between the bottom and sides of a boat.

Blocks Integral projections shaped on the surfaces of planks apparently to act as chocks to prevent movement of timbers fitted against them.

Butt Form of joint in which one timber is laid squarely against another without overlap. Also the lower or stump end of a tree-trunk or branch.

Capstan 'A cylinder or barrel revolving on a vertical axis, the power being supplied by movable bars inserted in horizontal sockets made round the top and pushed by men walking round' (OED)

Caulking Properly, stopping inserted in a seam after it has been assembled; used loosely here for the waterproofing process or material.

Cleat Here used for integral blocks or ridges perforated to allow the passage of timber or other material through the hole(s).

Cleat-system A group of cleats complete with transverse timbers, these in turn being grouped in multiple arrays.

Crook A curved timber which has grown into a shape useful for boat-building.

Flange A projecting rim.

Floor A transverse member across the bottom of a boat.

Frame A transverse member made up of more than one piece of timber.

Girth-lashing A binding of rope or similar material around the girth of a boat to hold the planks together.

Hog Distortion of a boat's hull in which the ends droop as when the middle is supported on the crest of a wave.

Hogging-stay A lengthwise rope attached to bow and stern and tightened by a tourniquet and props; to secure the hull against damage due to hogging.

Joint Generalized term for a variety of connections between timbers.

Keel The main longitudinal strength-member in a boat, usually formed from a plank or timber on edge.

Keel-plank Descriptive of the central length-wise member in the bottom structure of a Ferriby boat.

Lath A narrow strip of wood, used in the Ferriby boats for capping the seams.

Lay, laying Of rope, where more than one

strand of spun fibre is twisted with another spirally.

Logboat A boat whose hull is made from a hollowed tree-trunk, synonymous with '*dugout*'.

Luting Material inserted between two members of a boat's structure before they are assembled in order to make the seam watertight, as with the moss in the Ferriby case.

Mortise A rectilinear cavity cut in a timber to receive a tenon.

Ordnance datum (OD) The standard for mean tide-level for the British Isles taken at Newlyn, Cornwall. Levels for tides are shown as so many metres above (+) OD for highs and below (−) for lows. OD is also 'sea level' for heights on land.

Outer bottom plank Descriptive term for the planks fitted on each side of the keel-plank in a Ferriby boat to form the bottom-structure. In more recent boat-building they might be called 'garboard strakes'.

Plank A flat piece of timber: more than one plank may go to make up a strake (q.v.).

Saddle A lengthwise ridge with a shaped depression, thought to be to locate the end of a vertical post or mast.

Scarf A tapered or rectilinear joint between timbers of similar section at the join.

Seam The juncture of two members required to be watertight.

Sewing Description of edge-fastening of boat's planking by means of continuously threaded cord or similar fibrous material.

Sheer strake The top strake of planking in a boat.

Slot Term used for the angular space between upstanding blocks on planks thought to be contrived to accommodate and locate transverse timbers such as frames.

Stitch, stitching Used to describe the means of edge-fastening boat's planking by separate stitches of material such as withy or tree-root.

Strake Generally a single plank or combination of planks which stretches from one end of a boat to the other, in the Ferriby case confined to the planking of the sides (side-strakes, abbreviated to S-S1, S-S2, etc.).

Tenon 'The end of a member which has been worked so as to be a close fit in a cavity or mortise in another member' (McKee). A tenon may also be made of a separate piece of wood which fits into two opposing mortises.

Timber Generally any piece of wood used in the construction of a boat.

Transom Transverse board at the (squared) stern of a boat.

Winch Apparatus for hauling in which the barrel or drum on which rope or chain is wound is mounted horizontally in bearings on a carriage, power being applied by a crank-handle or short bars. (Synonym: *windlass*).

Bibliography

Adney, E. T. and Chapelle, H. I. (1964) *Bark Canoes and Skinboats of North America*, Washington, DC: Smithsonian Institution.

Åkerlund, H. (1963) *Nydamskeppen*, Sjöfartsmuseet, Göteborg.

Allison, J. and Godwin, H. (1947) 'Report on plant material associated with the Ferriby boats'. In Wright and Wright (1947) App.B.

Arnold, B. (1978) 'Gallo-Roman boat-finds in Switzerland'. In J. du Plat Taylor and H. Cleere (eds) *Roman Shipping and Trade: Britain and the Rhine Provinces*, CBA Research Report 24: 31–5.

Barley, M. W. (1936) 'Lincolnshire rivers in the Middle Ages', *Reports and Papers of the Associated Societies (Lincolnshire)* 1 (1):2.

Bass, G. F. (1972) *A History of Seafaring*, London: Thames Hudson.

Bisat, W. S. (1932) 'Glacial and post-glacial sections on the Humber shore at North Ferriby', *Transactions of the Hull Geological Society* 7 (3): 83–95.

Bound, M. (1985) 'Early observations on the construction of the pre-classical wreck at Campese Bay, Island of Giglio'. In S. McGrail and E. Kentley, (eds.) *Sewn Plank Boats*, Greenwich: NMM Arch. Series 10 (BAR International 276).

Brewster, T. C. M. (1963) *The Excavation of Staple Howe*, Scarborough: East Riding Research Committee.

Brogger, A. W. and Shetelig, H. (1971) *The Viking Ships*, London: Stanford.

Brusic, Z. and Domjan, M (1985) 'Liburnian boats – their construction and form'. In S. McGrail and E. Kentley (eds) *Sewn Plank Boats*, Greenwich: NMM Arch. Series 10 (BAR International 276).

Buckland, P. C., Beal, C. J. and Heal, V. S. E. (1990) 'Recent work on the archaeological and paleoenvironmental context of the Ferriby boats'. In S. Ellis and D. R. Crowther (eds) *Humber Perspectives*, Hull: Hull University Press.

Burgess, C. B. (1968) *Bronze Age Metalwork in Northern England*, Durham.

—— (1980) *The Age of Stonehenge*, London: Dent.

—— (1986) ' "Urnes of no small variety": collared urns reviewed', *PPS* 52: 339–51.

Casson, L. (1975) 'Bronze Age ships. The evidence of the Thera wall paintings', *IJNA* 4, 1:3–10.

Christensen, A. E. (1986) Personal communication.

Clark, J. G. D. (1952) *'Prehistoric Europe – the economic basis*, London: Methuen.

—— (1954) *Excavations at Starr Carr*, Cambridge: Cambridge University Press.

Clarke, R. S. (1986) Personal Communication.

Corder, P. and Pryce, T. D., (1938) 'Belgic and other early pottery found at North Ferriby, Yorks' *Ant. J.* 18:262–77.

Corder, P., Wright, C. W. and Wright, E. V. (1939) 'The pre-Roman settlement of the Parisi at North Ferriby', *The Naturalist* 1:237–43.

Crowther, D. R. (1987), 'Sediments and archaeology of the Humber foreshore'. In S. Ellis (ed.) *East Yorkshire Field Guide*, Cambridge: Quaternary Research Association.

Darrah, R. (1982) 'Working unseasoned wood'. In S. McGrail (ed.) *Woodworking Techniques before AD 1500*, Greenwich: NMM Arch. Series 7 (BAR International 129).

—— (1990) Personal communication.

Ellmers, D. (1984) 'Earliest evidence for skinboats in late Palaeolithic Europe'. In S. McGrail (ed.)

Aspects of Maritime Archaeology and Ethnology, Greenwich: NMM.

Farrell, A. W. (1979) 'Mast and sail in Scandinavia in the Bronze Age?', *MM* 65(1): 83.

Godwin, H. (1967) 'The ancient cultivation of hemp', *Ant.* 41(161): 42–9.

Greenhill, B. (1971) *Boats and Boatmen of Pakistan,* Newton Abbott: David & Charles.

—— (1976) *Archaeology of the Boat,* London: A & C Black.

Greenwell, W. (1877) *British Barrows,* Oxford: Clarendon Press.

Haggblom, A. (1982) 'Driftwood in Svalbard as an indicator of sea-ice conditions', *Geografiska Annaler* 64A: 81–94.

Hawkes, C. F. C. (1960) 'A scheme for the British Bronze Age' précis of address presented to Bronze Age Conference, CBA, London.

Heal, S. V. E. (1989) 'A Bronze Age wooden paddle from the R. Crouch, Canewdon, Essex'. In Wilkinson *et al. The Hullbridge Survey,* Essex County Council.

Hillam, J. (1981) 'Tree-ring analysis'. In S, McGrail (ed.) *The Brigg Raft,* Greenwich: NMM Arch. Series 6 (BAR British 89).

—— (1985) 'Dendrochronology of the North Ferriby boats'. In S. McGrail and E. Kentley (eds) *Sewn Plank Boats,* Greenwich: NMM Arch. Series 10 (BAR International 276).

Hoeg, O. A. (1977) 'Vidjer og viuspenniler', *Norveg* (Journal of Norwegian Ethnology) 20: 7–106.

Hornell, J. (1930) 'The tongue and groove seam of Gujerati boat-builders', *MM* 16 310–12.

—— (1946) *Water Transport,* Cambridge: Cambridge University Press.

Jenkins, N. (1980) *The Boat Beneath the Pyramid,* London: Thames & Hudson.

Johnstone, P. (1980) *The Sea-craft of Prehistory,* London: Routledge & Kegan Paul.

Kentley, E. (1985) 'Some aspects of the Masula surf boat'. In S. McGrail and E. Kentley (eds) *Sewn Plank Boats,* Greenwich: NMM Arch. Series 10 (BAR International 276).

Kentley, E. and Gunaratne, R. (1987) 'The *Madel paruwa* – a sewn boat with chine strakes', *IJNA* 16 (1) 35–48.

Landström, B. (1976) *The Ship,* London: Allen & Unwin (English edition).

Lipke, P. (1984) 'The Royal ship of Cheops', NMM Arch. Series 9 (BAR International 225).

Longworth, I. H. (1978) 'Comments on non-organic artifacts'. In E. V. Wright (1978).

McGrail, S. (1977) 'Axe, hoe or slice', *IJNA* 6: 62–4.

—— (1978) *Logboats of England and Wales,* Greenwich: NMM Arch. Series 2 (BAR British 51).

—— (1981a) *The Brigg 'Raft' and her Prehistoric Environment,* Greenwich: NMM Arch. Series 6 (BAR British 89).

—— (1981b) *The Ship,* London: NMM HMSO.

—— (1983) 'The interpretation of archaeological evidence for maritime structures'. In P. Annis (ed.) *Sea Studies,* Greenwich: NMM.

—— (1987a) *Ancient Boats in North West Europe,* London: Longman.

—— (1987b) 'Early boatbuilding techniques in Britain and Ireland', *IJNA* 16 (4): 343–54.

—— (1989) 'Prehistoric water transport in N.W. Europe', *MM* 75(4): 297–312.

McGrail, S. and Switsur, V. R. (1975) 'Early British boats and their chronology', *IJNA* 4 (2): 191–200.

McKee, E. (1972) *Clenched Lap or Clinker,* Greenwich: NMM.

Manby, T. G. (1974) 'Grooved ware sites in Yorkshire and the north of England', *BAR British Series* (Oxford) 9.

Millett, M. and McGrail, S. (1987) 'The archaeology of the Hasholme logboat', *Arch. J.* 144: 1–68.

Morrison, J. S. and Coates, J. F. (1986) *The Athenian Trireme,* Cambridge: Cambridge University Press.

Morrison, J. S. and Williams, R. T. (1968) *Greek Oared Ships, 900–322 BC,* Cambridge: Cambridge University Press.

Mortimer, J. R. (1905) *Forty Years Researches in British and Saxon Burial Mounds of East Yorkshire,* London: Brown.

Mullner, A. (1892) 'Ein Schiff im Laibacher Moore', *Argo* 1: 1–8.

Naskali, E. (1986) 'The reconstruction of the Rääkkylä boat', *Maritime Museum of Finland Annual Report 1984–5* 2–7.

Needham, J. (1971) 'Science and Civilisation in China', *Civil Engineering and Nautics* 4(3): 413; quoting G. R. G. Worcester, unpublished material no. 98.

Pomey, P. (1981) 'L'Epave de Bon-Porté et les bateaux cousus de Mediterranée', *MM* 67: 225–43.

Purcell, D. (1973) *The Building of Ely Cathedral*, Ely.

Rackham, O. (1982) Personal communication.

Rieck, F. and Crumlin-Pedersen, O. (1988) *Både fra Danmarks Old Tid*, Roskilde.

Rigby, V. (1989) 'Pottery from the North Ferriby boat-site'. In E. V. Wright, G. R. Hutchinson, and C. W. Gregson, 'A fourth boat-find from North Ferriby', *Arch. J.* 146.

Rosenberg, G. (1937) *Hjortspringfundet*, Copenhagen.

Severin, T. (1980) *The Sinbad Voyage*, London: Hutchinson.

Smith, M. A. (1959) 'Some Somerset hoards and their place in the Bronze Age of southern Britain', *PPS* 25: 144–87.

Smith, R. A. (1928) 'Pre-Roman remains at Scarborough', *Arch.* 77.

Stather, J. W. (1896) 'Drifts of the Humber Gap', *Proceedings of the Yorkshire Geological and Polytechnic Society* 13 (2): 210–20.

Stead, I. M. (1965) *The La Tène Cultures of Eastern Yorkshire*, York: Yorkshire Philosophical Society.

Switzur, V. R. and Wright, E. V. (1989) 'Radiocarbon dates for the boats from North Ferriby Humberside – a reappraisal', *Arch. J,* 146.

Thropp, J. (1887) 'An ancient raft found at Brigg, Lincolnshire', *Reports and Papers of the Associated Societies (Lincolnshire)* 19 (1): 95–7.

Varley, W. J. (1968) 'Barmston and the Holderness Crannogs', *East Riding Archaeologist* 1 (1): 12–27.

Wright, C. W. and Wright, E. V. (1933) 'Some notes on the Holocene deposits at North Ferriby', *The Naturalist* 1: 210–12.

Wright, C. W. and Wright, E. V. (1939) 'Submerged boat at North Ferriby', *Ant.* 151: 349–54.

Wright, E. V. (1976) 'The North Ferriby boats – a guidebook', *Maritime Monographs and Reports* 23, Greenwich: NMM.

Wright, E. V. (1977) 'Report on recent reexamination of the foreshore at the North Ferriby boat site and at Melton', unpublished typescript deposited at Hull Museums.

Wright, E. V. (1978) 'Artefacts from the boat-site at North Ferriby, Humberside, England', *PPS* 44: 187–202.

Wright, E. V. (1984) 'Practical experiments in boat-stitching'. In S. McGrail (ed.) *Aspects of Maritime Archaeology and Ethnology*, Greenwich: NMM, 57–84.

Wright, E. V. (1986) 'A Bronze Age beach-capstan?' *Oxford Journal of Archaeology* 5 (3): 309–21.

Wright, E. V. and Churchill, D. M. (1965) 'The boats from North Ferriby, Yorkshire', *PPS* 31: 1–24.

Wright, E. V. and Wright, C. W. (1947) 'Prehistoric boats from North Ferriby, E. Yorkshire', *PPS* 13: 114–38.

Wright, E. V., Hutchinson, G. R., and Gregson, C. W., (1989) 'A fourth boat-find at North Ferriby, Humberside', *Arch. J.* 146.

Index

Note: page numbers in **bold** type refer to illustrations. Where more than one illustration appears on the page, the relevant figure number is also given.